AMERICAN WOMEN
images and realities

AMERICAN WOMEN
Images and Realities

Advisory Editors
ANNETTE K. BAXTER
LEON STEIN

A Note About This Volume

Thomas Wentworth Higginson (1823-1911) was graduated from Harvard University at 17, second in his class. At 22, he announced himself a "disunion abolitionist," a declaration which did not ease his position as Unitarian minister. His belief in freedom was deeply personal: he fought with his fists to liberate the fugitive slave, Anthony Burns; he went west in behalf of free soil; he became a friend of John Brown and headed the first Negro regiment in the Civil War. In peacetime, he lived as a man of letters in Cambridge, championing woman's rights, befriending Emily Dickinson, contributing graceful, yet forceful pieces to the *Atlantic* and other publications. *Women and the Alphabet* is his plea for full education for women.

WOMEN
AND THE ALPHABET
A Series of Essays

THOMAS WENTWORTH HIGGINSON

ARNO PRESS
A New York Times Company
New York • 1972

Reprint Edition 1972 by Arno Press Inc.

Reprinted from a copy in The Columbia
University Library

American Women: Images and Realities
ISBN for complete set: 0-405-04445-3
See last pages of this volume for titles.

Manufactured in the United States of America

- - - - - - - - - - - -

Library of Congress Cataloging in Publication Data

Higginson, Thomas Wentworth, 1823-1911.
    Women and the alphabet.

    (American women: images and realities)
    Original ed. issued as v. 4 of The writings of
Thomas Wentworth Higginson.
    1. Woman--Social and moral questions--Addresses,
essays, lectures. 2. Education of women--Addresses,
essays, lectures. I. Title. II. Series.
HQ1419.H56 1972   301.41'2   72-2607
ISBN 0-405-04462-3

THE WRITINGS OF

THOMAS WENTWORTH HIGGINSON

VOLUME IV

WOMEN
AND THE ALPHABET

A Series of Essays

BY

THOMAS WENTWORTH HIGGINSON

BOSTON AND NEW YORK
HOUGHTON, MIFFLIN AND COMPANY
The Riverside Press, Cambridge
M DCCCC

PREFATORY NOTE

THE first essay in this volume, "Ought Women to learn the Alphabet?" appeared originally in the "Atlantic Monthly" of February, 1859, and has since been reprinted in various forms, bearing its share, I trust, in the great development of more liberal views in respect to the training and duties of women which has made itself manifest within forty years. There was, for instance, a report that it was the perusal of this essay which led the late Miss Sophia Smith to the founding of the women's college bearing her name at Northampton, Massachusetts.

The remaining papers in the volume formed originally a part of a book entitled "Common Sense About Women" which was made up largely of papers from the "Woman's Journal." This book was first published in 1881 and was reprinted in somewhat abridged form some years later in London (Sonnenschein). It must have attained a considerable circulation there, as the fourth (stereotyped) edition appeared in 1897. From this London reprint a German translation was made by Fräulein Eugenie Jacobi, under the title "Die Frauenfrage und der gesunde Menschenverstand" (Schupp: Neuwied and Leipzig, 1895).

T. W. H.

CAMBRIDGE, MASS.

CONTENTS

WOMEN AND THE ALPHABET

I

OUGHT WOMEN TO LEARN THE ALPHABET?

PARIS smiled, for an hour or two, in the year 1801, when, amidst Napoleon's mighty projects for remodelling the religion and government of his empire, the ironical satirist, Sylvain Maréchal, thrust in his "Plan for a Law prohibiting the Alphabet to Women." [1] Daring, keen, sarcastic, learned, the little tract retains to-day so much of its pungency, that we can hardly wonder at the honest simplicity of the author's friend and biographer, Madame Gacon Dufour, who declared that he must be insane, and soberly replied to him.

His proposed statute consists of eighty-two clauses, and is fortified by a "whereas" of a hundred and thirteen weighty reasons. He exhausts the range of history to show the frightful results which have followed this taste of

[1] *Projet d'une loi portant défense d'apprendre à lire aux femmes.*

fruit of the tree of knowledge ; quotes from the Encyclopédie, to prove that the woman who knows the alphabet has already lost a portion of her innocence ; cites the opinion of Molière, that any female who has unhappily learned anything in this line should affect ignorance, when possible ; asserts that knowledge rarely makes men attractive, and females never ; opines that women have no occasion to peruse Ovid's "Art of Love," since they know it all in advance ; remarks that three quarters of female authors are no better than they should be ; maintains that Madame Guion would have been far more useful had she been merely pretty and an ignoramus, such as Nature made her, — that Ruth and Naomi could not read, and Boaz probably would never have married into the family had they possessed that accomplishment, — that the Spartan women did not know the alphabet, nor the Amazons, nor Penelope, nor Andromache, nor Lucretia, nor Joan of Arc, nor Petrarch's Laura, nor the daughters of Charlemagne, nor the three hundred and sixty-five wives of Mohammed ; but that Sappho and Madame de Maintenon could read altogether too well ; while the case of Saint Brigitta, who brought forth twelve children and twelve books, was clearly exceptional, and afforded no safe precedent.

It would seem that the brilliant Frenchman

touched the root of the matter.   Ought women
to learn the alphabet ?   There the whole question lies.   Concede this little fulcrum, and
Archimedea will move the world before she
has done with it : it becomes merely a question
of time.   Resistance must be made here or
nowhere.   *Obsta principiis.*   Woman must be a
subject or an equal : there is no middle ground.
What if the Chinese proverb should turn out to
be, after all, the summit of wisdom, " For men,
to cultivate virtue is knowledge ; for women, to
renounce knowledge is virtue " ?

No doubt, the progress of events is slow, like
the working of the laws of gravitation generally.
Certainly there has been but little change in the
legal position of women since China was in its
prime, until within the last half century.   Lawyers admit that the fundamental theory of English and Oriental law is the same on this point :
Man and wife are one, and that one is the husband.   It is the oldest of legal traditions.   When
Blackstone declares that "the very being and
existence of the woman is suspended during the
marriage," and American Kent echoes that " her
legal existence and authority are in a manner
lost ; " when Petersdorff asserts that " the husband has the right of imposing such corporeal restraints as he may deem necessary," and Bacon
that "the husband hath, by law, power and

dominion over his wife, and may keep her by force within the bounds of duty, and may beat her, but not in a violent or cruel manner ;" when Mr. Justice Coleridge rules that the husband, in certain cases, "has a right to confine his wife in his own dwelling-house, and restrain her from liberty for an indefinite time," and Baron Alderson sums it all up tersely, "The wife is only the *servant* of her husband," — these high authorities simply reaffirm the dogma of the Gentoo code, four thousand years old and more : "A man, both day and night, must keep his wife so much in subjection that she by no means be mistress of her own actions. If the wife have her own free will, notwithstanding she be of a superior caste, she will behave amiss."

Yet behind these unchanging institutions, a pressure has been for centuries becoming concentrated, which, now that it has begun to act, is threatening to overthrow them all. It has not yet operated very visibly in the Old World, where, even in England, the majority of women have not till lately mastered the alphabet sufficiently to sign their own names in the marriage register. But in this country the vast changes of the last few years are already a matter of history. No trumpet has been sounded, no earthquake has been felt, while State after State has ushered into legal existence one half of the popu-

lation within its borders. Surely, here and now,
might poor M. Maréchal exclaim, the bitter fruits
of the original seed appear. The sad question
recurs, Whether women ought ever to have
tasted of the alphabet.

It is true that Eve ruined us all, according to
theology, without knowing her letters. Still
there is something to be said in defence of
that venerable ancestress. The Veronese lady,
Isotta Nogarola, five hundred and thirty-six of
whose learned epistles were preserved by De
Thou, composed a dialogue on the question,
Whether Adam or Eve had committed the
greater sin. But Ludovico Domenichi, in his
"Dialogue on the Nobleness of Women," maintains that Eve did not sin at all, because she
was not even created when Adam was told not
to eat the apple. It was "in Adam all died,"
he shrewdly says; nobody died in Eve: which
looks plausible. Be that as it may, Eve's daughters are in danger of swallowing a whole har-
vest of forbidden fruit, in these revolutionary
days, unless something be done to cut off the
supply.

It has been seriously asserted, that during
the last half century more books have been
written by women and about women than during all the previous uncounted ages. It may
be true; although, when we think of the innu-

merable volumes of *Mémoires* by French women
of the seventeenth and eighteenth centuries, —
each justifying the existence of her own ten
volumes by the remark, that all her contemporaries were writing as many, — we have our
doubts. As to the increased multitude of general treatises on the female sex, however, — its
education, life, health, diseases, charms, dress,
deeds, sphere, rights, wrongs, work, wages,
encroachments, and idiosyncrasies generally, —
there can be no doubt whatever; and the poorest of these books recognizes a condition of
public sentiment of which no other age ever
dreamed.

Still, literary history preserves the names of
some reformers before the Reformation, in this
matter. There was Signora Moderata Fonte,
the Venetian, who left a book to be published
after her death, in 1592, "Dei Meriti delle
Donne." There was her townswoman, Lucre-
zia Marinella, who followed, ten years after,
with her essay, "La Nobilità e la Eccelenza
delle Donne, con Difetti e Mancamenti degli
Uomini," — a comprehensive theme, truly!
Then followed the all-accomplished Anna Maria
Schurman, in 1645, with her "Dissertatio de
Ingenii Muliebris ad Doctrinam et meliores
Literas Aptitudine," with a few miscellaneous
letters appended in Greek and Hebrew. At

last came boldly Jacquette Guillaume, in 1665, and threw down the gauntlet in her title-page, "Les Dames Illustres ; où par bonnes et fortes Raisons il se prouve que le Sexe Feminin surpasse en toute Sorte de Genre le Sexe Masculin ; " and with her came Margaret Boufflet and a host of others ; and finally, in England, Mary Wollstonecraft, whose famous book, formidable in its day, would seem rather conservative now ; and in America, that pious and worthy dame, Mrs. H. Mather Crocker, Cotton Mather's grandchild, who, in 1848, published the first book on the "Rights of Woman" ever written on this side the Atlantic.

Meanwhile there have never been wanting men, and strong men, to echo these appeals. From Cornelius Agrippa and his essay (1509) on the excellence of woman and her preëminence over man, down to the first youthful thesis of Agassiz, "Mens Feminæ Viri Animo superior," there has been a succession of voices crying in the wilderness. In England, Anthony Gibson wrote a book, in 1599, called "A Woman's Woorth, defended against all the Men in the World, proving them to be more Perfect, Excellent, and Absolute in all Vertuous Actions than any Man of what Qualitie soever, *Interlarded with Poetry.*" *Per contra,* the learned Acidalius published a book in Latin, and afterwards in French, to prove that women are not reasonable creatures. Modern theologians are at worst merely sub-acid, and do not always say so, if they think so. Meanwhile most persons have been content to leave the world to go on its old course, in this matter as in others, and have thus acquiesced in that stern judicial decree with which Timon of Athens sums up all his curses upon womankind, — "If there sit twelve women at the table, let a dozen of them be — as they are."

Ancient or modern, nothing in any of these discussions is so valuable as the fact of the discussion itself. There is no discussion where there is no wrong. Nothing so indicates wrong as this morbid self-inspection. The complaints are a perpetual protest, the defences a perpetual confession. It is too late to ignore the question ; and, once opened, it can be settled only on absolute and permanent principles. There is a wrong ; but where ? Does woman already know too much, or too little ? Was she created for man's subject, or his equal ? Shall she have the alphabet, or not ?

Ancient mythology, which undertook to explain everything, easily accounted for the social and political disabilities of woman. Goguet quotes the story from Saint Augustine, who got it from Varro. Cecrops, building Athens, saw

starting from the earth an olive-plant and a
fountain, side by side. The Delphic oracle said
that this indicated a strife between Minerva
and Neptune for the honor of giving a name
to the city, and that the people must decide
between them. Cecrops thereupon assembled
the men, and the women also, who then had a
right to vote; and the result was that Minerva
carried the election by a glorious majority of
one. Then Attica was overflowed and laid
waste: of course the citizens attributed the
calamity to Neptune, and resolved to punish
the women. It was therefore determined that
in future they should not vote, nor should any
child bear the name of its mother.

Thus easily did mythology explain all trou-
blesome inconsistencies; but it is much that it
should even have recognized them as needing
explanation. The real solution is, however,
more simple. The obstacle to the woman's
sharing the alphabet, or indeed any other privilege, has been thought by some to be the fear
of impairing her delicacy, or of destroying her
domesticity, or of confounding the distinction
between the sexes. These may have been
plausible excuses. They have even been genuine, though minor, anxieties. But the whole
thing, I take it, had always one simple, intelli-
gible basis, — sheer contempt for the supposed

intellectual inferiority of woman. She was not
to be taught, because she was not worth teaching. The learned Acidalius aforesaid was in
the majority. According to Aristotle and the
Peripatetics, woman was *animal occasionatum*,
as if a sort of monster and accidental production. Mediæval councils, charitably asserting
her claims to the rank of humanity, still pro-
nounced her unfit for instruction. In the Hindoo dramas she did not even speak the same
language with her master, but used the dialect
of slaves. When, in the sixteenth century,
Françoise de Saintonges wished to establish
girls' schools in France, she was hooted in the
streets; and her father called together four
doctors, learned in the law, to decide whether
she was not possessed by demons, to think of
educating women, — *pour s'assurer qu'instruire
des femmes n'était pas un œuvre du démon.*

It was the same with political rights. The
foundation of the Salic Law was not any senti-
mental anxiety to guard female delicacy and
domesticity; it was, as stated by Froissart, a
blunt, hearty contempt: "The kingdom of
France being too noble to be ruled by a woman." And the same principle was reaffirmed
for our own institutions, in rather softened language, by Theophilus Parsons, in his famous
defence of the rights of Massachusetts men

(the "Essex Result," in 1778) : "Women, what age soever they are of, are not considered as having a sufficient acquired discretion [to exercise the franchise]."

In harmony with this are the various maxims and *bon-mots* of eminent men, in respect to women. Niebuhr thought he should not have educated a girl well, — he should have made her know too much. Lessing said, "The woman who thinks is like the man who puts on rouge, ridiculous." Voltaire said, "Ideas are like beards : women and young men have none." And witty Dr. Maginn carries to its extreme the atrocity, "We like to hear a few words of sense from a woman, as we do from a parrot, because they are so unexpected." Yet how can we wonder at these opinions, when the saints have been severer than the sages ? — since the pious Fénelon taught that true virgin delicacy was almost as incompatible with learning as with vice ; and Dr. Channing complained, in his "Essay on Exclusion and Denunciation," of "women forgetting the tenderness of their sex," and arguing on theology.

Now this impression of feminine inferiority may be right or wrong, but it obviously does a good deal towards explaining the facts it assumes. If contempt does not originally cause failure, it perpetuates it. Systematically discourage any individual, or class, from birth to death, and they learn, in nine cases out of ten, to acquiesce in their degradation, if not to claim it as a crown of glory. If the Abbé Choisi praised the Duchesse de Fontanges for being "beautiful as an angel and silly as a goose," it was natural that all the young ladies of the court should resolve to make up in folly what they wanted in charms. All generations of women having been bred under the shadow of intellectual contempt, they have, of course, done much to justify it. They have often used only for frivolous purposes even the poor opportunities allowed them. They have employed the alphabet, as Molière said, chiefly in spelling the verb *Amo*. Their use of science has been like that of Mlle. de Launay, who computed the decline in her lover's affection by his abbreviation of their evening walk in the public square, preferring to cross it rather than take the circuit ; "from which I inferred," she says, "that his passion had diminished in the ratio between the diagonal of a rectangular parallelogram and the sum of two adjacent sides." And their conception, even of art, has been too often on the scale of Properzia de Rossi, who carved sixty-five heads on a walnut, the smallest of all recorded symbols of woman's sphere.

All this might, perhaps, be overcome, if the

social prejudice which discourages women would only reward proportionately those who surmount the discouragement. The more obstacles, the more glory, if society would only pay in proportion to the labor; but it does not. Women being denied, not merely the training which prepares for great deeds, but the praise and compensation which follow them, have been weakened in both directions. The career of eminent men ordinarily begins with college and the memories of Miltiades, and ends with fortune and fame : woman begins under discouragement, and ends beneath the same. Single, she works with half preparation and half pay ; married, she puts name and wages into the keeping of her husband, shrinks into John Smith's "lady" during life, and John Smith's "relict" on her tombstone ; and still the world wonders that her deeds, like her opportunities, are inferior.

Evidently, then, the advocates of woman's claims — those who hold that "the virtues of the man and the woman are the same," with Antisthenes, or that "the talent of the man and the woman is the same," with Socrates in Xenophon's " Banquet " — must be cautious lest they attempt to prove too much. Of course, if women know as much as the men, without schools and colleges, there is no need of admitting them to those institutions. If they work as well on half pay, it diminishes the inducement to give them the other half. The safer position is, to claim that they have done just enough to show what they might have done under circumstances less discouraging. Take, for instance, the common remark, that women have invented nothing. It is a valid answer, that the only implements habitually used by woman have been the needle, the spindle, and the basket; and tradition reports that she herself invented all three. In the same way it may be shown that the departments in which women have equalled men have been the departments in which they have had equal training, equal encouragement, and equal compensation; as, for instance, the theatre. Madame Lagrange, the *prima donna*, after years of costly musical instruction, wins the zenith of professional success; she receives, the newspapers affirm, sixty thousand dollars a year, travelling expenses for ten persons, country-houses, stables, and liveries, besides an uncounted revenue of bracelets, bouquets, and *billets-doux*. Of course, every young *débutante* fancies the same thing within her own reach, with only a brief stage-vista between. On the stage there is no deduction for sex, and, therefore, woman has shown in that sphere an equal genius. But every female com-

mon-school teacher in the United States finds
the enjoyment of her four hundred dollars a
year to be secretly embittered by the knowledge that the young college stripling in the next
schoolroom is paid twice that sum for work
no harder or more responsible than her own,
and that, too, after the whole pathway of education has been obstructed for her, and smoothed
for him. These may be gross and carnal considerations; but Faith asks her daily bread,
and fancy must be fed. We deny woman her
fair share of training, of encouragement, of re-
muneration, and then talk fine nonsense about
her instincts and intuitions. We say sentimen-
tally with the Oriental proverbialist, "Every
book of knowledge is implanted by nature in
the heart of woman," — and make the compliment a substitute for the alphabet.

Nothing can be more absurd than to impose
entirely distinct standards, in this respect, on
the two sexes, or to expect that woman, any
more than man, will accomplish anything great
without due preparation and adequate stimulus.
Mrs. Patten, who navigated her husband's ship
from Cape Horn to California, would have failed
in the effort, for all her heroism, if she had not,
unlike most of her sex, been taught to use her
Bowditch's "Navigator." Florence Nightingale, when she heard of the distresses in the

Crimea, did not, as most people imagine, rise up and say, " I am a woman, ignorant but intuitive, with very little sense and information, but exceedingly sublime aspirations ; my strength lies in my weakness; I can do all things without knowing anything about them." Not at all: during ten years she had been in hard training for precisely such services ; had visited all the hospitals in London, Edinburgh, Dublin, Paris, Lyons, Rome, Brussels, and Berlin ; had studied under the Sisters of Charity, and been twice a nurse in the Protestant Institution at Kaiserswerth. Therefore she did not merely carry to the Crimea a woman's heart, as her stock in trade, but she knew the alphabet of her profession better than the men around her. Of course, genius and enthusiasm are, for both sexes, elements unforeseen and incalculable ; but, as a general rule, great achievements imply great preparations and favorable conditions.

To disregard this truth is unreasonable in the abstract, and cruel in its consequences. If an extraordinary male gymnast can clear a height of ten feet with the aid of a spring-board, it would be considered slightly absurd to ask a woman to leap eleven feet without one; yet this is precisely what society and the critics have always done. Training and wages and social approbation are very elastic springboards; and the whole course of history has seen these offered bounteously to one sex, and as sedulously withheld from the other. Let woman consent to be a doll, and there was no finery so gorgeous, no baby-house so costly, but she might aspire to share its lavish delights; let her ask simply for an equal chance to learn, to labor, and to live, and it was as if that same doll should open its lips, and propound Euclid's forty-seventh proposition. While we have all deplored the helpless position of indigent women, and lamented that they had no alternative beyond the needle, the wash-tub, the school-room, and the street, we have usually resisted their admission into every new occupation, denied them training, and cut their compensation down. Like Charles Lamb, who atoned for coming late to the office in the morning by going away early in the afternoon, we have, first, half educated women, and then, to restore the balance, only half paid them. What innumerable obstacles have been placed in their way as female physicians; what a complication of difficulties has been encountered by them, even as printers, engravers, and designers! In London, Mr. Bennett was once mobbed for lecturing to women on watchmaking. In this country, we have known grave professors refuse to address lyceums which thought fit to employ an occasional female lecturer. Mr. Comer stated that it was "in the face of ridicule and sneers" that he began to educate American women as bookkeepers many years ago; and it was a little contemptible in Miss Muloch to revive the same satire in "A Woman's Thoughts on Women," when she must have known that in half the retail shops in Paris her own sex rules the ledger, and Mammon knows no Salic law.

We find, on investigation, what these considerations would lead us to expect, that eminent women have commonly been exceptional in training and position, as well as in their genius. They have excelled the average of their own sex because they have shared the ordinary advantages of the other sex. Take any department of learning or skill; take, for instance, the knowledge of languages, the universal alphabet, philology. On the great stairway at Padua stands the statue of Elena Cornaro, professor of six languages in that once renowned university. But Elena Cornaro was educated like a boy, by her father. On the great door of the University of Bologna is inscribed the epitaph of Clotilda Tambroni, the honored correspondent of Porson, and the first Greek scholar of southern Europe in her day. But Clotilda Tambroni was educated like a boy, by

Emanuele Aponte. How fine are those prefatory words, "by a Right Reverend Prelate," to that pioneer book in Anglo-Saxon lore, Elizabeth Elstob's grammar: "Our earthly possessions are indeed our patrimony, as derived to us by the industry of our fathers; but the language in which we speak is our mother tongue, and who so proper to play the critic in this as the females?" Yet this particular female obtained the rudiments of her rare education from her mother, before she was eight years old, in spite of much opposition from her right reverend guardians. Adelung declares that all modern philology is founded on the translation of a Russian vocabulary into two hundred different dialects by Catherine II. But Catherine shared, in childhood, the instructors of her brother, Prince Frederick, and was subject to some reproach for learning, though a girl, so much more rapidly than he did. Christina of Sweden ironically reproved Madame Dacier for her translation of Callimachus: "Such a pretty girl as you are, are you not ashamed to be so learned?" But Madame Dacier acquired Greek by contriving to do her embroidery in the room where her father was teaching her stupid brother; and her queenly critic had herself learned to read Thucydides, harder Greek than Callimachus, before she was four-

teen. And so down to our own day, who knows
how many mute, inglorious Minervas may have
perished unenlightened, while Margaret Fuller
Ossoli and Elizabeth Barrett Browning were
being educated "like boys."

This expression simply means that they had
the most solid training which the times afforded.
Most persons would instantly take alarm at the
very words; that is, they have so little faith in
the distinctions which Nature has established,
that they think, if you teach the alphabet, or
anything else, indiscriminately to both sexes,
you annul all difference between them. The
common reasoning is thus: "Boys and girls
are acknowledged to be very unlike. Now,
boys study Greek and algebra, medicine and
bookkeeping. Therefore girls should not." As
if one should say: "Boys and girls are very
unlike. Now, boys eat beef and potatoes.
Therefore, obviously, girls should not."

The analogy between physical and spiritual
food is precisely in point. The simple truth is,
that, amid the vast range of human powers and
properties, the fact of sex is but one item.
Vital and momentous in itself, it does not con-
stitute the whole organism, but only a part.
The distinction of male and female is special,
aimed at a certain end; and, apart from that
end, it is, throughout all the kingdoms of Na-

ture, of minor importance. With but trifling exceptions, from infusoria up to man, the female animal moves, breathes, looks, listens, runs, flies, swims, pursues its food, eats it, digests it, in precisely the same manner as the male: all instincts, all characteristics, are the same, except as to the one solitary fact of parentage. Mr. Ten Broeck's race-horses, Pryor and Prioress, were foaled alike, fed alike, trained alike, and finally ran side by side, competing for the same prize. The eagle is not checked in soaring by any consciousness of sex, nor asks the sex of the timid hare, its quarry. Nature, for high purposes, creates and guards the sexual distinction, but keeps it subordinate to those still more important.

Now all this bears directly upon the alphabet. What sort of philosophy is that which says, "John is a fool; Jane is a genius: nevertheless, John, being a man, shall learn, lead, make laws, make money; Jane, being a woman, shall be ignorant, dependent, disfranchised, underpaid"? Of course, the time is past when one would state this so frankly, though Comte comes quite near it, to say nothing of the Mormons; but this formula really lies at the bottom of the reasoning one hears every day. The answer is, Soul before sex. Give an equal chance, and let genius and industry do the rest. *La car-*

rière ouverte aux talens! Every man for himself, every woman for herself, and the alphabet
for us all.

Thus far, my whole course of argument has
been defensive and explanatory. I have shown
that woman's inferiority in special achievements,
so far as it exists, is a fact of small importance,
because it is merely a corollary from her historic
position of degradation. She has not excelled,
because she has had no fair chance to excel.
Man, placing his foot upon her shoulder, has
taunted her with not rising. But the ulterior
question remains behind. How came she into
this attitude originally? Explain the explanation, the logician fairly demands. Granted that
woman is weak because she has been systematically degraded : but why was she degraded?
This is a far deeper question, — one to be met
only by a profounder philosophy and a positive
solution. We are coming on ground almost
wholly untrod, and must do the best we can.

I venture to assert, then, that woman's social
inferiority has been, to a great extent, in the
past a legitimate thing. To all appearance,
history would have been impossible without it,
just as it would have been impossible without
an epoch of war and slavery. It is simply a
matter of social progress, — a part of the succession of civilizations. The past has been

inevitably a period of ignorance, of engrossing
physical necessities, and of brute force, — not
of freedom, of philanthropy, and of culture.
During that lower epoch, woman was necessarily an inferior, degraded by abject labor, even
in time of peace, — degraded uniformly by war,
chivalry to the contrary notwithstanding. Behind all the courtesies of Amadis and the Cid
lay the stern fact, — woman a child or a toy.
The flattering troubadours chanted her into a
poet's paradise; but alas! that kingdom of heaven suffered violence, and the violent took it
by force. The truth simply was, that her time
had not come. Physical strength must rule for
a time, and she was the weaker. She was very
properly refused a feudal grant, by reason, say
"Les Coustumes de Normandie," of her unfit-
ness for war or policy: *C'est l'homme ki se
bast et ki conseille.* Other authorities put it
still more plainly : " A woman cannot serve the
emperor or feudal lord in war, on account of
the decorum of her sex; nor assist him with
advice, because of her limited intellect ; nor
keep his counsel, owing to the infirmity of her
disposition." All which was, no doubt, in the
majority of cases, true ; and the degradation of
woman was simply a part of a system which
has, indeed, had its day, but has bequeathed its
associations.

From this reign of force, woman never freed herself by force. She could not fight, or would not. Bohemian annals, to be sure, record the legend of a literal war between the sexes, in which the women's army was led by Libussa and Wlasla, and which finally ended with the capture, by the army of men, of Castle Dziewin, Maiden's Tower, whose ruins are still visible near Prague. The armor of Libussa is still shown at Vienna; and the guide calls attention to the long-peaked toes of steel, with which, he avers, the tender princess was wont to pierce the hearts of her opponents, while careering through the battle. And there are abundant instances in which women have fought side by side with men, and on equal terms. The ancient British women mingled in the wars of their husbands, and their princesses were trained to the use of arms in the Maiden's Castle at Edinburgh, in the Isle of Skye. The Moorish wives and maidens fought in defence of their European peninsula; and the Portuguese women fought on the same soil, against the armies of Philip II. The king of Siam has, at present, a body-guard of four hundred women : they are armed with lance and rifle, are admirably disciplined, and their commander (appointed after saving the king's life at a tiger-hunt) ranks as one of the royal family, and has ten elephants

at her service. When the all-conquering Daho-
mian army marched upon Abbeokuta, in 1851,
they numbered ten thousand men and six thousand women. The women were, as usual, placed
foremost in the assault, as being most reliable;
and of the eighteen hundred bodies left dead
before the walls, the vast majority were of women. The Hospital of the Invalides, in Paris,
has sheltered, for half a century, a fine specimen of a female soldier, "Lieutenant Madame
Bulan," who lived to be more than eighty years
old, had been decorated by Napoleon's own
hand with the cross of the Legion of Honor,
and was credited on the hospital books with
"seven years' service, seven campaigns, three
wounds, several times distinguished, especially
in Corsica, in defending a fort against the English." But these cases, though interesting to
the historian, are still exceptional; and the instinctive repugnance they inspire is a condem-
nation, not of women, but of war.

The reason, then, for the long subjection of
woman has been simply that humanity was
passing through its first epoch, and her full
career was to be reserved for the second. As
the different races of man have appeared suc-
cessively upon the stage of history, so there
has been an order of succession of the sexes.
Woman's appointed era, like that of the Teu-

tonic races, was delayed, but not omitted. It is not merely true that the empire of the past has belonged to man, but that it has properly belonged to him; for it was an empire of the muscles, enlisting, at best, but the lower powers of the understanding. There can be no question that the present epoch is initiating an empire of the higher reason, of arts, affections, aspirations; and for that epoch the genius of woman has been reserved. The spirit of the age has always kept pace with the facts, and outstripped the statutes. Till the fulness of time came, woman was necessarily kept a slave to the spinning-wheel and the needle; now higher work is ready; peace has brought invention to her aid, and the mechanical means for her emancipation are ready also. No use in releasing her till man, with his strong arm, had worked out his preliminary share in civilization. "Earth waits for her queen" was a favorite motto of Margaret Fuller Ossoli; but it would be more correct to say that the queen has waited for her earth, till it could be smoothed and prepared for her occupancy. Now Cinderella may begin to think of putting on her royal robes.

Everybody sees that the times are altering the whole material position of woman; but most people do not appear to see the inevitable

social and moral changes which are also involved. As has been already said, the woman
of ancient history was a slave to physical necessities, both in war and peace. In war she could
do too little; in peace she did too much, under
the material compulsions which controlled the
world. How could the Jews, for instance, elevate woman? They could not spare her from
the wool and the flax, and the candle that goeth
not out by night. In Rome, when the bride
first stepped across her threshold, they did not
ask her, Do you know the alphabet? they asked
simply, Can you spin? There was no higher
epitaph than Queen Amalasontha's, — *Domum
servavit, lanam fecit.* In Bœotia, brides were
conducted home in vehicles whose wheels were
burned at the door, in token that they were
never to leave the house again. Pythagoras
instituted at Crotona an annual festival for the
distaff; Confucius, in China, did the same for
the spindle; and these celebrated not the freedom, but the serfdom, of woman.

And even into modern days this same tyrannical necessity has lingered. "Go spin, you
jades! go spin!" was the only answer vouch-
safed by the Earl of Pembroke to the twice-
banished nuns of Wilton. Even now, travellers
agree that throughout civilized Europe, with
the partial exception of England and France,

the profound absorption of the mass of women in household labors renders their general elevation impossible. But with us Americans, and in this age, when all these vast labors are being more and more transferred to arms of brass and iron ; when Rochester grinds the flour and Lowell weaves the cloth, and the fire on the hearth has gone into black retirement and mourning ; when the wiser a virgin is, the less she has to do with oil in her lamp ; when the needle has made its last dying speech and confession in the "Song of the Shirt," and the sewing-machine has changed those doleful marches to delightful measures, — how is it possible for the blindest to help seeing that a new era is begun, and that the time has come for woman to learn the alphabet ?

Nobody asks for any abolition of domestic labor for women, any more than of outdoor labor for men. Of course, most women will still continue to be mainly occupied with the indoor care of their families, and most men with their external support. All that is desirable for either sex is such an economy of labor, in this respect, as shall leave some spare time to be appropriated in other directions. The argument against each new emancipation of woman is precisely that always made against the liberation of serfs and the enfranchisement of plebe-

ians, — that the new position will take them
from their legitimate business. "How can he
[or she] get wisdom that holdeth the plough
[or the broom], — whose talk is of bullocks [or
of babies]?" Yet the American farmer has
already emancipated himself from these fancied
incompatibilities ; and so will the farmer's wife.
In a nation where there is no leisure class and
no peasantry, this whole theory of exclusion is
an absurdity. We all have a little leisure, and
we must all make the most of it. If we will
confine large interests and duties to those who
have nothing else to do, we must go back to
monarchy at once. If otherwise, then the alphabet, and its consequences, must be open to
woman as to man. Jean Paul says nobly, in
his "Levana," that, "before and after being a
mother, a woman is a human being, and neither
maternal nor conjugal relation can supersede
the human responsibility, but must become its
means and instrument." And it is good to
read the manly speech, on this subject, of John
Quincy Adams, quoted at length in Quincy's
life of him, in which, after fully defending the
political petitions of the women of Plymouth,
he declares that "the correct principle is that
women are not only justified, but exhibit the
most exalted virtue, when they do depart from
the domestic circle, and enter on the concerns

of their country, of humanity, and of their
God."

There are duties devolving on every human
being, — duties not small nor few, but vast and
varied, — which spring from home and private
life, and all their sweet relations. The support
or care of the humblest household is a function
worthy of men, women, and angels, so far as it
goes. From these duties none must shrink,
neither man nor woman; the loftiest genius
cannot ignore them; the sublimest charity
must begin with them. They are their own
exceeding great reward; their self-sacrifice is
infinite joy; and the selfishness which discards
them is repaid by loneliness and a desolate old
age. Yet these, though the most tender and
intimate portion of human life, do not form its
whole. It is given to noble souls to crave other
interests also, added spheres, not necessarily
alien from these; larger knowledge, larger action also; duties, responsibilities, anxieties,
dangers, all the aliment that history has given
to its heroes. Not home less, but humanity
more. When the high-born English lady in
the Crimean hospital, ordered to a post of almost
certain death, only raised her hands to heaven,
and said, "Thank God!" she did not renounce
her true position as woman: she claimed it.
When the queen of James I. of Scotland, already

immortalized by him in stately verse, won a
higher immortality by welcoming to her fair
bosom the dagger aimed at his; when the
Countess of Buchan hung confined in her iron
cage, outside Berwick Castle, in penalty for
crowning Robert the Bruce; when the stainless
soul of Joan of Arc met God, like Moses, in a
burning flame, — these things were as they
should be. Man must not monopolize these
privileges of peril, the birthright of great souls.
Serenades and compliments must not replace
the nobler hospitality which shares with woman
the opportunity of martyrdom.   Great administrative duties also, cares of state, for which one
should be born gray-headed, how nobly do these
sit upon a woman's brow! Each year adds to
the storied renown of Elizabeth of England,
greatest sovereign of the greatest of historic
nations.   Christina of Sweden, alone among the
crowned heads of Europe (so says Voltaire),
sustained the dignity of the throne against
Richelieu and Mazarin.   And these queens
most assuredly did not sacrifice their womanhood in the process; for her Britannic Majesty's
wardrobe included four thousand gowns; and
Mlle. de Montpensier declares that when Christina had put on a wig of the latest fashion, "she
really looked extremely pretty."

Les races se féminisent, said Buffon, — "The

world is growing more feminine." It is a compliment, whether the naturalist intended it or not. Time has brought peace; peace, invention; and the poorest woman of to-day is born to an inheritance of which her ancestors never dreamed. Previous attempts to confer on women social and political equality, — as when Leopold, Grand Duke of Tuscany, made them magistrates; or when the Hungarian revolutionists made them voters; or when our own New Jersey tried the same experiment in a guarded fashion in early times, and then revoked the privilege, because (as in the ancient fable) the women voted the wrong way; — these things were premature, and valuable only as recognitions of a principle. But in view of the rapid changes now going on, he is a rash man who asserts the "Woman Question" to be anything but a mere question of time. The fulcrum has been already given in the alphabet, and we must simply watch, and see whether the earth does not move.

There is the plain fact: woman must be either a subject or an equal; there is no middle ground. Every concession to a supposed principle only involves the necessity of the next concession for which that principle calls. Once yield the alphabet, and we abandon the whole long theory of subjection and coverture: tradi-

tion is set aside, and we have nothing but reason
to fall back upon. Reasoning abstractly, it
must be admitted that the argument has been,
thus far, entirely on the women's side, inasmuch
as no man has yet seriously tried to meet them
with argument. It is an alarming feature of
this discussion, that it has reversed, very generally, the traditional positions of the sexes:
the women have had all the logic; and the
most intelligent men, when they have attempted
the other side, have limited themselves to satire
and gossip. What rational woman can be really
convinced by the nonsense which is talked in
ordinary society around her, — as, that it is
right to admit girls to common schools, and
equally right to exclude them from colleges;
that it is proper for a woman to sing in public,
but indelicate for her to speak in public; that a
post-office box is an unexceptionable place to
drop a bit of paper into, but a ballot-box terri-
bly dangerous? No cause in the world can
keep above water, sustained by such contradic-
tions as these, too feeble and slight to be dignified by the name of fallacies. Some persons
profess to think it impossible to reason with a
woman, and such critics certainly show no disposition to try the experiment.

But we must remember that all our American
institutions are based on consistency, or on no-

thing : all claim to be founded on the principles of natural right ; and when they quit those, they are lost.   In all European monarchies it is the theory that the mass of the people are children to be governed, not mature beings to govern themselves ; this is clearly stated and consistently applied.   In the United States we have formally abandoned this theory for one half of the human race, while for the other half it flourishes with little change.   The moment the claims of woman are broached, the democrat becomes a monarchist.   What Americans commonly criticise in English statesmen, namely, that they habitually evade all arguments based on natural right, and defend every legal wrong on the ground that it works well in practice, is the precise defect in our habitual view of woman.   The perplexity must be resolved somehow.   Most men admit that a strict adherence to our own principles would place both sexes in precisely equal positions before law and constitution, as well as in school and society.   But each has his special quibble to apply, showing that in this case we must abandon all the general maxims to which we have pledged ourselves, and hold only by precedent.   Nay, he construes even precedent with the most ingenious rigor ; since the exclusion of women from all direct contact with affairs can be made far

more perfect in a republic than is possible in a
monarchy, where even sex is merged in rank,
and the female patrician may have far more
power than the male plebeian. But, as matters
now stand among us, there is no aristocracy but
of sex : all men are born patrician, all women
are legally plebeian ; all men are equal in having political power, and all women in having
none. This is a paradox so evident, and such
an anomaly in human progress, that it cannot
last forever, without new discoveries in logic,
or else a deliberate return to M. Maréchal's
theory concerning the alphabet.

Meanwhile, as the newspapers say, we anx-
iously await further developments. According
to present appearances, the final adjustment lies
mainly in the hands of women themselves.
Men can hardly be expected to concede either
rights or privileges more rapidly than they are
claimed, or to be truer to women than women
are to each other. In fact, the worst effect of a
condition of inferiority is the weakness it leaves
behind ; even when we say, " Hands off ! " the
sufferer does not rise. In such a case, there is
but one counsel worth giving. More depends
on determination than even on ability. Will,
not talent, governs the world. Who believed
that a poetess could ever be more than an An-
not Lyle of the harp, to soothe with sweet melo-

dies the leisure of her lord, until in Elizabeth
Barrett Browning's hands the thing became a
trumpet? Where are gone the sneers with
which army surgeons and parliamentary orators opposed Mr. Sidney Herbert's first proposition to send Florence Nightingale to the
Crimea? In how many towns was the current
of popular prejudice against female orators
reversed by one winning speech from Lucy
Stone! Where no logic can prevail, success
silences. First give woman, if you dare, the
alphabet, then summon her to her career : and
though men, ignorant and prejudiced, may oppose its beginnings, they will at last fling
around her conquering footsteps more lavish
praises than ever greeted the opera's idol, —
more perfumed flowers than ever wooed, with
intoxicating fragrance, the fairest butterfly of
the ball-room.

II

PHYSIOLOGY

"Allein, bevor und nachdem man Mutter ist, ist Man ein
Mensch ; die mütterliche Bestimmung aber, oder gar die hee-
liche, kann nicht die menschliche überwiegen oder ersetzen,
sondern sie muss das Mittel, nicht der Zweck derselben sein."
—J. P. F. RICHTER : Levana, § 89.

"But, before and after being a mother, one is a human
being; and neither the motherly nor the wifely destination
can overbalance or replace the human, but must become its
means, not its end."

TOO MUCH   Lord Melbourne, speaking of the
NATURAL   fine ladies in London who were
HISTORY
fond of talking about their ailments,
used to complain that they gave him too much
of their natural history. There are a good
many writers — usually men — who, with the
best intentions, discuss woman as if she had
merely a physical organization, and as if she
existed only for one object, the production and
rearing of children. Against this some protest
may well be made.

Doubtless there are few things more important to a community than the health of its
women. The Sandwich Island proverb says :—

"If strong is the frame of the mother,
The son will give laws to the people."

And, in nations where all men give laws, all men need mothers of strong frames.

Moreover, there is no harm in admitting that all the rules of our structure are imperative; that soul and body, whether of man or woman, are made in harmony, so that each part of our nature must accept the limitations of the other. A man's soul may yearn to the stars; but so long as the body cannot jump so high, he must accept the body's veto. It is the same with any veto interposed in advance by the physical structure of woman. Nobody objects to this general principle. It is only when clerical gentlemen or physiological gentlemen undertake to go a step farther, and put in that veto on their own responsibility, that it is necessary to say, "Hands off, gentlemen! Precisely because women are women, they, not you, are to settle that question."

One or two points are clear. Every specialist is liable to overrate his own specialty; and the man who thinks of woman only as a wife and mother is apt to forget, that, before she was either of these, she was a human being. "Women, as such," says an able writer, "are constituted for purposes of maternity and the continuation of mankind." Undoubtedly, and so were men, as such, constituted for paternity. But very much depends on what relative importance we assign to the phrase, "as such." Even an essay so careful, so moderate, and so free from coarseness, as that here quoted, suggests, after all, a slight one-sidedness, — perhaps a natural reaction from the one-sidedness of those injudicious reformers who allow themselves to speak slightingly of "the merely animal function of child-bearing." Higher than either — wiser than both put together — is that noble statement with which Jean Paul begins his fine essay on the education of girls in "Levana." "Before being a wife or mother, one is a human being; and neither motherly nor wifely destination can overbalance or replace the human, but must become its means, not end. As above the poet, the painter, or the hero, so above the mother, does the human being rise preëminent."

Here is sure anchorage. We can hold to this. And, fortunately, all the analogies of nature sustain this position. Throughout nature the laws of sex rule everywhere; but they rule a kingdom of their own, always subordinate to the greater kingdom of the vital functions. Every creature, male or female, finds in its sexual relations only a subordinate part of its existence. The need of food, the need of exercise, the joy of living, these come first, and absorb the bulk of its life, whether the individual be male or female. This *Antiope* butterfly, that flits at this moment past my window, — the first of the season, — spends almost all its existence in a form where the distinction of sex lies dormant : a few days, I might almost say a few hours, comprise its whole sexual consciousness, and the majority of its race die before reaching that epoch. The law of sex is written absolutely through the whole insect world. Yet everywhere it is written as a secondary and subordinate law. The life which is common to the sexes is the principal life ; the life which each sex leads, "as such," is a minor and subordinate thing.

The same rule pervades nature. Two riders pass down the street before my window. One rides a horse, the other a mare. The animals were perhaps foaled in the same stable, of the same progenitors. They have been reared alike, fed alike, trained alike, ridden alike ; they need the same exercise, the same grooming ; nine tenths of their existence are the same, and only the other tenth is different. Their whole organization is marked by the distinction of sex ; but, though the marking is ineffaceable, the distinction is not the first or most important fact.

If this be true of the lower animals, it is far

more true of the higher. The mental and moral laws of the universe touch us first and chiefly as human beings. We eat our breakfasts as human beings, not as men or women; and it is the same with nine tenths of our interests and duties in life. In legislating or philosophizing for woman, we must neither forget that she has an organization distinct from that of man, nor must we exaggerate the fact. Not "first the womanly and then the human," but first the human and then the womanly, is to be the order of her training.

DARWIN, HUXLEY, AND BUCKLE   When any woman, old or young, asks the question, Which among all modern books ought I to read first? the answer is plain. She should read Buckle's lecture before the Royal Institution upon "The Influence of Woman on the Progress of Knowledge." It is one of two papers contained in a thin volume called "Essays by Henry Thomas Buckle." As a means whereby a woman may become convinced that her sex has a place in the intellectual universe, this little essay is almost indispensable. Nothing else quite takes its place.

Darwin and Huxley seem to make woman simply a lesser man, weaker in body and mind, — an affectionate and docile animal, of inferior

grade. That there is any aim in the distinction
of the sexes, beyond the perpetuation of the
race, is nowhere recognized by them, so far as
I know. That there is anything in the intellectual sphere to correspond to the physical
difference ; that here also the sexes are equal
yet diverse, and each the natural completion and
complement of the other, — this neither Huxley
nor Darwin explicitly recognizes. And with
the utmost admiration for their great teachings
in other ways, I must think that here they are
open to the suspicion of narrowness.

Huxley wrote in " The Reader," in 1864, a
short paper called " Emancipation — Black and
White," in which, while taking generous ground
in behalf of the legal and political position of
woman, he yet does it pityingly, *de haut en bas*,
as for a creature hopelessly inferior, and so
heavily weighted already by her sex that she
should be spared all further trials. Speaking
through an imaginary critic, who seems to represent himself, he denies " even the natural equality of the sexes," and declares " that in every
excellent character, whether mental or physical,
the average woman is inferior to the average
man, in the sense of having that character less
in quantity and lower in quality." Finally he
goes so far as " to defend the startling paradox
that even in physical beauty man is the supe-

rior." He admits that for a brief period of early youth the case may be doubtful, but claims that after thirty the superior beauty of man is unquestionable. Thus reasons Huxley; the whole essay being included in his volume of "Lay Sermons, Addresses, and Reviews." [1]

Darwin's best statements on the subject may be found in his "Descent of Man." [2] He is, as usual, more moderate and guarded than Huxley. He says, for instance: "It is generally admitted that with women the powers of intuition, of rapid perception, and perhaps of imitation, are more strongly marked than in man; but some, at least, of these faculties are characteristic of the lower races, and therefore of a past and lower state of civilization." Then he passes to the usual assertion that man has thus far attained to a higher eminence than woman. " If two lists were made of the most eminent men and women in poetry, painting, sculpture, music, — comprising composition and performance, — history, science, and philosophy, with half a dozen names under each subject, the two lists would not bear comparison." But the obvious answer, that nearly every name on his list, upon the masculine side, would probably be taken from periods when woman was excluded from any fair competition, — this he does not seem

[1] Pp. 22, 23, Am. ed.   [2] Vol. ii. p. 311, Am. ed.

to recognize at all. Darwin, of all men, must admit that superior merit generally arrives later, not earlier, on the scene ; and the question for him to answer is, not whether woman equalled man in the first stages of the intellectual "struggle for life," but whether she is not gaining on him now.

If, in spite of man's enormous advantage in the start, woman is already overtaking his very best performances in several of the highest intellectual departments, — as, for instance, prose fiction and dramatic representation, — then it is mere dogmatism in Mr. Darwin to deny that she may yet do the same in other departments. We in this generation have actually seen this success achieved by Rachel and Ristori in the one art, by " George Sand " and " George Eliot " in the other. Woman is, then, visibly gaining on man in the sphere of intellect ; and, if so, Mr. Darwin, at least, must accept the inevitable inference.

But this is arguing the question on the superficial facts merely. Buckle goes deeper, and looks to principles. That superior quickness of women, which Darwin dismisses so lightly as something belonging to savage epochs, is to Buckle the sign of a quality which he holds essential, not only to literature and art, but to science itself. Go among ignorant women, he says, and you will find them more quick and intelligent than equally ignorant men. A woman will usually tell you the way in the street more readily than a man can; a woman can always understand a foreigner more easily; and Dr. Currie says in his letters, that when a laborer and his wife came to consult him, the man always got all the information from the wife. Buckle illustrates this at some length, and points out that a woman's mind is by its nature deductive and quick; a man's mind, inductive and slow; that each has its value, and that science profoundly needs both.

"I will endeavor," he says, "to establish two propositions. First, that women naturally prefer the deductive method to the inductive. Secondly, that women, by encouraging in men deductive habits of thought, have rendered an immense though unconscious service to the progress of science, by preventing scientific investigators from being as exclusively inductive as they would otherwise be."

Then he shows that the most important scientific discoveries of modern times — as of the law of gravitation by Newton, the law of the forms of crystals by Haüy, and the metamorphosis of plants by Goethe — were all essentially the results of that *a priori* or deductive method "which, during the last two centuries,

Englishmen have unwisely despised." They
were all the work, in a manner, of the imagination, — of the intuitive or womanly quality of
mind. And nothing can be finer or truer than
the words in which Buckle predicts the benefits
that are to come from the intellectual union of
the sexes for the work of the future. " In that
field which we and our posterity have yet to
traverse, I firmly believe that the imagination
will effect quite as much as the understanding.
Our poetry will have to reinforce our logic,
and we must feel quite as much as we must
argue. Let us, then, hope that the imaginative
and emotional minds of one sex will continue
to accelerate the great progress by acting upon
and improving the colder and harder minds of
the other sex. By this coalition, by this union
of different faculties, different tastes, and different methods, we shall go on our way with
the greater ease."

THE SPIRIT   When Mr. John Smauker and the
OF SMALL   Bath footmen invited Sam Weller
TYRANNY
to their " swarry," consisting of a
boiled leg of mutton, each guest had some expression of contempt and wrath for the humble
little green-grocer who served them, — " in the
true spirit," Dickens says, " of the very smallest tyranny." The very fact that they were

subject to being ordered about in their own persons gave them a peculiar delight in issuing tyrannical orders to others : just as sophomores in college torment freshmen because other sophomores once teased the present tormentors themselves; and Irishmen denounce the Chinese for underbidding them in the labor market, precisely as they were themselves denounced by native-born Americans thirty years ago. So it has sometimes seemed to me that the men whose own positions and claims are really least commanding are those who hold most resolutely that women should be kept in their proper place of subordination.

A friend of mine maintains the theory that men large and strong in person are constitutionally inclined to do justice to women, as fearing no competition from them in the way of bodily strength ; but that small and weak men are apt to be vehemently opposed to anything like equality in the sexes. He quotes in defence of his theory the big soldier in London who justified himself for allowing his little wife to chastise him, on the ground that it pleased her and did not hurt him ; and on the other hand cites the extreme domestic tyranny of the dwarf Quilp. He declares that in any difficult excursion among woods and mountains, the guides and the able-bodied men are often willing

to have women join the party, while it is sure
to be opposed by those who doubt their own
strength or are reluctant to display their weakness. It is not necessary to go so far as my
friend goes; but many will remember some fact
of this kind, making such theories appear not
quite so absurd as at first.

Thus it seems from the "Life and Letters"
of Sydney Dobell, the English poet, that he
was opposed both to woman suffrage and woman authorship, believing the movement for
the former to be a "blundering on to the perdi-
tion of womanhood." It appears that against
all authorship by women his convictions yearly
grew stronger, he regarding it as "an error and
an anomaly." It seems quite in accordance
with my friend's theory to hear, after this, that
Sydney Dobell was slight in person and a life-
long invalid; nor is it surprising, on the same
theory, that his poetry took no deep root, and
that it will not be likely to survive long, except
perhaps in his weird ballad of "Ravelston."
But he represents a large class of masculine
intellects, of secondary and mediocre quality,
whose opinions on this subject are not so much
opinions as instinctive prejudices against a
competitor who may turn out their superior.
Whether they know it, or not, their aversion to
the authorship of women is very much like the

conviction of a weak pedestrian, that women are not naturally fitted to take long walks; or the opinion of a man whose own accounts are in a muddle, that his wife is constitutionally unfitted to understand business.

It is a pity to praise either sex at the expense of the other. The social inequality of the sexes was not produced so much by the voluntary tyranny of man, as by his great practical advantage at the outset; human history necessarily beginning with a period when physical strength was sole ruler. It is unnecessary, too, to consider in how many cases women may have justified this distrust; and may have made themselves as obnoxious as Horace Walpole's maids of honor, whose coachman left his savings to his son on condition that he should never marry a maid of honor. But it is safe to say that on the whole the feeling of contempt for women, and the love to exercise arbitrary power over them, is the survival of a crude impulse which the world is outgrowing, and which is in general least obvious in the manliest men. That clear and able English writer, Walter Bagehot, well describes "the contempt for physical weakness and for women which marks early society. The non-combatant population is sure to fare ill during the ages of combat. But these defects, too, are cured or lessened; women have now marvellous means of winning their way in the world; and mind without muscle has far greater force than muscle without mind." [1]

THE NOBLE SEX   A highly educated American woman of my acquaintance once employed a French tutor in Paris to assist her in teaching Latin to her little grandson. The Frenchman brought with him a Latin grammar, written in his own language, with which my friend was quite pleased, until she came to a passage relating to the masculine gender in nouns, and claiming grammatical precedence for it on the ground that the male sex is the noble sex, — "*le sexe noble.*" "Upon that," she said, "I burst forth in indignation, and the poor teacher soon retired. But I do not believe," she added, "that the Frenchman has the slightest conception, up to this moment, of what I could find in that phrase to displease me."

I do not suppose he could. From the time when the Salic Law set French women aside from the royal succession, on the ground that the kingdom of France was "too noble to be ruled by a woman," the claim of nobility has been all on one side. The State has strengthened the Church in this theory, the Church

1 *Physics and Politics*, p. 79.

has strengthened the State ; and the result of all is, that French grammarians follow both these high authorities. When even the good Père Hyacinthe teaches, through the New York "Independent," that the husband is to direct the conscience of his wife, precisely as the father directs that of his child, what higher philosophy can you expect of any Frenchman than to maintain the claims of "*le sexe noble*" ?

We see the consequence, even among the most heterodox Frenchmen. Rejecting all other precedents and authorities, the poor Communists still held to this. Consider, for instance, this translation of a marriage contract under the Commune, which lately came to light in a trial reported in the " Gazette des Tribunaux : " —

FRENCH REPUBLIC.

The citizen Anet, son of Jean Louis Anet, and the *citoyenne* Maria Saint ; she engaged to follow the said citizen everywhere and to love him always. — ANET. MARIA SAINT.

Witnessed by the under-mentioned citizen and *citoyenne*. — FOURIER. LAROCHE.

PARIS, April 22, 1871.

What a comfortable arrangement is this ! Poor *citoyenne* Maria Saint, even when all human laws have suspended their action, still holds by her grammar, still must annex herself to *le sexe noble.* She still must follow citizen Anet as the feminine pronoun follows the masculine, or as a verb agrees with its nominative case in number and in person. But with what a lordly freedom from all obligation does citizen Anet, representative of this nobility of sex, accept the allegiance! The citizeness may "follow him," certainly, — so long as she is not in the way, — and she must "love him always ;" but he is not bound. Why should he be? It would be quite ungrammatical.

Yet, after all is said and done, there is a brutal honesty in this frank subordination of the woman according to the grammar. It has the same merit with the old Russian marriage consecration : "Here, wolf, take thy lamb," which at least put the thing clearly, and made no nonsense about it. I do not know that anywhere in France the wedding ritual is now so severely simple as this, but I know that in some French villages the bride is still married in a mourning-gown. I should think she would be.

THE TRUTH ABOUT OUR GRANDMOTHERS   Every young woman of the present generation, so soon as she ventures to have a headache or a set of nerves, is immediately confronted by indignant critics with her grandmother. If the grandmother is living, the fact of her existence is appealed to : if there is only a departed grandmother to remember, the maiden is confronted with a ghost. That ghost is endowed with as many excellences as those with which Miss Betsey Trotwood endowed the niece that never had been born ; and just as David Copperfield was reproached with the virtues of his unborn sister who "would never have run away," so that granddaughter with the headache is reproached with the ghostly perfections of her grandmother, who never had a headache — or, if she had, it is luckily forgotten. It is necessary to ask, sometimes, what was really the truth about our grandmothers ? Were they such models of bodily perfection as is usually claimed ?

If we look at the early colonial days, we are at once met by the fact, that although families were then often larger than is now common, yet this phenomenon was by no means universal, and was balanced by a good many childless homes. Of this any one can satisfy himself by looking over any family history ; and he can also satisfy himself of the fact, — first pointed out, I believe, by Mrs. Dall, — that third and fourth marriages were then obviously and unquestionably more common than now. The inference would seem to be, that there is a little illusion about the health of those days, as there

is about the health of savage races. In both
cases, it is not so much that the average health
is greater under rude social conditions, as that
these conditions kill off the weak, and leave
only the strong. Modern civilized society, on
the other hand, preserves the health of many
men and women — and permits them to marry,
and become parents — who under the severities
of savage life or of pioneer life would have died,
and given way to others.

On this I will not dwell; because these pri-
meval ladies were not strictly our grandmothers,
being farther removed. But of those who were
our grandmothers, — the women of the Revolutionary and post-Revolutionary epochs, — we
happen to have very definite physiological observations recorded; not very flattering, it is
true, but frank and searching. What these
good women are in the imagination of their descendants, we know. Mrs. Stowe describes them
as "the race of strong, hardy, cheerful girls
that used to grow up in country places, and
made the bright, neat New England kitchens of
olden times;" and adds, "This race of women,
pride of olden time, is daily lessening; and in
their stead come the fragile, easily fatigued,
languid girls of a modern age, drilled in book-
learning, ignorant of common things."

What, now, was the testimony of those who

saw our grandmothers in the flesh? As it happens, there were a good many foreigners, generally Frenchmen, who came to visit the new Republic during the presidency of Washington. Let us take, for instance, the testimony of the two following.

The Abbé Robin was a chaplain in Rochambeau's army during the Revolution, and wrote thus in regard to the American ladies in his "Nouveau Voyage dans l'Amérique Septentrionale," published in 1782 : —

"They are tall and well-proportioned ; their features are generally regular ; their complexions are generally fair and without color. . . . At twenty years of age the women have no longer the freshness of youth. At thirty-five or forty they are wrinkled and decrepit. The men are almost as premature."

Again : The Chevalier Louis Félix de Beaujour lived in the United States from 1804 to 1814, as consul-general and *chargé d'affaires ;* and wrote a book, immediately after, which was translated into English under the title, "A Sketch of the United States at the Commencement of the Present Century." In this he thus describes American women : —

"The women have more of that delicate beauty which belongs to their sex, and in general have finer features and more expression in their physi-

ognomy. Their stature is usually tall, and nearly
all are possessed of a light and airy shape, — the
breast high, a fine head, and their color of a daz-
zling whiteness. Let us imagine, under this brillant
form, the most modest demeanor, a chaste and
virginal air, accompanied by those single and un-
affected graces which flow from artless nature, and
we may have an idea of their beauty ; but this
beauty fades and passes in a moment. At the age
of twenty-five their form changes, and at thirty the
whole of their charms have disappeared."

These statements bring out a class of facts,
which, as it seems to me, are singularly ignored
by some of our physiologists. They indicate
that the modification of the American type began early, and was, as a rule, due to causes
antedating the fashions or studies of the present day. Here are our grandmothers and
great-grandmothers as they were actually seen
by the eyes of impartial or even flattering critics.
These critics were not Englishmen, accustomed
to a robust and ruddy type of women, but
Frenchmen, used to a type more like the American. They were not mere hasty travellers ;
for the one lived here ten years, and the other
was stationed for some time at Newport, R. I.,
in a healthy locality, noted in those days for
the beauty of its women. Yet we find it their
verdict upon these grandmothers of nearly a

hundred years ago, that they showed the same delicate beauty, the same slenderness, the same pallor, the same fragility, the same early decline, with which their granddaughters are now reproached.

In some respects, probably, the physical habits of the grandmothers were better : but an examination of their portraits will satisfy any one that they laced more tightly than their descendants, and wore their dresses lower in the neck ; and as for their diet, we have the testimony of another French traveller, Volney, who was in America from 1795 to 1798, that "if a premium were offered for a regimen most destructive to the teeth, the stomach, and the health in general, none could be devised more efficacious for these ends than that in use among this people." And he goes on to give particulars, showing a far worse condition in respect to cookery and diet than now prevails in any decent American society.

We have therefore strong evidence that the essential change in the American type was effected in the last century, not in this. Dr. E. H. Clarke says, "A century does not afford a period long enough for the production of great changes. That length of time could not transform the sturdy German *fräulein* and robust English damsel into the fragile American miss."

And yet it is pretty clear that the first century and a half of our colonial life had done just this for our grandmothers. And, if so, our physiologists ought to conform their theories to the facts.

THE PHY-   I was talking the other day with
SIQUE OF   a New York physician, long retired
AMERICAN
WOMEN   from practice, who after an absence
            of a dozen years in Europe has
returned within a year to this country. He volunteered the remark, that nothing had so impressed him since his return as the improved health of Americans. He said that his wife had been equally struck with it ; and that they had noticed it especially among the inhabitants of cities, among the more cultivated classes, and in particular among women.

It so happened, that within twenty-four hours almost precisely the same remark was made to me by another gentleman of unusually cosmopolitan experience, and past middle age. He further fortified himself by a similar assertion made him by Charles Dickens, in comparing his second visit to this country with his first. In answer to an inquiry as to what points of difference had most impressed him, Dickens said, " Your people, especially the women, look better fed than formerly."

It is possible that in all these cases the witnesses may have been led to exaggerate the original evil, while absent from the country, and so may have felt some undue reaction on their arrival. One of my informants went so far as to express confidence that among his circle of friends in Boston and in London a dinner party of half a dozen Americans would outweigh an English party of the same number. Granting this to be too bold a statement, and granting the unscientific nature of all these assertions, they still indicate a probability of their own truth until refuted by facts on the other side. They are further corroborated by the surprise expressed by Huxley and some other recent Englishmen at finding us a race more substantial than they had supposed.

The truth seems to be, that Nature is endeavoring to take a new departure in the American, and to produce a race more finely organized, more sensitive, more pliable, and of more nervous energy, than the races of Northern Europe; that this change of type involves some risk to health in the process, but promises greater results whenever the new type shall be established. I am confident that there has been within the last half-century a great improvement in the physical habits of the more cultivated classes, at least, in this country, —

better food, better air, better habits as to bath-
ing and exercise. The great increase of athletic
games; the greatly increased proportion of seaside and mountain life in summer; the thicker
shoes and boots of women and little girls, per-
mitting them to go out more freely in all
weathers, — these are among the permanent
gains. The increased habit of dining late, and
of taking only a lunch at noon, is of itself an
enormous gain to the professional and mercantile classes, because it secures time for eating
and for digestion. Even the furnaces in houses,
which seemed at first so destructive to the very
breath of life, turn out to have given a new
lease to it; and open fires are being rapidly
reintroduced as a provision for enjoyment and
health, when the main body of the house has
been tempered by the furnace. There has
been, furthermore, a decided improvement in
the bread of the community, and a very general introduction of other farinaceous food. All
this has happened within my own memory, and
gives *a priori* probability to the alleged improvement in physical condition within twenty
years.

And, if these reasonings are still insufficient
on the one side, it must be remembered that
the facts of the census are almost equally in-
adequate when quoted on the other. If, for

instance, all the young people of a New Hampshire village take a fancy to remove to Wisconsin, it does not show that the race is dying out because their children swell the birth-rate of Wisconsin instead of New Hampshire. If in a given city the births among the foreign-born population are twice as many in proportion as among the American, we have not the whole story until we learn whether the deaths are not twice as many also. If so, the inference is that the same recklessness brought the children into the world and sent them out of it; and no physiological inference whatever can be drawn. It was clearly established by the medical commission of the Boston Board of Health, a few years ago, that "the general mortality of the foreign element is much greater than that of the native element of our population." "This is found to be the case," they add, "throughout the United States as well as in Boston."

So far as I can judge, all our physiological tendencies are favorable rather than otherwise: and the transplantation of the English race seems now likely to end in no deterioration, but in a type more finely organized, and more comprehensive and cosmopolitan; and this without loss of health, of longevity, or of physical size and weight. And, if this is to hold

true, it must be true not only of men, but of
women.

THE LIMI-   Are there any inevitable limita-
TATIONS   tions of sex?
OF SEX
     Some reformers, apparently, think
that there are not, and that the best way to help
woman is to deny the fact of limitations.   But
I think the great majority of reformers would
take a different ground, and would say that the
two sexes are mutually limited by nature. They
would doubtless add that this very fact is an
argument for the enfranchisement of woman:
for, if woman is a mere duplicate of man, man
can represent her; but if she has traits of her
own, absolutely distinct from his, then he cannot represent her, and she should have a voice
and a vote of her own.

     To this last body of believers I belong.   I
think that all legal or conventional obstacles
should be removed, which debar woman from
determining for herself, as freely as man deter-
mines, what the real limitations of sex are, and
what restrictions are merely conventional. But,
when all is said and done, there is no doubt
that plenty of limitations will remain on both
sides.

     That man has such limitations is clear.   No
matter how finely organized he may be, how

sympathetic, how tender, how loving, there is yet a barrier, never to be passed, that separates him from the most precious part of the woman's kingdom. All the wondrous world of mother-hood, with its unspeakable delights, its holy of holies, remains forever unknown by him ; he may gaze, but never enter. That halo of pure devotion, which makes a Madonna out of so many a poor and ignorant woman, can never touch his brow. Many a man loves children more than many a woman : but, after all, it is not he who has borne them ; to that peculiar sacredness of experience he can never arrive. But never mind whether the loss be a great one or a small one : it is distinctly a limitation ; and to every loving mother it is a limitation so important that she would be unable to weigh all the privileges and powers of manhood against this peculiar possession of her child.

Now, if this be true, and if man be thus dis-tinctly limited by the mere fact of sex, can the woman complain that she also should have some natural limitations? Grant that she should have no unnecessary restrictions ; and that the course of human progress is constantly setting aside, as unnecessary, point after point that was once held essential. Still, if she finds — as she undoubtedly will find — that some natural barriers and hindrances remain at last, and that she can no more do man's whole work in the world than he can do hers, why should she complain? If he can accept his limitations, she must be prepared also to accept hers.

Some of our physiological reformers declare that a girl will be perfectly healthy if she can only be sensibly dressed, and can "have just as much outdoor exercise as the boys, and of the same sort, if she choose it." But I have observed that matter a good deal, and have watched the effect of boyish exercise on a good many girls; and I am satisfied that so far from being safely turned loose, as boys can be, they need, for physical health, the constant supervision of wise mothers. Otherwise the very exposure that only hardens the boy may make the girl an invalid for life. The danger comes from a greater sensitiveness of structure, — not weakness, properly so called, since it gives, in certain ways, more power of endurance, — a greater sensitiveness which runs through all a woman's career, and is the expensive price she pays for the divine destiny of motherhood. It is another natural limitation.

No wise person believes in any "reform against Nature," or that we can get beyond the laws of Nature. If I believed the limitations of sex to be inconsistent with woman suffrage for instance, I should oppose it; but I do

not see why a woman cannot form political
opinions by her baby's cradle, as well as her
husband in his workshop, while her very love
for the child commits her to an interest in good
government. Our duty is to remove all the
artificial restrictions we can. That done, it will
not be hard for man or woman to acquiesce in
the natural limitations.

III

TEMPERAMENT

Ἀνδρὸς καὶ γυναικὸς ἡ αὐτὴ ἀρετή. — ANTISTHENES in Diogenes Laertius, vi. 1, 5.

"Virtue in man and woman is the same."

THE INVISI- The Invisible Lady, as advertised
BLE LADY in all our cities a good many years
ago, was a mysterious individual who remained
unseen, and had apparently no human organs
except a brain and a tongue. You asked questions of her, and she made intelligent answers;
but where she was, you could no more discover
than you could find the man inside the Automaton Chess-Player. Was she intended as a
satire on womankind, or as a sincere representation of what womankind should be? To many
men, doubtless, she would have seemed the
ideal of her sex, could only her brain and tongue
have disappeared like the rest of her faculties.
Such men would have liked her almost as well
as that other mysterious personage on the London signboard, labelled "The Good Woman,"

and represented by a female figure without a
head.

It is not that any considerable portion of
mankind actually wishes to abolish woman from
the universe. But the opinion dies hard that
she is best off when least visible. These appeals which still meet us for "the sacred pri-
vacy of woman" are only the Invisible Lady on
a larger scale. In ancient Bœotia, brides were
carried home in vehicles whose wheels were
burned at the door in token that they would
never again be needed. In ancient Rome, it
was a queen's epitaph, "She stayed at home,
and spun," — *Domum servavit, lanam fecit.* In
Turkey, not even the officers of justice can
enter the apartments of a woman without her
lord's consent. In Spain and Spanish America,
the veil replaces the four walls of the house,
and is a portable seclusion. To be visible is at
best a sign of peasant blood and occupations ;
to be high-bred is to be invisible.

In the Azores I found that each peasant
family endeavored to secure for one or more
of its daughters the pride and glory of living
unseen. The other sisters, secure in innocence,
tended cattle on lonely mountain-sides, or toiled
bare-legged up the steep ascents, their heads
crowned with orange-baskets. The chosen sister was taught to read, to embroider, and to

dwell indoors ; if she went out it was only under escort, and with her face buried in a hood of almost incredible size, affording only a glimpse of the poor pale cheeks, quite unlike the rosy vigor of the damsels on the mountain-side. The girls, I was told, did not covet this privilege of seclusion ; but let us be genteel, or die.

Now all that is left of the Invisible Lady among ourselves is only the remnant of this absurd tradition. In the seaside town where I write, ladies of fashion usually go veiled in the streets, and so general is the practice that little girls often veil their dolls. They all suppose it to be done for complexion or for ornament ; just as people still hang straps on the backs of their carriages, not knowing that it is a relic of the days when footmen stood there and held on. But the veil represents a tradition of seclusion, whether we know it or not ; and the dread of hearing a woman speak in public, or of seeing a woman vote, represents precisely the same tradition. It is entitled to no less respect, and no more.

Like all traditions, it finds something in human nature to which to attach itself. Early girlhood, like early boyhood, needs to be guarded and sheltered, that it may mature unharmed. It is monstrous to make this an excuse for keeping a woman, any more than a man, in a condition of perpetual subordination and seclusion. The young lover wishes to lock up his angel in a little world of her own, where none may intrude. The harem and the seraglio are simply the embodiment of this desire. But the maturer man and the maturer race have found that the beloved being should be something more.

After this discovery is made, the theory of the Invisible Lady disappears. It is less of a shock for an American to hear a woman speak in public than it is for an Oriental to see her show her face in public at all. Once open the door of the harem, and she has the freedom of the house : the house includes the front door, and the street is but a prolonged doorstep. With the freedom of the street comes inevitably a free access to the platform, the tribunal, and the pulpit. You might as well try to stop the air in its escape from a punctured balloon, as to try, when woman is once out of the harem, to put her back there. Ceasing to be an Invisible Lady, she must become a visible force : there is no middle ground. There is no danger that she will not be anchored to the cradle, when cradle there is ; but it will be by an elastic cable, that will leave her as free to think and vote as to pray. No woman is less a mother because she cares for all the concerns

of the world into which her child is born. It
was John Quincy Adams who said, defending
the political petitions of the women of Plymouth, that "women are not only justified, but
exhibit the most exalted virtue, when they do
depart from the domestic circle, and enter on
the concerns of their country, of humanity, and
of their God."

SACRED   In the preface to that ill-named
OBSCURITY but delightful book, the "Remains
of the late Mrs. Richard Trench," there is a
singular remark by the editor, her son. He says
that "the adage is certainly true in regard to
the British matron, *Bene vixit quæ bene latuit*,"
the meaning of this phrase being, "She has
lived well who has kept herself well out of
sight." Applying this to his beloved mother,
he further expresses a regret at disturbing her
"sacred obscurity." Then he goes on to dis-
turb it pretty effectually by printing a thick
octavo volume of her most private letters.

It is a great source of strength and advantage to reformers, that there are always men
preserved to be living examples of this good
old Oriental doctrine of "sacred obscurity."
Just as Mr. Darwin needs for the demonstration of his theory that the lower orders of creation should still be present in visible form

for purposes of comparison, so every reformer needs to fortify his position by showing examples of the original attitude from which society has been gradually emerging. If there had been no Oriental seclusion, many things in the present position of woman would be inexplicable. But when we point to that ; when we show that even in the more enlightened Eastern countries it is still held indecorous to allude to the feminine members of a man's family ; when we see among the Christian nations of Southern Europe many lingering traits of this same habit of seclusion ; and when we find an archdeacon of the English Church still clinging to the theory, even while exhibiting his mother's family letters to the whole world, — we more easily understand the course of development.

These reassertions of the Oriental theory are simply reversions, as a naturalist would say, to the original type. They are instances of "atavism," like the occasional appearance of six fingers on one hand in a family where the great-great-grandfather happened to possess that ornament. Such instances can always be found, when one takes the pains to look for them. Thus a critic, discussing in the "Atlantic Monthly " Mr. Mahaffy's book on " Social Life in Greece," is surprised that this writer should quote, in proof of the degradation of woman in Athens, the remark attributed to Pericles, "That woman is best who is least spoken of among men, whether for good or for evil." "In our opinion," adds the reviewer, "that remark was wise then, and is wise now." The Oriental theory is not then, it seems, extinct ; and we are spared the pains of proving that it ever existed.

If this theory be true, how falsely has the admiration of mankind been given! If the most obscure woman is best, the most conspicuous must undoubtedly be worst. Tried by this standard, how unworthy must have been Elizabeth Barrett Browning, how reprehensible must be Dorothea Dix, what a model of all that is discreditable is Rosa Bonheur, what a crowning instance of human depravity is Florence Nightingale ! Yet how consoling the thought, that, while these disreputable persons were thus wasting their substance in the riotous performance of what the world weakly styled good deeds, there were always women who saw the folly of such efforts ; women who by steady devotion to eating, drinking, and sleeping continued to keep themselves in sacred obscurity, and to prove themselves the ornaments of their sex, inasmuch as no human being ever had occasion to mention their names !

But alas for human inconsistency ! As for

this inverse-ratio theory, — this theory of virtue so exalted that it has never been known or felt or mentioned among men, — it is to be observed that those who hold it are the first to desert it when stirred by an immediate occasion. Just as a slaveholder, in the old times, after demonstrating to you that freedom was a curse to the negro, would instantly turn round, and inflict this greatest of all curses on some slave who had saved his life; so, I fear, would one of these philosophers, if he were profoundly impressed with any great action done by a woman, give the lie to all his theories, and celebrate her fame. In spite of all his fine principles, if he happened to be rescued from drowning by Grace Darling, he would put her name in the newspaper; if he were tended in hospital by Clara Barton, he would sound her praise; and if his mother wrote as good letters as did Mrs. Trench, he would probably print them to the extent of five hundred pages, as the archdeacon did, and all his gospel of silence would exhale itself in a single sigh of regret in the preface.

VIRTUES IN COMMON   A young friend of mine, who was educated at one of the very best schools for girls in New York city, told me that one day her teacher requested the older girls

to write out a list of virtues suitable to manly
character, which they did. A month or more
later, when this occurrence was well forgotten,
the same teacher bade them write out a list of
womanly virtues, she making no reference to
the other list. Then she made each girl compare her lists ; and they all found with surprise
that there was no substantial difference between
them. The only variation, in most cases, was,
that they had put in a rather vague special virtue of "manliness" in the one case, and "womanliness" in the other ; a sort of miscellaneous
department or "odd drawer," apparently, in
which to group all traits not easily analyzed.

The moral is that, as tested by the common
sense of these young people, duty is duty, and
the difference between ethics for men and ethics
for women lies simply in practical applications,
not in principles.

Who can deny that the philosopher Antisthenes was right when he said, "The virtues of
the man and the woman are the same"? Not
the Christian, certainly ; for he accepts as his
highest standard the being who in all history
best united the highest qualities of both sexes.
Not the metaphysician ; for his analysis deals
with the human mind as such, not with the
mind of either sex. Not the evolutionist ; for
he is accustomed to trace back qualities to their

source, and cannot deny that there is in each
sex at least a "survival" of every good and
every bad trait. We may say that these qualities are, or may be, or ought to be, distributed
unequally between the sexes; but we cannot
reasonably deny that each sex possesses a share
of every quality, and that what is good in one
sex is also good in the other. Man may be the
braver, and yet courage in a woman may be
nobler than cowardice. Woman may be the
purer, and yet purity may be noble in a man.

So clear is this, that some of the very coarsest
writers in all literature, and those who have
been severest upon women, have yet been
obliged to acknowledge it. Take, for instance,
Dean Swift, who writes : —

" I am ignorant of any one quality that is amiable in a woman, which is not equally so in a man.
I do not except even modesty and gentleness of
nature; nor do I know one vice or folly which is
not equally detestable in both."

Mrs. Jameson, in her delightful " Commonplace Book," illustrates this admirably by one
or two test cases. She takes, for instance, from
one of Humboldt's letters a much-admired passage on manly character : —

" Masculine independence of mind I hold to be
in reality the first requisite for the formation of a

character of real manly worth. The man who allows himself to be deceived and carried away by his own weakness may be a very amiable person in other respects, but cannot be called a good man : such beings should not find favor in the eyes of a woman, for a truly beautiful and purely feminine nature should be attracted only by what is highest and noblest in the character of man."

"Take now this same bit of moral philosophy," she says, "and apply it to the feminine character, and it reads quite as well : —

"'Feminine independence of mind I hold to be in reality the first requisite for the formation of a character of real feminine worth. The woman who allows herself to be deceived and carried away by her own weakness may be a very amiable person in other respects, but cannot be called a good woman ; such beings should not find favor in the eyes of a man, for a truly beautiful and purely manly nature should be attracted only by what is highest and noblest in the character of woman.'"

I have never been able to perceive that there was a quality or grace of character which really belonged exclusively to either sex, or which failed to win honor when wisely exercised by either. It is not thought necessary to have separate editions of books on ethical science, the one for man, the other for woman, like almanacs calculated for different latitudes. The

books that vary are not the scientific works,
but little manuals of practical application, —
"Duties of Men," "Duties of Women." These
vary with times and places : where women do
not know how to read, no advice on reading
will be found in the women's manuals ; where
it is held wrong for women to uncover the face,
it will be laid down in these manuals as a sin.
But ethics are ethics : the great principles of
morals, as proclaimed either by science or by
religion, do not fluctuate for sex ; their basis is
in the very foundations of right itself.

This grows clearer when we remember that
it is equally true in mental science. There is
not one logic for men, and another for women ;
a separate syllogism, a separate induction : the
moment we begin to state intellectual principles, that moment we go beyond sex. We deal
then with absolute truth. If an observation is
wrong, if a process of reasoning is bad, it makes
no difference who brings it forward. Any list
of mental processes, any inventory of the con-
tents of the mind, would be identical, so far as
sex goes, whether compiled by a woman or a
man. These things, like the circulation of the
blood or the digestion of food, belong clearly to
the ground held in common. The London
"Spectator" well said some time since, —

"After all, knowledge is knowledge ; and there

is no more a specifically feminine way of describing
correctly the origin of the Lollard movement, or
the character of Spenser's poetry, than there is a
specifically feminine way of solving a quadratic
equation, or of proving the forty-seventh problem
of Euclid's first book."

All we can say in modification of this is, that
there is, after all, a foundation for the rather
vague item of "manliness" and "womanliness"
in these schoolgirl lists of duties. There is a
difference, after all is said and done; but it is
something that eludes analysis, like the differing perfume of two flowers of the same genus
and even of the same species. The method of
thought must be essentially the same in both
sexes; and yet an average woman will put more
flavor of something we call instinct into her
mental action, and the average man something
more of what we call logic into his. Whipple
tells us that not a man guessed the plot of
Dickens's "Great Expectations," while many
women did; and this certainly indicates some
average difference of quality or method. So
the average opinions of a hundred women, on
some question of ethics, might very probably
differ from the average of a hundred men, while
it yet remains true that "the virtues of the man
and the woman are the same."

INDIVIDUAL Blackburn, in his entertaining
DIFFER- book, "Artists and Arabs," draws
ENCES
a contrast between Frith's painting
of the "Derby Day" and Rosa Bonheur's
"Horse Fair,"—"the former pleasing the eye
by its cleverness and prettiness, the latter im-
pressing the spectator by its power and its
truthful rendering of animal life. The difference between the two painters is probably more
one of education than of natural gifts. But
whilst the style of the former is grafted on a
fashion, the latter is founded on a rock, — the
result of a close study of nature, chastened by
classic feeling and a remembrance, it may be,
of the friezes of the Parthenon."

Now it is to be observed that this description
runs precisely counter to the popular impression
as to the work of the two sexes. Novelists like
Charles Reade, for instance, who have apparently seen precisely one woman in their lives,
and hardly more than one man, and who keep
on sketching these two figures most felicitously
and brilliantly thenceforward, would be apt to
assign these qualities of the artist very differ-
ently. Their typical man would do the truthful and powerful work, and everybody would
say, "How manly!" Their woman would please
by cleverness and prettiness, and everybody
would say, "How womanly!" Yet Blackburn

shows us that these qualities are individual, not sexual; that they result from temperament, or, he thinks, still more from training. If Rosa Bonheur does better work than Frith, it is not because she is a woman, nor is it in spite of that ; but because, setting sex aside, she is a better artist.

This is not denying the distinctions of sex, but only asserting that they are not so exclusive and all-absorbing as is supposed. It is easy to name other grounds of difference which entirely ignore those of sex, striking directly across them, and rendering a different classification necessary. It is thus with distinctions of race or color, for instance. An Indian man and woman are at many points more like to each other than is either to a white person of the same sex. A black-haired man and woman, or a fair-haired man and woman, are to be classified together in these physiological aspects. So of differences of genius : a man and woman of musical temperament and training have more in common than has either with a person who is of the same sex, but who cannot tell one note from another. So two persons of ardent or imaginative temperament are thus far alike, though the gulf of sex divides them ; and so are two persons of cold or prosaic temperament. In a mixed school the teacher cannot class together intel-

lectually the boys as such, and the girls as such:
bright boys take hold of a lesson very much as
bright girls do, and slow girls as slow boys.
Nature is too rich, too full, too varied, to be
content with a single basis of classification: she
has a hundred systems of grouping, according
to sex, age, race, temperament, training, and so
on; and we get but a narrow view of life when
we limit our theories to one set of distinctions.

As a matter of social philosophy, this train
of thought logically leads to coeducation, impartial suffrage, and free coöperation in all the
affairs of life. As a matter of individual duty,
it teaches the old moral to "act well your part."
No wise person will ever trouble himself or
herself much about the limitations of sex in intellectual labor. Rosa Bonheur was not trying
to work like a woman, or like a man, or unlike
either, but to do her work thoroughly and well.
He or she who works in this spirit works nobly,
and gives an example which will pass beyond
the bounds of sex, and help all. The Abbé
Liszt, the most gifted of modern pianists, told a
friend of mine, his pupil, that he had learned
more of music from hearing Madame Malibran
sing, than from anything else whatever.

ANGELIC SUPERIORITY   It is better not to base any plea for woman on the ground of her angelic superiority. The argument proves too much. If she is already so perfect, there is every inducement to let well alone. It suggests the expediency of conforming man's condition to hers, instead of conforming hers to man's. If she is a winged creature, and man can only crawl, it is his condition that needs mending.

Besides, one may well be a little incredulous of these vast claims. Granting some average advantage to woman, it is not of such completeness as to base much argument upon it. The minister, looking on his congregation, rarely sees an unmixed angel, either at the head or at the foot of any pew. The domestic servant rarely has the felicity of waiting on an absolute saint at either end of the dinner-table. The lady's-maid has to compare her little observations of human infirmity with those of the valet de chambre. The lover worships the beloved, whether man or woman; but marriage bears rather hard on the ideal in either case; and those who pray out of the same book, "Have mercy upon us, miserable sinners," are not supposed to be offering up petitions for each other only.

We all know many women whose lives are

made wretched by the sins and follies of their husbands. There are also many men whose lives are turned to long wretchedness by the selfishness, the worldliness, or the bad temper of their wives. Domestic tyranny belongs to neither sex by monopoly. If man tortures or depresses woman, she also has a fearful power to corrupt and deprave man. On the other hand, to quote old Antisthenes once more, "the virtues of the man and woman are the same." A refined man is more refined than a coarse woman. A child-loving man is infinitely tenderer and sweeter toward children than a hard and unsympathetic woman. The very qualities that are claimed as distinctively feminine are possessed more abundantly by many men than by many of what is called the softer sex.

Why is it necessary to say all this? Because there is always danger that we who believe in the equality of the sexes should be led into over-statements, which will react against ourselves. It is not safe to say that the ballot-box would be reformed if intrusted to feminine votes alone. Had the voters of the South been all women, it would have plunged earlier into the gulf of secession, dived deeper, and come up even more reluctantly. Were the women of Spain to rule its destinies unchecked, the Pope

would be its master, and the Inquisition might
be reëstablished. For all that we can see, the
rule of women alone would be as bad as the
rule of men alone. It would be as unsafe to
give women the absolute control of man as to
make man the master of woman.

Let us be a shade more cautious in our reasonings. Woman needs equal rights, not because she is man's better half, but because she
is his other half. She needs them, not as an
angel, but as a fraction of humanity. Her political education will not merely help man, but
it will help herself. She will sometimes be
right in her opinions, and sometimes be altogether wrong; but she will learn, as man learns,
by her own blunders. The demand in her behalf is that she shall have the opportunity to
make mistakes, since it is by that means she
must become wise.

In all our towns there is a tendency toward
"mixed schools." We rarely hear of the sexes
being separated in a school after being once
united; but we constantly hear of their being
brought together after separation. This union is
commonly, but mistakenly, recommended as an
advantage to the boys alone. I once heard an
accomplished teacher remonstrate against this
change, when thus urged. "Why should my
girls be sacrificed," she said, "to improve your

boys ?" Six months after, she had learned by
experience. "Why," she asked, "did you rest
the argument on so narrow a ground? Since
my school consisted half of boys, I find with
surprise that the change has improved both
sexes. My girls are more ambitious, more obe-
dient, and more ladylike. I shall never distrust
the policy of mixed schools again."

What is true of the school is true of the
family and of the state. It is not good for
man, or for woman, to be alone. Granting the
woman to be, on the whole, the more spiritually
minded, it is still true that each sex needs the
other. When the rivet falls from a pair of scis-
sors, we do not have them mended because
either half can claim angelic superiority over
the other half, but because it takes two halves
to make a whole.

VICARIOUS   There is a story in circulation —
HONORS   possibly without authority — to the
effect that a certain young lady has ascended
so many Alps that she would have been chosen
a member of the English Alpine Club but for
her misfortune in respect to sex. As a matter
of personal recognition, however, and, as it
were, of approximate courtesy, her dog, who
has accompanied her in all her trips, and is not
debased by sex, has been elected into the club.

She has therefore an opportunity for exercising in behalf of her dog that beautiful self-abnegation which is said to be a part of woman's nature, impelling her always to prefer that her laurels should be worn by somebody else.

The dog probably made no objection to these vicarious honors ; nor is any objection made by the young gentlemen who reply eloquently to the toast, " The Ladies," at public dinners, or who kindly consent to be educated at masculine colleges on "scholarships" perhaps founded by women. Those who receive the emoluments of these funds must reflect within themselves, occasionally, how grand a thing is this power of substitution given to women, and how pleasant are its occasional results to the substitute. It is doubtless more blessed to give than to receive, but to receive without giving has also its pleasures. Very likely the holder of the scholarship, and the orator who rises with his hand on his heart to "reply in behalf of the ladies," may do their appointed work well ; and so did the Alpine dog. Yet, after all, but for the work done by his mistress, the dog would have won no more honor from the Alpine Club than if he had been a chamois.

Nothing since Artemus Ward and his wife's relations has been finer than the generous way in which fathers and brothers disclaim all desire

for profits or honors on the part of their feminine relatives. In a certain system of schools
once known to me, the boys had prizes of
money on certain occasions, but the successful
girls at those times received simply a testimo-
nial of honor for each; "the committee being
convinced," it was said, "that this was more
consonant with the true delicacy and generosity
of woman's nature." So in the new arrangements for opening the University of Copenhagen to young women, Karl Blind writes to
the New York "Evening Post," that it is ex-
pressly provided that they shall not "share in
the academic benefices and stipends which have
been set apart for male students." Half of
these charities may, for aught that appears,
have been established originally by women, like
the American scholarships already mentioned.
Women, however, can avail themselves of them
only by deputy, as the Alp-climbing young lady
is represented by her dog.

It is all a beautiful tribute to the disinterestedness of woman. The only pity is that this
virtue, so much admired, should not be recipro-
cated by showing the like disinterestedness toward her. It does not appear that the butchers
and bakers of Copenhagen propose to reduce
in the case of women students "the benefices
and stipends" which are to be paid for daily

food. Young ladies at the university are only prohibited from receiving money, not from needing it. Nor will any of the necessary fatigues of Alpine climbing be relaxed for any young lady because she is a woman. The fatigues will remain in full force, though the laurels be denied. The mountain-passes will make small account of the "tenderness and delicacy of her sex." When the toil is over she will be regarded as too delicate to be thanked for it ; but, by way of compensation, the Alpine Club will allow her to be represented by her dog.

THE GOS-   "The silliest man who ever lived,"
PEL OF HU- wrote Fanny Fern once, "has al-
MILIATION
            ways known enough, when he says
his prayers, to thank God he was not born a woman." President —— of —— College is not a silly man at all, and he is devoting his life to the education of women ; yet he seems to feel as vividly conscious of his superior position as even Fanny Fern could wish. If he had been born a Jew, he would have thanked God, in the appointed ritual, for not having made him a woman. If he had been a Mohammedan, he would have accepted the rule which forbids "a fool, a madman, or a woman" to summon the faithful to prayer. Being a Christian clergyman,

with several hundred immortal souls, clothed in female bodies, under his charge, he thinks it his duty, at proper intervals, to notify his young ladies, that, though they may share with men the glory of being sophomores, they still are in a position, as regards the other sex, of hopeless subordination. This is the climax of his discourse, which in its earlier portions contains many good and truthful things : —

"And, as the woman is different from the man, so is she relative to him. This is true on the other side also. They are bound together by mutual relationship so intimate and vital that the existence of neither is absolutely complete except with reference to the other. But there is this difference, that the relation of woman is, characteristically, that of subordination and dependence. This does not imply inferiority of character, of capacity, of value, in the sight of God or man; and it has been the glory of woman to have accepted the position of formal inferiority assigned her by the Creator, with all its responsibilities, its trials, its possible outward humiliations and sufferings, in the proud consciousness that it is not incompatible with an essential superiority; that it does not prevent her from occupying, if she will, an inward elevation of character, from which she may look down with pitying and helpful love on him she calls her lord. Jesus said, 'Ye know that the princes of the Gentiles exercise dominion over them, and they that are

great exercise authority upon them. But it shall
not be so among you ; but whosoever will be great
among you, let him be your minister ; and whosoever will be chief among you, let him be your servant, even as the Son of man came, not to be min-
istered unto, but to minister, and to give his life a
ransom for many.' Surely woman need not hesitate
to estimate her status by a criterion of dignity
sustained by such authority. She need not shrink
from a position which was sought by the Son of
God, and in whose trials and griefs she will have his
sympathy and companionship."

There is a comforting aspect to this discourse,
after all. It holds out the hope, that a particu-
larly noble woman may not be personally inferior to a remarkably bad husband, but " may
look down with pitying and helpful love on him
she calls her lord." The drawback is not
only that it insults woman by a reassertion of
a merely historical inferiority, which is steadily
diminishing, but that it fortifies this by precisely the same talk about the dignity of subordination which has been used to buttress
every oppression since the world began. Never
yet was there a pious slaveholder who did not
quote to his slaves, on Sunday, precisely the
same texts with which President —— favors
his meek young pupils. Never yet was there a
slaveholder who would not shoot through the

head anybody who should attempt to place
him in that beautiful position of subjection
whose spiritual merits he had just been proclaiming. When it came to that, he was like
Thoreau, who believed resignation to be a virtue, but preferred "not to practice it unless it
was quite necessary."

Thus, when the Rev. Charles C. Jones of
Savannah used to address the slaves on their
condition, he proclaimed the beauty of obedience
in a way to bring tears to their eyes. And this,
he frankly assures the masters, is the way to
check insurrection and advance their own "pe-
cuniary interests." He says of the slave, that
under proper religious instruction "his conscience is enlightened and his soul is awed;
. . . to God he commits the ordering of his lot,
and in his station renders to all their dues,
obedience to whom obedience, and honor to
whom honor. *He dares not wrest from God his
own care and protection.* While he sees a preference in the various conditions of men, he re-
members the words of the apostle : 'Art thou
called being a servant? care not for it; but if
thou mayest be free, use it rather. For he that is
called in the Lord, being a servant, is the Lord's
freeman : likewise also he that is called, being
free, is Christ's servant.' "[1]

[1] *Religious Instruction of the Negroes.* Savannah, 1842,
pp. 208–211.

I must say that the Rev. Mr. Jones's preaching seems to me precisely as good as Dr. ——'s, and that a sensible woman ought to be as much influenced by the one as was Frederick Douglass by the other — that is, not at all. Let the preacher try "subordination" himself, and see how he likes it. The beauty of service, such as Jesus praised, lay in the willingness of the service: a service that is serfdom loses all beauty, whether rendered by man or by woman. My objection to separate schools and colleges for women is that they are too apt to end in such instructions as this.

CELERY AND CHERUBS   There was once a real or imaginary old lady who had got the metaphor of Scylla and Charybdis a little confused. Wishing to describe a perplexing situation, this lady said, —

"You see, my dear, she was between Celery on one side and Cherubs on the other! You know about Celery and Cherubs, don't you? They was two rocks somewhere; and if you did n't hit one, you was pretty sure to run smack on the other."

This describes, as a clever writer in the New York "Tribune" declares, the present condition of women who "agitate." Their Celery and Cherubs are tears and temper.

It is a good hit, and we may well make a note of it. It is the danger of all reformers, that they will vibrate between discouragement and anger. When things go wrong, what is it one's impulse to do? To be cast down, or to be stirred up; to wring one's hands, or clench one's fists, — in short, tears or temper.

"Mother," said a resolute little girl of my acquaintance, "if the dinner was all spoiled, I would n't sit down, and cry! I 'd say, 'Hang it!'" This cherub preferred the alternative of temper, on days when the celery turned out badly. Probably her mother was addicted to the other practice, and exhibited the tears.

But as this alternative is found to exist for both sexes, and on all occasions, why charge it especially on the woman-suffrage movement? Men are certainly as much given to ill temper as women; and, if they are less inclined to tears, they make it up in sulks, which are just as bad. Nicholas Nickleby, when the pump was frozen, was advised by Mr. Squeers to "content himself with a dry polish;" and so there is a kind of dry despair into which men fall, which is quite as forlorn as any tears of women. How many a man has doubtless wished at such times that the pump of his lachrymal glands could only thaw out, and he could give his emotions something more than a "dry polish"! The unspeakable comfort some women feel in sitting for ten minutes with a handkerchief over their eyes! The freshness, the heartiness, the new life visible in them, when the crying is done, and the handkerchief comes down again!

And, indeed, this simple statement brings us to the real truth, which should have been more clearly seen by the writer who tells this story. She is wrong in saying, "It is urged that men and women stand on an equality, are exactly alike." Many of us urge the "equality:" very few of us urge the "exactly alike." An apple and an orange, a potato and a tomato, a rose and a lily, the Episcopal and the Presbyterian churches, Oxford and Cambridge, Yale and Harvard, — we may surely grant equality in each case, without being so exceedingly foolish as to go on and say that they are exactly alike.

And precisely here is the weak point of the whole case, as presented by this writer. Women give way to tears more readily than men? Granted. Is their sex any the weaker for it? Not a bit. It is simply a difference of temperament: that is all. It involves no inferiority. If you think that this habit necessarily means weakness, wait and see! Who has not seen women break down in tears during some domestic calamity, while the "stronger sex" were

calm; and who has not seen those same women, that temporary excitement being over,
rise up and dry their eyes, and be thenceforth
the support and stay of their households, and
perhaps bear up the "stronger sex" as a stream
bears up a ship? I said once to an experienced
physician, watching such a woman, "That woman is really great." — "Of course she is," he
answered; "did you ever see a woman who was
not great, when the emergency required?"

Now, will women carry this same quality of
temperament into their public career? Doubtless: otherwise they would cease to be women.
Will it be betraying confidence if I own that I
have seen two of the very bravest women of
my acquaintance — women who have swayed
great audiences — burst into tears, during a
committee meeting, at a moment of unexpected
adversity for "the cause"? How pitiable! our
critical observers would have thought. In five
minutes that April shower had passed, and
those women were as resolute and unconquer-
able as Queen Elizabeth: they were again the
natural leaders of those around them; and the
cool and tearless men who sat beside them were
nothing — men were "a lost art," as some one
says — compared with the inexhaustible moral
vitality of those two women.

No: the dangers of "Celery and Cherubs"

are exaggerated. For temper, women are as
good as men, and no better. As for tears, long
may they flow! They are symbols of that
mighty distinction of sex which is as efface-
able and as essential as the difference between
land and sea.

THE NEED   In the interesting Buddhist book,
OF CAV-   "The Wheel of the Law," trans-
ALRY   lated by Henry Alabaster, there is
an account of a certain priest who used to bless
a great king, saying, "May your majesty have
the firmness of a crow, the audacity of a woman,
the endurance of a vulture, and the strength of
an ant." The priest then told anecdotes illus-
trating all of these qualities. Who has not
known occasions wherein some daring woman
has been the Joan of Arc of a perfectly hopeless cause, taken it up where men shrank, carried it through where they had failed, and con-
quered by weapons which men would never have
thought of using, and would have lacked faith
to employ even if put into their hands? The
wit, the resources, the audacity of women, have
been the key to history and the staple of novels,
ever since that larger novel called history began
to be written.

How is it done? Who knows the secret of
their success? All that any man can say is

that the heart takes a large share in the magic.
Rogers asserts in his "Table-Talk," that often,
when doubting how to act in matters of importance, he had received more useful advice from
women than from men. "Women have the
understanding of the heart," he said, "which is
better than that of the head." Then this instinct, that begins from the heart, reaches other
hearts also, and through that controls the will.
"Win hearts," said Lord Burleigh to Queen
Elizabeth, "and you have hands and purses;"
and the greatest of English sovereigns, in spite
of ugliness and rouge, in spite of coarseness
and cruelty and bad passions, was adored by
the nation that she first made great.

It seems to me that women are a sort of cavalry force in the army of mankind. They are
not always to be relied upon for that steady
"hammering away," which was Grant's one
method; but there is a certain Sheridan quality
about them, light-armed, audacious, quick, irresistible. They go before the main army; their
swift wits go scouting far in advance; they are
the first to scent danger, or to spy out chances
of success. Their charge is like that of a Tar-
tar horde, or the wild sweep of the Apaches.
They are upon you from some wholly unexpected quarter; and this respectable, systematic, well-drilled masculine force is caught and

rolled over and over in the dust, before the man
knows what has hit him. Even if repelled
and beaten off, this formidable cavalry is uncon-
quered: routed and in confusion to-day, it
comes back upon you to-morrow — fresh, alert,
with new devices, bringing new dangers. In
dealing with it, as the French complained of
the Arabs in Algiers, "Peace is not to be pur-
chased by victory." And, even if all seems
lost, with what a brilliant final charge it will
cover a retreat!

Decidedly, we need cavalry. In older countries, where it has been a merely undisciplined
and irregular force, it has often done mischief;
and public men, from Demosthenes down, have
been lamenting that measures which the statesman has meditated a whole year may be overturned in a day by a woman. Under our
American government we have foolishly attempted to leave out this arm of the service
altogether; and much of the alleged dulness
of our American history has come from this
attempt. Those who have been trained in the
various reforms where woman has taken an
equal part — the anti-slavery reform especially
— know well how much of the energy, the
dash, the daring, of those movements have
come from her. A revolution with a woman
in it is stronger than the established order that

omits her. It is not that she is superior to man, but she is different from man; and we can no more spare her than we could spare the cavalry from an army.

THE REA-   It is a part of the necessary the-
SON FIRM,   ory of republican government, that
THE TEM-
PERATE   every class and race shall be judged
WILL   by its highest types, not its lowest.
The proposition of the French revolutionary statesman, to begin the work of purifying the world by arresting all the cowards and knaves, is liable to the objection that it would find victims in every circle. Republican government begins at the other end, and assumes that the community generally has good intentions at least, and some common sense, however it may be with individuals. Take the very quality which the newspapers so often deny to women, — the quality of steadiness. "In fact, men's great objection to the entrance of the female mind into politics is drawn from a suspicion of its unsteadiness on matters in which the feelings could by any possibility be enlisted." Thus says the New York "Nation." Let us consider this implied charge against women, and consider it not by generalizing from a single instance, — "just like a woman," as the editors would doubtless say, if a woman had done it, —

but by observing whole classes of that sex, taken together.

These classes need some care in selection, for the plain reason that there are comparatively few circles in which women have yet been allowed enough freedom of scope, or have acted sufficiently on the same plane with men, to furnish a fair estimate of their probable action, were they enfranchised. Still there occur to me three such classes, — the anti-slavery women, the Quaker women, and the women who conduct philanthropic operations in our large cities. If the alleged unsteadiness of women is to be felt in public affairs, it would have been felt in these organizations. Has it been so felt?

Of the anti-slavery movement I can personally testify — and I have heard the same point fully recognized among my elders, such as Garrison, Phillips, and Quincy — that the women contributed their full share, if not more than their share, to the steadiness of that movement, even in times when the feelings were most excited, as, for instance, in fugitive-slave cases. Who that has seen mobs practically put down, and mayors cowed into decency, by the silent dignity of those rows of women who sat, with their knitting, more imperturbable than the men, can read without a smile these doubts of the " steadiness " of that sex? Again, among

Quaker women, I have asked the opinion of prominent Friends, as of John G. Whittier, whether it has been the experience of that body that women were more flighty and unsteady than men in their official action; and have been uniformly answered in the negative. And finally, as to benevolent organizations, a good test is given in the fact, — first pointed out, I believe, by that eminently practical philanthropist, Rev. Augustus Woodbury of Providence, — that the whole tendency has been, during the last twenty years, to put the management, even the financial control, of our benevolent societies, more and more into the hands of women, and that there has never been the slightest reason to reverse this policy. Ask the secretaries of the various boards of State Charities, or the officers of the Social Science Associations, if they have found reason to complain of the want of steadfast qualities in the " weaker sex." Why is it that the legislation of Massachusetts has assigned the class requiring the steadiest of all supervision — the imprisoned convicts — to " five commissioners of prisons, two of whom shall be women " ? These are the points which it would be worthy of our journals to consider, instead of hastily generalizing from single instances. Let us appeal from the typical woman of the editorial picture,

— fickle, unsteady, foolish, — to the nobler conception of womanhood which the poet Wordsworth found fulfilled in his own household : —

> " A being breathing thoughtful breath,
> A traveller betwixt life and death ;
> *The reason firm, the temperate will ;*
> *Endurance, foresight, strength and skill ;*
> A perfect woman, nobly planned
> To warn, to comfort, to command,
> And yet a spirit still, and bright
> With something of an angel light."

ALLURES TO BRIGHTER WORLDS, AND LEADS THE WAY   When a certain legislature had " School Suffrage " under consider-ation, the other day, the suggestion was made by one of the pithiest and quaintest of the speakers, that men were always better for the society of women, and therefore ought to vote in their company. "If all of us," he said, "would stay away from all places where we cannot take our wives and daughters with us, we should keep better com-pany than we now do." This expresses a feel-ing which grows more and more common among the better class of men, and which is the key to much progress in the condition of women. There can be no doubt that the increased asso-ciation of the sexes in society, in school, in lit-erature, tends to purify these several spheres of action. Yet, when we come to philosophize on this, there occur some perplexities on the way.

For instance, the exclusion of woman from all these spheres was in ancient Greece almost complete; yet the leading Greek poets, as Homer and the tragedians, are exceedingly chaste in tone, and in this respect beyond most of the great poets of modern nations. Again, no European nation has quite so far sequestered and subordinated women as has Spain; and yet the whole tone of Spanish literature is conspicuously grave and decorous. This plainly indicates that race has much to do with the matter, and that the mere admission or exclusion of women is but one among several factors. In short, it is easy to make out a case by a rhetorical use of the facts on one side; but, if we look at all the facts, the matter presents greater difficulties.

Again, it is to be noted that in several countries the first women who have taken prominent part in literature have been as bad as the men; as, for instance, Marguerite of Navarre and Mrs. Aphra Behn. This might indeed be explained by supposing that they had to gain entrance into literature by accepting the dissolute standards which they found prevailing. But it would probably be more correct to say that these standards themselves were variable, and that their variation affected, at certain periods, women as well as men. Marguerite of Navarre wrote religious books as well as merry stories ; and we know from Lockhart's Life of Scott, that ladies of high character in Edinburgh used to read Mrs. Behn's tales and plays aloud, at one time, with delight, — although one of the same ladies found, in her old age, that she could not read them to herself without blushing. Shakespeare puts coarse repartees into the mouths of women of stainless virtue. George Sand is not considered an unexceptionable writer ; but she tells us in her autobiography that she found among her grandmother's papers poems and satires so indecent that she could not read them through, and yet they bore the names of *abbés* and gentlemen whom she remembered in her childhood as models of dignity and honor. Voltaire inscribes to ladies of high rank, who doubtless regarded it as a great compliment, verses such as not even a poet of the English "fleshly school" would now print at all. In "Poems by Eminent Ladies," — published in 1755 and reprinted in 1774, — there are one or two poems as gross and disgusting as anything in Swift ; yet their authors were thought reputable women. Allan Ramsay's "Tea-Table Miscellany" — a collection of English and Scottish songs — was first published in 1724 ; and in his preface to the sixteenth edition the editor attributes its great success, especially among the ladies, to the fact that he has carefully excluded all grossness, "that the modest voice and ear of the fair singer might meet with no affront;" and adds, "the chief bent of all my studies being to attain their good graces." There is no doubt of the great popularity enjoyed by the book in all circles; yet it contains a few songs which the most licentious newspaper would not now publish. The inference is irresistible, from this and many other similar facts, that the whole tone of manners and decency has very greatly improved among the European races within a century and a half.

I suspect the truth to be, that, besides the visible influence of race and religion, there has been an insensible and almost unconscious improvement in each sex, with respect to these matters, as time has passed on; and that the mutual desire to please has enabled each sex to help the other, — the sex which is naturally the more refined taking the lead. But I should lay more stress on this mutual influence, and less on mere feminine superiority, than would be laid by many. It is often claimed by teachers that co-education helps not only boys, but also girls, to develop greater propriety of manners. When the sexes are wholly separate, or associate on terms of entire inequality, no such good influence occurs : the more equal the association, the better for both parties. After all, the Divine model is to be found in the family ; and the best ingenuity cannot improve much upon it.

IV

THE HOME

"In respect to the powers and rights of married women, the law is by no means abreast of the spirit of the age. Here are seen the old fossil footprints of feudalism. The law relating to woman tends to make every family a barony or a monarchy or a despotism, of which the husband is the baron, king, or despot, and the wife the dependent, serf, or slave. That this is not always the fact, is not due to the law, but to the enlarged humanity which spurns the narrow limits of its rules. The progress of civilization has changed the family from a barony to a republic; but the law has not kept pace with the advance of ideas, manners, and customs." — W. W. STORY's Treatise on Contracts not under Seal, § 84, third edition, p. 89.

WANTED —
HOMES
We see advertisements, occasionally, of "Homes for Aged Women," and more rarely "Homes for Aged Men." The question sometimes suggests itself, whether it would not be better to begin the provision earlier, and see that homes are also provided, in some form, for the middle-aged and even the young. The trouble is, I suppose, that as it takes two to make a bargain, so it takes at least two to make a home; and unluckily it takes only one to spoil it.

Madame Roland once defined marriage as
an institution where one person undertakes to
provide happiness for two ; and many failures
are accounted for, no doubt, by this false basis.
Sometimes it is the man, more often the woman, of whom this extravagant demand is
made. There are marriages which have proved
a wreck almost wholly through the fault of the
wife. Nor is this confined to wedded homes
alone. I have known a son who lived alone,
patiently and uncomplainingly, with that sad-
dest of all conceivable companions, a drunken
mother. I have known another young man
who supported in his own home a mother and
sister, both habitual drunkards. All these were
American-born, and all of respectable social
position. A house shadowed by such misery is
not a home, though it might have proved such
but for the sins of women. Such instances are,
however, rare and occasional compared with the
cases where the same offence in the husband
makes ruin of the home.

Then there are the cases where indolence,
or selfishness, or vanity, or the love of social
excitement, in the woman, unfits her for home
life. Here we come upon ground where perhaps woman is the greater sinner. It must be
remembered, however, that against this must
be balanced the neglect produced by club-life,

or by the life of society-membership, in a man. A brilliant young married belle in London once told me that she was glad her husband was so fond of his club, for it amused him every night while she went to balls. " Married men do not go much into society here," she said, " unless they are regular flirts, — which I do not think my husband would ever be, for he is very fond of me, — so he goes every night to his club, and gets home about the same time that I do. It is a very nice arrangement." It is perhaps needless to add that they are long since divorced.

It is common to denounce club-life in our large cities as destructive of the home. The modern club is simply a more refined substitute for the old-fashioned tavern, and is on the whole an advance in morals as well as manners. In our large cities a man in a certain social coterie belongs to a club, if he can afford it, as a means of contact with his fellows, and to have various conveniences which he cannot so economically obtain at home. A few haunt clubs constantly; the many use them occasionally. More absorbing than these, perhaps, are the secret societies which have so revived among us since the war, and which consume time so fearfully. There was a case mentioned in the newspapers lately of a man who belonged to some twenty of these associations ; and when he died, and each wished to conduct his funeral, great was the strife! In the small city where I write there are seventeen secret societies down in the directory, and I suppose as many more not so conspicuous. I meet men who assure me that they habitually attend a society meeting every evening of the week except Sunday, when they go to church meeting. These are rarely men of leisure ; they are usually mechanics or business men of some kind, who are hard at work all day, and never see their families except at meal-times. Their case is far worse, so far as absence from home is concerned, than that of the " club-men " of large cities ; for these are often men of leisure, who, if married, at least make home one of their lounging-places, which such secret-society men do not.

I honestly believe that this melancholy desertion of the home is largely due to the traditional separation between the alleged spheres of the sexes. The theory still prevails largely, that home is the peculiar province of the woman, that she has almost no duties out of it ; and hence, naturally enough, that the husband has almost no duties in it. If he is amused there, let him stay there ; but, as it is not his recognized sphere of duty, he is not actually violating any duty by absenting himself. This theory even pervades our manuals of morals, of metaphysics, and of popular science ; and it is not every public teacher who has the manliness, having once stated it, to modify his statement, as did the venerable President Hopkins of Williams College, when lecturing the other day to the young ladies of Vassar.

" I would," he said, "at this point correct my teaching in 'The Law of Love' to the effect that home is peculiarly the sphere of woman, and civil government that of man. *I now regard the home as the joint sphere of man and woman, and the sphere of civil government more of an open question as between the two.* It is, however, to be lamented that the present agitation concerning the rights of woman is so much a matter of 'rights' rather than of 'duties,' as the reform of the latter would involve the former."

If our instructors in moral philosophy will only base their theory of ethics as broadly as this, we shall no longer need to advertise "Homes Wanted ; " for the joint efforts of men and women will soon provide them.

THE ORIGIN OF CIVILIZATION   Nothing throws more light on the whole history of woman than the first illustration in Sir John Lubbock's " Origin of Civilization." A young girl, almost naked, is being dragged furiously along the ground by a party of naked savages, armed literally to the teeth, while those of another band grasp her by the arm, and almost tear her asunder in the effort to hold her back. These last are her brothers and her friends; the others are—her enemies? As you please to call them. They are her future husband and his kinsmen, who have come to aid him in his wooing.

This was the primitive rite of marriage. Vestiges of it still remain among savage nations. And all the romance and grace of the most refined modern marriage — the orange-blossoms, the bridal veil, the church service, the wedding feast — these are only the "bright consummate flower" reared by civilization from that rough seed. All the brutal encounter is softened into this. Nothing remains of the barbarism except the one word "obey," and even that is going.

Now, to say that a thing is going, is to say that it will presently be gone. To say that anything is changed, is to say that it is to change further. If it never has been altered, perhaps it will not be; but a proved alteration of an inch in a year opens the way to an indefinite modification. The study of the glaciers, for instance, began with the discovery that they

had moved; and from that moment no one
doubted that they were moving all the time.
It is the same with the position of woman.
Once open your eyes to the fact that it has
changed, and who is to predict where the matter shall end? It is sheer folly to say, "Her
relative position will always be what it has
been," when one glance at Sir John Lubbock's
picture shows that there is no fixed "has been,"
but that her original position was long since
altered and revised. Those who still use this
argument are like those who laughed at the
lines of stakes which Agassiz planted across
the Aar glacier in 1840. But the stakes settled
the question, and proved the motion. *Però si
muove:* "But it moves."

The motion once proved, the whole range of
possible progress is before us. The amazement
of that Chinese visitor in Boston, the other
day, when he saw a woman addressing a mis-
sionary meeting; the astonishment of all English visitors when young ladies teach classes in
geometry and Latin, in our high schools; the
surprise of foreigners at seeing the rough throng
in the Cooper Institute reading-room submit to
the sway of one young woman with a crochet-
needle — all these simply testify to the fact that
the stakes have moved. That they have yet
been carried halfway to the end, who knows?

What a step from the horrible nuptials of those savage days to the poetic marriage of Robert Browning and Elizabeth Barrett — the " Sonnets from the Portuguese " on one side, the " One Word More " on the other! But who can say that the whole relation between man and woman reached its climax there, and that where the past has brought changes so vast the future is to add nothing? Who knows that, when "the world's great bridals come," people may not look back with pity, even on this era of the Brownings? Perhaps even Elizabeth Barrett promised to obey!

At any rate, it is safe to say that each step concedes the probability of another. Even from the naked barbarian to the veiled Oriental, from the savage hut to the carefully enshrined harem, there is a step forward. One more step in the spiral line of progress has brought us to the unveiled face and comparatively free movements of the English or American woman. From the kitchen to the public lecture-room, from that to the lecture-platform, and from that again to the ballot-box, — these are far slighter steps than those which gradually lifted the savage girl of Sir John Lubbock's picture into the possession of the alphabet and the dignity of a home. So easy are these future changes beside those of the past, that to doubt their possibility is as if Agassiz, after tracing year by year the motion of his Alpine glacier, should deny its power to move one inch farther into the sunny valley, and there to melt harmlessly away.

THE LOW-WATER MARK — We constantly see it assumed, in arguments against any step in the elevation of woman, that her position is a thing fixed permanently by nature, so that there can be in it no great or essential change. Every successive modification is resisted as "a reform against nature;" and this argument from permanence is always that which appears most convincing to conservative minds. Let us see how the facts confirm it.

A story is going the rounds of the newspapers in regard to a Russian peasant and his wife. For some act of disobedience the peasant took the law into his own hands; and his mode of discipline was to tie the poor creature naked to a post in the street, and to call on every passer-by to strike her a blow. Not satisfied with this, he placed her on the ground, and tied heavy weights on her limbs until one arm was broken. When finally released, she made a complaint against him in court. The court discharged him on the ground that he had not exceeded the legal authority of a husband.

Encouraged by this, he caused her to be arrested in return ; and the same court sentenced her to another public whipping for disobedience.

No authority was given for this story in the newspaper where I saw it ; but it certainly did not first appear in a woman-suffrage newspaper, and cannot therefore be a manufactured "outrage." I use it simply to illustrate the low-water mark at which the position of woman may rest, in the largest Christian nation of the world. All the refinements, all the education, all the comparative justice, of modern society, have been gradually upheaved from some such depth as this. When the gypsies described by Leland treat even the ground trodden upon by a woman as impure, they simply illustrate the low plane from which all the elevation of woman has begun. All these things show that the position of that sex in society, so far from being a thing in itself permanent, has been in reality the most changing of all factors in the social problem. And this inevitably suggests the question, Are we any more sure that her present position is finally and absolutely fixed than were those who observed it at any previous time in the world's history ? Granting that her condition was once at low-water mark, who is authorized to say that it has yet reached high tide ?

It is very possible that this Russian wife, once scourged back to submission, ended her days in the conviction, and taught it to her daughters, that such was a woman's rightful place. When an American woman of to-day says, " I have all the rights I want," is she on any surer ground? Grant that the difference is vast between the two. How do we know that even the later condition is final, or that anything is final but entire equality before the laws? It is not many years since William Story — in a legal work inspired and revised by his father, the greatest of American jurists — wrote this indignant protest against the injustice of the old common law : —

" In respect to the powers and rights of married women, the law is by no means abreast of the spirit of the age. Here are seen the old fossil footprints of feudalism. The law relating to woman tends to make every family a barony or a monarchy, or a despotism, of which the husband is the baron, king, or despot, and the wife the dependent, serf, or slave. That this is not always the fact is not due to the law, but to the enlarged humanity which spurns the narrow limits of its rules. The progress of civilization has changed the family from a barony to a republic; but the law has not kept pace with the advance of ideas, manners, and customs. And, although public opinion is a check to legal rules on the subject, the rules are feudal and stern. Yet

the position of woman throughout history serves as
the criterion of the freedom of the people or an age.
When man shall despise that right which is founded
only on might, woman will be free and stand on an
equal level with him, — a friend and not a dependent." [1]

We know that the law is greatly changed
and ameliorated in many places since Story
wrote this statement; but we also know how
almost every one of these changes was resisted:
and who is authorized to say that the final and
equitable fulfilment is yet reached?

OBEY   After witnessing the marriage
ceremony of the Episcopal Church,
the other day, I walked down the aisle with the
young rector who had officiated. It was natural
to speak of the beauty of the Church service on
an occasion like that; but, after doing this, I
felt compelled to protest against the unrighteous pledge to obey. "I hope," I said, "to live
to see that word expunged from the Episcopal
service, as it has been from that of the Meth-
odists. The Roman Catholics, you know, have
never had it."

"Why do you object?" he asked. "Is it
because you know that they will not obey?"

1 Story's *Treatise on the Law of Contracts not under Seal*,
§ 84, p. 89.

"Because they ought not," I said.

"Well," said he, after a few moments' reflection, and looking up frankly, "I do not think they ought!"

Here was a young clergyman of great earnestness and self-devotion, who included it among the sacred duties of his life to impose upon ignorant young girls a solemn obligation, which he yet thought they ought not to incur, and did not believe that they would keep. There could hardly be a better illustration of the confusion in the public mind, or the manner in which "the subjection of woman" is being outgrown, or the subtile way in which this subjection has been interwoven with sacred ties, and baptized "duty."

The advocates of woman suffrage are constantly reproved for using the terms "subjection," "oppression," and "slavery," as applied to woman. They simply commit the same sin as that committed by the original abolitionists. They are "as harsh as truth, as uncompromising as justice." Of course they talk about oppression and emancipation. It is the word *obey* that constitutes the one, and shows the need of the other. Whoever is pledged to obey is technically and literally a slave, no matter how many roses surround the chains. All the more so if the slavery is self-imposed, and sur-

rounded by all the prescriptions of religion.
Make the marriage tie as close as church or
state can make it ; but let it be equal, impartial.
That it may be so, the word *obey* must be
abandoned or made reciprocal. Where invariable obedience is promised, equality is gone.

That there may be no doubt about the meaning of this word in the marriage covenant, the
usages of nations often add symbolic explana-
tions. These are generally simple, and brutal
enough to be understood. The Hebrew ceremony, when the bridegroom took off his slipper
and struck the bride on the neck as she crossed
his threshold, was unmistakable. As my black
sergeant said, when a white prisoner questioned
his authority, and he pointed to the *chevrons*
on his sleeve, "Dat mean guv'ment." All
these forms mean simply government also.
The ceremony of the slipper has now no recognition, except when people fling an old shoe
after the bride, which is held by antiquarians to
be the same observance. But it is all preserved
and concentrated into a single word, when the
bride promises to obey.

The deepest wretchedness that has ever been
put into human language, or that has exceeded
it, has grown out of that pledge. There is no
misery on earth like that of a pure and refined
woman who finds herself owned, body and soul,

by a drunken, licentious, brutal man. The
very fact that she is held to obedience by a
spiritual tie makes it worse. Chattel slavery
was not so bad; for, though the master might
pervert religion for his own satisfaction, he
could not impose upon the slave. Never yet
did I see a negro slave who thought it a duty
to obey his master; and therefore there was
always some dream of release. But who has
not heard of some delicate and refined woman,
one day of whose torture was equivalent to
years of that possible to an obtuse frame, —
who had the door of escape ready at hand for
years, and yet died a lingering death rather
than pass through it; and this because she had
promised to obey!

It is said of one of the most gifted women
who ever trod American soil, — she being of
English birth, — that, before she obtained the
divorce which separated her from her profligate
husband, she once went for counsel to the wife
of her pastor. She unrolled before her the
long catalogue of merciless outrages to which
she had been subject, endangering finally her
health, her life, and that of her children born
and to be born. When she turned at last for
advice to her confessor, with the agonized inquiry, " What is it my duty to do? " — " Do? "
said the stern adviser: " Lie down on the floor,

and let your husband trample on you if he will.
That is a woman's duty."

The woman who gave this advice was not
naturally inhuman nor heartless: she had simply been trained in the school of obedience.
The Jesuit doctrine, that a priest should be as
a corpse, *perinde ac cadaver*, in the hands of a
superior priest, is not worse. Woman has no
right to delegate, nor man to assume, a responsibility so awful. Just in proportion as it is
consistently carried out, it trains men from
boyhood into self-indulgent tyrants ; and, while
some women are transformed by it to saints,
others are crushed into deceitful slaves. That
this was the result of chattel slavery, this nation has at length learned. We learn more
slowly the profounder and more subtle moral
evil that follows from the unrighteous promise
to obey.

WOMAN
IN THE
CHRYSALIS
When the bride receives the ring
upon her finger, and utters — if she
utters it — the promise to obey, she
sees a poetic beauty in the rite. Turning of
her own free will from her maiden liberty, she
voluntarily takes the yoke of service upon her.
This is her view ; but is this the historic fact in
regard to marriage ? Not at all. The pledge
of obedience — the whole theory of inequality

in marriage — is simply what is left to us of a former state of society, in which every woman, old or young, must obey somebody. The state of tutelage, implied in such a marriage, is merely what is left of the old theory of the "Perpetual Tutelage of Women," under the Roman law.

Roman law, from which our civil law is derived, has its foundation evidently in patriarchal tradition. It recognized at first the family only, and that family was held together by paternal power (*patria potestas*). If the father died, his powers passed to the son or grandson, as the possible head of a new family; but these powers could never pass to a woman, and every woman, of whatever age, must be under somebody's legal control. Her father dying, she was still subject through life to her nearest male relations, or to her father's nominees, as her guardians. She was under perpetual guardianship, both as to person and property. No years, no experience, could make her anything but a child before the law.

In Oriental countries the system was still more complete. "A man," says the Gentoo Code of Laws, "must keep his wife so much in subjection that she by no means be mistress of her own action. If the wife have her own free will, notwithstanding she be of a superior caste, she will behave amiss." But this author-

ity, which still exists in India, is not merely
conjugal. The husband exerts it simply as
being the wife's legal guardian. If the woman
be unmarried or a widow, she must be as rig-
orously held under some other guardianship.
It is no uncommon thing for a woman in India
to be the ward of her own son. Lucretia Mott
or Florence Nightingale would there be in personal subjection to somebody. Any man of
legal age would be recognized as a fit custodian
for them, but there must be a man.

With some variation of details at different
periods, the same system prevailed essentially
at Rome, down to the time when Rome became
Christian. Those who wish for particulars will
find them in an admirable chapter (the fifth) of
Maine's "Ancient Law." At one time the
husband was held to possess the *patria potestas*, or paternal power, in its full force. By law
"the woman passed *in manum viri*, that is, she
became the daughter of her husband." All she
had became his, and after his death she was
retained in the same strict tutelage by any
guardians his will might appoint. Afterwards,
to soften this rigid bond, the woman was regarded in law as being temporarily deposited by
her family with her husband; the family appointed guardians over her; and thus, between
the two tyrannies, she won a sort of independ-

ence. Then came Christianity, and swept away the merely parental authority for married women, concentrating all upon the husband. Hence our legislation bears the mark of a double origin, and woman is half recognized as an equal and half as a slave.

It is necessary to remember, therefore, that all the relation of subjection in marriage is merely the residue of an unnatural system, of which all else is long since outgrown. It would have seemed to an ancient Roman a matter of course that a woman should, all her life long, obey the guardians set over her person. It still seems to many people a matter of course that she should obey her husband. To others among us, on the contrary, both these theories of obedience seem barbarous, and the one is merely a relic of the other.

We cannot disregard the history of the Theory of Tutelage. If we could believe that a chrysalis is always a chrysalis, and a butterfly always a butterfly, we could easily leave each to its appropriate sphere; but when we see the chrysalis open, and the butterfly come half out of it, we know that sooner or later it must spread wings, and fly. The theory of tutelage implies the chrysalis. Woman is the butterfly. Sooner or later she will be wholly out.

TWO AND　　A young man of very good brains
TWO　　　　was telling me, the other day, his
dreams of his future wife. Rattling on, more
in joke than in earnest, he said, "She must be
perfectly ignorant, and a bigot : she must know
nothing, and believe everything. I should wish
to have her from the adjoining room call to me,
'My dear, what do two and two make?'"

It did not seem to me that his demand would
be so very hard to fill, since bigotry and ignorance are to be had almost anywhere for the
asking ; and, as for two and two, I should say
that it had always been the habit of women to
ask that question of some man, and to rest
easily satisfied with the answer. They have
generally called, as my friend wished, from
some other room, saying, "My dear, what do
two and two make?" and the husband or father
or brother has answered and said, "My dear,
they make four for a man, and three for a
woman."

At any given period in the history of woman,
she has adopted man's whim as the measure of
her rights ; has claimed nothing ; has sweetly
accepted anything ; the law of two-and-two itself should be at his discretion. At any given
moment, so well was his interpretation received,
that it stood for absolute right. In Rome a
woman, married or single, could not testify in

court ; in the middle ages, and down to quite
modern times, she could not hold real estate ;
thirty years ago she could not, in New England,
obtain a collegiate education ; even now she
can only vote for school officers.

The first principles of republican government
are so rehearsed and re-rehearsed, that one
would think they must become "as plain as
that two and two make four." But we find
throughout, that, as Emerson said of another
class of reasoners, "Their two is not the real
two ; their four is not the real four." We find
different numerals and diverse arithmetical rules
for the two sexes ; as, in some Oriental countries, men and women speak different dialects of
the same language.

In novels the hero often begins by dreaming,
like my friend, of an ideal wife, who shall be
ignorant of everything, and have only brains
enough to be bigoted. Instead of sighing, like
Falstaff, " Oh for a fine young thief, of the age
of two and twenty or thereabouts ! " the hero
sighs for a fine young idiot of similar age.
When the hero is successful in his search and
wooing, the novelist sometimes mercifully removes the young woman early, like David Copperfield's Dora, she bequeathing the bereaved
husband, on her deathbed, to a woman of sense.
In real life these convenient interruptions do

not commonly occur, and the foolish youth re-
grets through many years that he did not select
an Agnes instead.

The acute observer Stendhal says, —

" In Paris, the highest praise for a marriageable
girl is to say, 'She has great sweetness of character
and the disposition of a lamb.' Nothing produces
more impression on fools who are looking out for
wives. I think I see the interesting couple, two
years after, breakfasting together on a dull day,
with three tall lackeys waiting upon them! "

And he adds, still speaking in the interest of
men : —

" Most men have a period in their career when
they might do something great, a period when nothing seems impossible. The ignorance of women
spoils for the human race this magnificent opportunity : and love, at the utmost, in these days, only
inspires a young man to learn to ride well, or to
make a judicious selection of a tailor." [1]

Society, however, discovers by degrees that
there are conveniences in every woman's knowing the four rules of arithmetic for herself.
Two and two come to the same amount on a
butcher's bill, whether the order be given by
a man or a woman ; and it is the same in all

[1] *De L'Amour*, par de Stendhal (Henri Beyle). Paris,
1868 [written in 1822], pp. 182, 198.

affairs or investments, financial or moral. We shall one day learn that with laws, customs, and public affairs it is the same. Once get it rooted in a woman's mind, that for her, two and two make three only, and sooner or later the accounts of the whole human race fail to balance.

A MODEL HOUSE-HOLD   There is an African bird called the hornbill, whose habits are in some respects a model. The female builds her nest in a hollow tree, lays her eggs, and broods on them. So far, so good. Then the male feels that he must also contribute some service; so he walls up the hole closely, giving only room for the point of the female's bill to protrude. Until the eggs are hatched, she is thenceforth confined to her nest, and is in the mean time fed assiduously by her mate, who devotes himself entirely to this object. Dr. Livingstone has seen these nests in Africa, Layard and others in Asia, and Wallace in Sumatra.

Personally I have never seen a hornbill's nest. The nearest approach I ever made to it was when in Fayal I used to pass near a gloomy mansion, of which the front windows were walled up, and only one high window was visible in the rear, beyond the reach of eyes from any neighboring house. In this cheerful abode, I

was assured, a Portuguese lady had been for
many years confined by her jealous husband.
It was long since any neighbor had caught a
glimpse of her, but it was supposed that she
was alive. There is no reason to doubt that
her husband fed her well. It was simply a case
of human hornbill, with the imprisonment made
perpetual.

I have more than once asked lawyers whether,
in communities where the old common law prevailed, there was anything to prevent such an
imprisonment of a married woman; and they
have always answered, "Nothing but public
opinion." Where the husband has the legal
custody of the wife's person, no *habeas corpus*
can avail against him. The hornbill household
is based on a strict application of the old common law. A Hindoo household was a hornbill household: "a woman, of whatsoever age,
should never be mistress of her own actions,"
said the code of Menu. An Athenian household was a hornbill's nest, and great was the
outcry when some Aspasia broke out of it.
When the remonstrant petitions legislatures
against the emancipation of woman, we seem
to hear the twittering of the hornbill mother,
imploring to be left inside.

Under some forms, the hornbill theory becomes respectable. There are many peaceful

families, innocent though torpid, where the only dream of existence is to have plenty of quiet, plenty of food, and plenty of well-fed children. For them this African household is a sufficient model. The wife is "a home body." The husband is "a good provider." These are honest people, and have a right to speak. The hornbill theory is only dishonest when it comes — as it often comes — from women who lead the life, not of good stay-at-home fowls, but of paroquets and hummingbirds, — who sorrowfully bemoan the active habits of enlightened women, while they themselves

> "Bear about the mockery of woe
> To midnight dances and the public show."

It is from these women, in Washington, New York, and elsewhere, that the loudest appeal for the hornbill standard of domesticity proceeds. Put them to the test, and give them their chicken-salad and champagne through a hole in the wall only, and see how they like it.

But even the most honest and peaceful conservatives will one day admit that the hornbill is not the highest model. Plato thought that "the soul of our grandame might haply inhabit the body of a bird;" but Nature has kindly provided various types of bird-households to suit all varieties of taste. The bright orioles, filling the summer boughs with color and with song,

are as truly domestic in the freedom of their
airy nest as the poor hornbills who ignorantly
make home into a dungeon. And certainly
each new generation of orioles, spreading free
wings from that pendent cradle, affords a happier
illustration of judicious nurture than is to be
found in the uncouth little offspring of the hornbills, which Wallace describes as " so flabby and
semi-transparent as to resemble a bladder of
jelly, furnished with head, legs, and rudimentary
wings, but with not a sign of a feather, except
a few lines of points indicating where they
would come."

A SAFE-
GUARD
FOR THE
FAMILY

Many German - Americans are
warm friends of woman suffrage ;
but the editors of " Puck," it seems,
are not. In a certain number of that
comic journal, there was an unfavorable cartoon
on this reform ; and in a following number, — the
number, by the way, which contains that amusing illustration of the vast seaside hotels of the
future, with the cheering announcement, " Only
one mile to the barber's shop," and "Take the
cars to the dining-room," — a lady came to the
rescue, and bravely defended woman suffrage.
It seems that the original cartoon depicted in
the corner a pretty family scene, representing
father, mother, and children seated happily to-

gether, with the melancholy motto, "Nevermore, nevermore!" And when the correspondent, Mrs. Blake, very naturally asks what this touching picture has to do with woman suffrage, Puck says, "If the husband in our 'pretty family scene' should propose to vote for the candidate who was obnoxious to his wife, would this 'pretty family scene' continue to be a domestic paradise, or would it remind the spectator of the region in which Dante spent his 'fortnight off'?"

It is beautiful to see how much anxiety there is to preserve the family. Every step in the modification of the old common law, whereby the wife was, in Baron Alderson's phrase, "the servant of her husband," was resisted as tending to endanger the family. The proposal that the wife should control her own earnings, so that her husband should not have the right to collect them in order to pay his gambling debts, was declared by English advocates, in the celebrated case of the Hon. Mrs. Norton, the poetess, to imperil all the future peace of British households. Even the liberal-minded "Punch," about the time Girton College was founded in England, expressed grave doubts whether the harmony of wedded unions would not receive a blow, from the time when wives should be liable to know more Greek than their husbands. Yet

the marriage relation has withstood these inno-
vations.   It has not been impaired, either by
separate rights, private earnings, or independent
Greek: can it be possible that a little voting
will overthrow it?

The very ground on which woman suffrage
is opposed by its enemies might assuage these
fears.   If, as we are told, women will not take
the pains to vote except upon the strongest
inducements, who has so good an opportunity
as the husband to bring those inducements to
bear? and, if so, what is the separation?   Or
if, as we are told, women will merely reflect
their husbands' political opinions, why should
they dispute about them?   The mere suggestion of a difference deep enough to quarrel for,
implies a real difference of convictions or interests, and indicates that there ought to be an
independent representation of each; unless we
fall back, once for all, on the common-law tradition that man and wife are one, and that one is
the husband.   Either the antagonisms which
occur in politics are comparatively superficial,
in which case they would do no harm; or else
they touch matters of real interest and principle, in which case every human being has a
right to independent expression, even at a good
deal of risk.   In either case, the objection falls
to the ground.

We have fortunately a means of testing, with some fairness of estimate, the probable amount of this peril. It is generally admitted — and certainly no German-American will deny — that the most fruitful sources of hostility and war in all times have been religious, not political. All merely political antagonism, certainly all which is possible in a republic, fades into insignificance before this more powerful dividing influence. Yet we leave all this great explosive force in unimpeded operation, — at any moment it may be set in action, in any one of those "pretty family scenes" which "Puck" depicts, — while we are solemnly warned against admitting the comparatively mild peril of a political difference! It is like cautioning a manufacturer of dynamite against the danger of meddling with mere edge-tools. Even with all the intensity of feeling on religious matters, few families are seriously divided by them ; and the influence of political differences would be still more insignificant.

The simple fact is that there is no better basis for union than mutual respect for each other's opinions ; and this can never be obtained without an intelligent independence. "I would rather have a thorn in my side than an echo," said Emerson of friendship ; and the same is true of married life. It is the echoes, the

nonentities, of whom men grow tired; it is the
women with some flavor of individuality who
keep the hearts of their husbands. This is
only applying in a higher sense what Shakespeare's Cleopatra saw. When her handmaidens are questioning how to hold a lover,
and one says, —

"Give way to him in all: cross him in nothing," —

Cleopatra, from the depth of an unequalled experience, retorts, —

"Thou speakest like a fool: the way to lose him!"

And what "the serpent of old Nile" said, the
wives of the future, who are to be wise as ser-
pents and harmless as doves, may well ponder.
It takes two things different to make a union;
and part of that difference may as well lie in
matters political as anywhere else.

WOMEN AS   An able lawyer of Boston, argu-
ECONO-   ing the other day before a legisla-
MISTS   tive committee in favor of giving to
the city council a check upon the expenditures
of the school committee, gave as one reason that
this body would probably include more women
henceforward, and that women were ordinarily
more lavish than men in their use of money.
The truth of this assumption was questioned at
the time; and, the more I think of it, the more

contrary it is to my whole experience. I should
say that women, from the very habit of their
lives, are led to be more particular about details,
and more careful as to small economies. The
very fact that they handle less money tends to
this. When they are told to spend money, as
they often are by loving or ambitious husbands,
they no doubt do it freely : they have naturally
more taste than men, and quite as much love
of luxury. In some instances in this country
they spend money recklessly and wickedly, like
the heroines of French novels ; but as, even in
brilliant Paris, the women of the middle classes
are notoriously better managers than the men,
so we often see, in our scheming America, the
same relative superiority. Often have I heard
young men say, "I never knew how to econo-
mize until after my marriage ;" and who has
not seen multitudes of instances where women
accustomed to luxury have accepted poverty
without a murmur for the sake of those whom
they loved ?

I remember a young girl, accustomed to the
gayest society of New York, who engaged herself to a young naval officer, against the advice
of the friends of both. One of her near relatives said to me, "Of all the young girls I have
ever known, she is the least fitted for a poor
man's wife." Yet from the very moment of

her marriage she brought their joint expenses within his scanty pay, and even saved a little money from it. Everybody knows such instances. We hear men denounce the extravagance of women, while those very men spend on wine and cigars, on clubs and horses, twice what their wives spend on their toilet. If the wives are economical, the husbands perhaps urge them on to greater lavishness. "Why do you not dress like Mrs. So-and-so?" — "I can't afford it." — "But *I* can afford it;" and then, when the bills come in, the talk of extravagance recommences. At one time in Newport, that lady among the summer visitors who was reported to be Worth's best customer was also well known to be quite indifferent to society, and to go into it mainly to please her husband, whose social ambition was notorious.

It has often happened to me to serve in organizations where both sexes were represented, and where expenditures were to be made for business or pleasure. In these I have found, as a rule, that the women were more careful, or perhaps I should say more timid, than the men, less willing to risk anything : the bolder financial experiments came from the men, as one might expect. In talking the other day with the secretary of an important educational enterprise, conducted by women, I was sur-

prised to find that it was cramped for money,
though large subscriptions were said to have
been made to it. On inquiry it appeared that
these ladies, having pledged themselves for four
years, had divided the amount received into
four parts, and were resolutely limiting themselves, for the first year, to one quarter part of
what had been subscribed. No board of men
would have done so. Any board of men would
have allowed far more than a quarter of the
sum for the first year's expenditures, justly reasoning that if the enterprise began well it would
command public confidence, and bring in additional subscriptions as time went on. I would
appeal to any one whose experience has been in
joint associations of men and women, whether
this is not a fair statement of the difference between their ways of working. It does not prove
that women are more honest than men, but
that their education or their nature makes
them more cautious in expenditure.

The habits of society make the dress of a
fashionable woman far more expensive than
that of a man of fashion. Formerly it was not
so ; and, so long as it was not so, the extravagance of men in this respect quite equalled
that of women. It now takes other forms, but
the habit is the same. The waiters at any
fashionable restaurant will tell you that what is

a cheap dinner for a man would be a dear dinner for a woman. Yet after all, the test is not in any particular class of expenditures, but in the business-like habit. Men are of course more business-like in large combinations, for they are more used to them ; but for the small details of daily economy women are more watchful. The cases where women ruin their husbands by extravagance are exceptional. As a rule, the men are the bread-winners ; but the careful saving and managing and contriving come from the women.

GREATER INCLUDES LESS   I was once at a little musical party in New York, where several accomplished amateur singers were present, and with them the eminent professional, Miss Adelaide Phillipps. The amateurs were first called on. Each chose some difficult operatic passage, and sang her best. When it came to the great opera-singer's turn, instead of exhibiting her ability to eclipse those rivals on her own ground, she simply seated herself at the piano, and sang "Kathleen Mavourneen" with such thrilling sweetness that the young Irish girl who was setting the supper-table in the next room forgot all her plates and teaspoons, threw herself into a chair, put her apron over her face, and sobbed as if her heart would break.

All the training of Adelaide Phillipps — her magnificent voice, her stage experience, her skill in effects, her power of expression — went into the performance of that simple song. The greater included the less. And thus all the intellectual and practical training that any woman can have, all her public action and her active career, will make her, if she be a true woman, more admirable as a wife, a mother, and a friend. The greater includes the less for her also.

Of course this is a statement of general facts and tendencies. There must be among women, as among men, an endless variety of individual temperaments. There will always be plenty whose career will illustrate the infirmities of genius, and whom no training can convince that two and two make four. But the general fact is sure. As no sensible man would seriously prefer for a wife a Hindoo or Tahitian woman rather than one bred in England or America, so every further advantage of education or opportunity will only improve, not impair, the true womanly type.

Lucy Stone once said, "Woman's nature was stamped and sealed by the Almighty, and there is no danger of her unsexing herself while his eye watches her." Margaret Fuller said, "One hour of love will teach a woman more of her

true relations than all your philosophizing."
These were the testimony of women who had
studied Greek, and were only the more womanly
for the study. They are worth the opinions of
a million half-developed beings like the Duchess
de Fontanges, who was described as being "as
beautiful as an angel and as silly as a goose."
The greater includes the less. Your view from
the mountain-side may be very pretty, but she
who has taken one step higher commands your
view and her own also. It was no dreamy recluse,
but the accomplished and experienced Stendhal,
who wrote, "The joys of the gay world do not
count for much with happy women." [1]

If a highly educated man is incapable and un-
practical, we do not say that he is educated too
well, but not well enough. He ought to know
what he knows, and other things also. Never
yet did I see a woman too well educated to be a
wife and a mother; but I know multitudes who
deplore, or have reason to deplore, every day of
their lives, the untrained and unfurnished minds
that are so ill-prepared for these sacred duties.
Every step towards equalizing the opportunities
of men and women meets with resistance, of
course; but every step, as it is accomplished,

[1] *De l'Amour*, par de Stendhal (Henri Beyle): "Les
plaisirs du grand monde n'en sont pas pour les femmes
heureuses," p. 189.

leaves men still men, and women still women.
And as we who heard Adelaide Phillipps felt
that she had never had a better tribute to her
musical genius than this young Irish girl's
tears, so the true woman will feel that all her
college training for instance, if she has it, may
have been well invested, even for the sake of
the baby on her knee. And it is to be remembered, after all, that each human being lives to
unfold his or her own powers, and do his or her
own duties first, and that neither woman nor
man has the right to accept a merely secondary
and subordinate life. A noble woman must be
a noble human being; and the most sacred
special duties, as of wife or mother, are all included in this, as the greater includes the less.

A COPART-
NERSHIP
Marriage, considered merely in its
financial and business relations, may
be regarded as a permanent copartnership.

Now, in an ordinary copartnership there is
very often a complete division of labor among
the partners. If they manufacture locomotive-
engines, for instance, one partner perhaps
superintends the works, another attends to
mechanical inventions and improvements, another travels for orders, another conducts the
correspondence, another receives and pays out
the money. The latter is not necessarily the

head of the firm. Perhaps his place could be
more easily filled than some of the other posts.
Nevertheless, more money passes through his
hands than through those of all the others put
together. Now, should he, at the year's end,
call together the inventor and the superintend-
ent and the traveller and the correspondent,
and say to them, " I have earned all this money
this year, but I will generously give you some
of it," — he would be considered simply impertinent, and would hardly have a chance to
repeat the offence the year after.

Yet precisely what would be called folly in
this business partnership is constantly done by
men in the copartnership of marriage, and is
there called " common sense " and " social science " and " political economy."

For instance, a farmer works himself half to
death in the hayfield, and his wife meanwhile
is working herself wholly to death in the dairy.
The neighbors come in to sympathize after her
demise ; and during the few months' interval before his second marriage they say approvingly,
" He was always a generous man to his folks !
He was a good provider !"   But where was the
room for generosity, any more than the member of any other firm is to be called generous,
when he keeps the books, receipts the bills, and
divides the money ?

In case of the farming business, the share of the wife is so direct and unmistakable that it can hardly be evaded. If anything is earned by the farm, she does her distinct and important share of the earning. But it is not necessary that she should do even that, to make her, by all the rules of justice, an equal partner, entitled to her full share of the financial proceeds.

Let us suppose an ordinary case. Two young people are married, and begin life together. Let us suppose them equally poor, equally capable, equally conscientious, equally healthy. They have children. Those children must be supported by the earning of money abroad, by attendance and care at home. If it requires patience and labor to do the outside work, no less is required inside. The duties of the household are as hard as the duties of the shop or office. If the wife took her husband's work for a day, she would probably be glad to return to her own. So would the husband if he undertook hers. Their duties are ordinarily as distinct and as equal as those of two partners in any other copartnership. It so happens that the outdoor partner has the handling of the money; but does that give him a right to claim it as his exclusive earnings? No more than in any other business operation.

He earned the money for the children and

the household. She disbursed it for the children and the household. The very laws of nature, by giving her the children to bear and rear, absolve her from the duty of their support, so long as he is alive who was left free by nature for that purpose. Her task on the average is as hard as his : nay, a portion of it is so especially hard that it is distinguished from all others by the name "labor." If it does not earn money, it is because it is not to be measured in money, while it exists, — nor to be replaced by money, if lost. If a business man loses his partner, he can obtain another : and a man, no doubt, may take a second wife ; but he cannot procure for his children a second mother. Indeed, it is a palpable insult to the whole relation of husband and wife when one compares it, even in a financial light, to that of business partners. It is only because a constant effort is made to degrade the practical position of woman below even this standard of comparison, that it becomes her duty to claim for herself at least as much as this.

There was a tradition in a town where I once lived, that a certain Quaker, who had married a fortune, was once heard to repel his wife, who had asked him for money in a public place, with the response, " Rachel, where is that ninepence I gave thee yesterday ? " When I read

in "Scribner's Monthly" an article deriding
the right to representation of the Massachusetts
women who pay two millions of tax on one hundred and thirty-two million dollars of property,
— asserting that they produced nothing of it ;
that it was only " men who produced this
wealth, and bestowed it upon these women ; "
that it was " all drawn from land and sea by the
hands of men whose largess testifies alike of
their love and their munificence," — I must say
that I am reminded of Rachel's ninepence.

ONE RE-   When we look through any busi-
SPONSIBLE ness directory, there seem to be
HEAD   almost as many copartnerships as
single dealers ; and three quarters of these copartnerships appear to consist of precisely two
persons, no more, no less. These partners are,
in the eye of the law, equal. It is not found
necessary, under the law, to make a general
provision that in each case one partner should
be supreme and the other subordinate. In
many cases, by the terms of the copartnership
there are limitations on one side and special
privileges on the other, — marriage settlements,
as it were ; but the general law of copartnership is based on the presumption of equality.
It would be considered infinitely absurd to require that, as the general rule, one party or the

other should be in a state of *coverture*, during which the very being and existence of the one should be suspended, or entirely merged and incorporated into that of the other.

And yet this requirement, which would be an admitted absurdity in the case of two business partners, is precisely that which the English common law still lays down in case of husband and wife. The words which I employed to describe it, in the preceding sentence, are the very phrases in which Blackstone describes the legal position of women. And though the English common law has been, in this respect, greatly modified and superseded by statute law; yet, when it comes to an argument on woman suffrage, it is constantly this same tradition to which men and even women habitually appeal, — the necessity of a single head to the domestic partnership, and the necessity that the husband should be that head. This is especially true of English men and women ; but it is true of Americans as well. Nobody has stated it more tersely than Fitzjames Stephen, in his " Liberty, Equality, and Fraternity" (p. 216), when arguing against Mr. Mill's view of the equality of the sexes.

" Marriage is a contract, one of the principal objects in which is the government of a family.

" This government must be vested, either by law

or by contract, in the hands of one of the two married persons."

[Then follow some collateral points, not bearing on the present question.]

" Therefore if marriage is to be permanent, the
government of the family must be put by law and
by morals into the hands of the husband, for no one
proposes to give it to the wife."

This argument he calls "as clear as that of
a proposition in Euclid." He thinks that the
business of life can be carried on by no other
method. How is it, then, that when we come
to what is called technically and especially the
"business" of every day, this whole fine-spun
theory is disregarded, and men come together
in partnership on the basis of equality?

Nobody is farther than I from regarding
marriage as a mere business partnership. But
it is to be observed that the points wherein it
differs from a merely mercantile connection are
points that should make equality more easy,
not more difficult. The tie between two ordinary business partners is merely one of interest : it is based on no sentiments, sealed by no
solemn pledge, enriched by no home associations, cemented by no new generation of young
life. If a relation like this is found to work
well on terms of equality, — so well that a large

part of the business of the world is done by it,
— is it not absurd to suppose that the same
equal relation cannot exist in the married partnership of husband and wife ? And if law, custom, society, all recognize this fact of equality
in the one case, why, in the name of common-
sense, should they not equally recognize it in
the other ?

And, again, it may often be far easier to assign a sphere to each partner in marriage than
in business ; and therefore the double headship
of a family will involve less need of collision.
In nine cases out of ten, the external support
of the family will devolve upon the husband,
unquestioned by the wife ; and its internal economy upon the wife, unquestioned by the husband. No voluntary distribution of powers and
duties between business partners can work so
naturally, on the whole, as this simple and easy
demarcation, with which the claim of suffrage
makes no necessary interference. It may require angry discussion to decide which of two
business partners shall buy, and which shall
sell ; which shall keep the books, and which do
the active work, and so on ; but all this is usually settled in married life by the natural order
of things. Even in regard to the management
of children, where collision is likely to come, if
anywhere, it can commonly be settled by that

happy formula of Jean Paul's, that the mother usually supplies the commas and the semi-colons in the child's book of life, and the father the colons and periods. And as to matters in general, the simple and practical rule, that each question that arises should be decided by that partner who has personally most at stake in it, will, in ninety-nine times out of a hundred, carry the domestic partnership through without ship-wreck. Those who cannot meet the hundredth case by mutual forbearance are in a condition of shipwreck already.

ASKING FOR MONEY One of the very best wives and mothers I have ever known once said to me, that, whenever her daughters should be married, she should stipulate in their behalf with their husbands for a regular sum of money to be paid them, at certain intervals, for their personal expenditures. Whether this sum was to be larger or smaller, was a matter of secondary importance, — that must depend on the income, and the style of living; but the essential thing was, that it should come to the wife regularly, so that she should no more have to make a special request for it than her husband would have to ask her for a dinner. This lady's own husband was, as I happened to know, of a most generous disposition, was devotedly attached to her, and denied her nothing. She herself was a most accurate and careful manager. There was everything in the household to make the financial arrangements flow smoothly. Yet she said to me, "I suppose no man can possibly understand how a sensitive woman shrinks from *asking* for money. If I can prevent it, my daughters shall never have to ask for it. If they do their duty as wives and mothers they have a right to their share of the joint income, within reasonable limits ; for certainly no money could buy the services they render. Moreover, they have a right to a share in determining what those reasonable limits are."

Now, it so happened that I had myself gone through an experience which enabled me perfectly to comprehend this feeling. In early life I was for a time in the employ of one of my relatives, who paid me a fair salary but at no definite periods : I was at liberty to ask him for money up to a certain amount whenever I needed it. This seemed to me, in advance, a most agreeable arrangement ; but I found it quite otherwise. It proved to be very disagreeable to apply for money : it made every dollar seem a special favor ; it brought up all kinds of misgivings, as to whether he could spare it without inconvenience, whether he really thought

my services worth it, and so on. My employer
was a thoroughly upright and noble man, and I
was much attached to him. I do not know that
he ever refused or demurred when I made my
request. The annoyance was simply in the
process of asking; and this became so great,
that I often underwent serious inconvenience
rather than do it. Finally, at the year's end, I
surprised my relative very much by saying that
I would accept, if necessary, a lower salary, on
condition that it should be paid on regular days,
and as a matter of business. The wish was at
once granted, without the reduction; and he
probably never knew what a relief it was to
me.

Now, if a young man is liable to feel this
pride and reluctance toward an employer, even
when a kinsman, it is easy to understand how
many women may feel the same, even in regard
to a husband. And I fancy that those who feel
it most are often the most conscientious and
high-minded women. It is unreasonable to say
of such persons, "Too sensitive! Too fastidious!" For it is just this quality of finer sensitiveness which men affect to prize in a woman,
and wish to protect at all hazards. The very
fact that a husband is generous; the very fact
that his income is limited, — these may bring
in conscience and gratitude to increase the re-

straining influence of pride, and make the wife less willing to ask money of such a husband than if he were a rich man or a mean one. The only dignified position in which a man can place his wife is to treat her at least as well as he would treat a housekeeper, and give her the comfort of a perfectly clear and definite arrangement as to money matters. She will not then be under the necessity of nerving herself to solicit from him as a favor what she really needs and has a right to spend. Nor will she be torturing herself, on the other side, with the secret fear lest she has asked too much and more than they can really spare. She will, in short, be in the position of a woman and a wife, not of a child or a toy.

I have carefully avoided using the word " allowance " in what has been said, because that word seems to imply the untrue and mean assumption that the money is all the husband's to give or withhold as he will. Yet I have heard this sort of phrase from men who were living on a wife's property or a wife's earnings ; from men who nominally kept boarding-houses, working a little, while their wives worked hard, — or from farmers, who worked hard, and made their wives work harder. Even in cases where the wife has no direct part in the money-making, the indirect part she performs, if she takes faithful charge of her household, is so essential, so beyond all compensation in money, that it is an utter shame and impertinence in the husband when he speaks of "giving" money to his wife as if it were an act of favor. It is no more an act of favor than when the business manager of a firm pays out money to the unseen partner who directs the indoor business or runs the machinery. Be the joint income more or less, the wife has a claim to her honorable share, and that as a matter of right, without the daily ignominy of sending in a petition for it.

WOMAN-   I always groan in spirit when any
HOOD AND   advocate of woman suffrage, carried
MOTHER-
HOOD   away by zeal, says anything disrespectful about the nursery. It is contrary to the general tone of feeling among reformers, I am sure, to speak of this priceless institution as a trivial or degrading sphere, unworthy the emancipated woman. It is rarely that anybody speaks in this way; but a single such utterance hinders progress more than any arguments of the enemy. For every thoughtful person sees that the cares of motherhood, though not the whole duty of woman, are an essential part of that duty, wherever they occur; and that no theory of womanly life is good for

anything which undertakes to leave out the cradle. Even her school education is based on this fact, were it only on Stendhal's theory that the sons of a woman who reads Gibbon and Schiller will be more likely to show talent than those of one who only tells her beads and reads Mme. de Genlis. And so clearly is this understood among us, that, when we ask for suffrage for woman, it is almost always claimed that she needs it for the sake of her children. To secure her in her right to them; to give her a voice in their education; to give her a vote in the government beneath which they are to live, — these points are seldom omitted in our statement of her claims. Anything else would be an error.

But there is an error at the other extreme, which is still greater. A woman should no more merge herself in her child than in her husband. Yet we often hear that she should do just this. What is all the public sphere of woman, it is said, — what good can she do by all her speaking and writing and action, — compared with that she does by properly training the soul of one child? It is not easy to see the logic of this claim.

For what service is that child to render in the universe, except that he, too, may write and speak and act for that which is good and true?

And if the mother foregoes all this that the child, in growing up, may simply do what the mother has left undone, the world gains nothing. In sacrificing her own work to her child's, moreover, she exchanges a present good for a prospective and merely possible one. If she does this through overwhelming love, we can hardly blame her; but she cannot justify it before reason and truth. Her child may die, and the service to mankind be done by neither. Her child may grow up with talents unlike hers, or with none at all; as the son of Howard was selfish, the son of Chesterfield a boor, and the son of Wordsworth in the last degree prosaic.

Or the special occasion when she might have done great good may have passed before her boy or girl grows up to do it. If Mrs. Child had refused to write "An Appeal for that Class of Americans called Africans," or Mrs. Stowe had laid aside "Uncle Tom's Cabin," or Florence Nightingale had declined to go to the Crimea, on the ground that a woman's true work was through the nursery, and they must all wait for that, the consequence would be that these things would have remained undone. The brave acts of the world must be performed when occasion offers, by the first brave soul who feels moved to do them, man or woman.

If all the children in all the nurseries are thereby helped to do other brave deeds when their turn comes, so much the better. But when a great opportunity offers for direct aid to the world, we have no right to transfer that work to other hands — not even to the hands of our own children. We must do the work, and train the children besides.

I am willing to admit, therefore, that the work of education, in any form, is as great as any other work; but I fail to see why it should be greater. Usefulness is usefulness : there is no reason why it should be postponed from generation to generation, or why it is better to rear a serviceable human being than to be one in person. Carry the theory consistently out : if each mother must simply rear her daughter that she in turn may rear somebody else, then from each generation the work will devolve upon a succeeding generation, so that it will be only the last woman who will personally do any service, except that of motherhood ; and when her time comes it will be too late for any service at all.

If it be said, "But some of these children will be men, who are necessarily of more use than women," I deny the necessity. If it be said, "The children may be many, and the mother, who is but one, may well be sacrificed," it might be replied that, as one great act may be worth many smaller ones, so all the numerous children and grandchildren of a woman like Lucretia Mott may not collectively equal the usefulness of herself alone. If she, like many women, had held it her duty to renounce all other duties and interests from the time her motherhood began, I think that the world, and even her children, would have lost more than could ever have been gained by her more complete absorption in the nursery.

The true theory seems a very simple one. The very fact that during one half the years of a woman's average life she is made incapable of child-bearing shows that there are, even for the most prolific and devoted mothers, duties other than the maternal. Even during the most absorbing years of motherhood, the wisest women still try to keep up their interest in society, in literature, in the world's affairs — were it only for their children's sake. Multitudes of women will never be mothers ; and those more fortunate may find even the usefulness of their motherhood surpassed by what they do in other ways. If maternal duties interfere in some degree with all other functions, the same is true, though in a far less degree, of those of a father. But there are those who combine both spheres. The German poet Wieland claimed to be the

parent of fourteen children and forty books;
and who knows by which parentage he served
the world the best?

A GERMAN   Many Americans will remember
POINT OF   the favorable impression made by
VIEW   Professor Christlieb of Germany,
when he attended the meeting of the Evangelical Alliance in New York some years ago.
His writings, like his presence, show a most
liberal spirit; and perhaps no man has ever
presented the more advanced evangelical theology of Germany in so attractive a light. Yet
I heard a story of him the other day, which
either showed him in an aspect quite undesirable, or else gave an unpleasant view of the
social position of women in Germany.

The story was to the effect that a young
American student recently called on Professor
Christlieb with a letter of introduction. The
professor received him cordially, and soon en-
tered into conversation about the United States.
He praised the natural features of the country,
and the enterprising spirit of our citizens, but
expressed much solicitude about the future of
the nation. On being asked his reasons, he
frankly expressed his opinion that "the Spirit
of Christ" was not here. Being still further
pressed to illustrate his meaning, he gave, as

instances of this deficiency, not the Crédit
Mobilier or the Tweed scandal, but such alarming facts as the following. He seriously declared that, on more than one occasion, he had
heard an American married woman say to her
husband, "Dear, will you bring me my shawl?"
and the husband had brought it. He further
had seen a husband return home at evening,
and enter the parlor where his wife was sitting,
— perhaps in the very best chair in the room, —
and the wife not only did not go and get his
dressing-gown and slippers, but she even remained seated, and left him to find a chair as
he could. These things, as Professor Christlieb
pointed out, suggested a serious deficiency of
the spirit of Christ in the community.

With our American habits and interpreta-
tions, it is hard to see this matter just as the
professor sees it. One would suppose that, if
there is any meaning in the command, "Bear
ye one another's burdens, and so fulfil the law
of Christ," a little of such fulfilling might
sometimes be good for the husband, as for the
wife. And though it would undoubtedly be
more pleasing to see every wife so eager to receive her husband that she would naturally
spring from her chair and run to kiss him in
the doorway, yet, where such devotion was wanting, it would be but fair to inquire which of

the two had done the more fatiguing day's work, and to whom the easy-chair justly belonged. The truth is, I suppose, that the good professor's remark indicated simply a "survival" in his mind, or in his social circle, of a barbarous tradition, under which the wife of a Mexican herdsman cannot eat at the table with her "lord and master," and the wife of a German professor must vacate the best armchair at his approach.

If so, it is not to be regretted that we in this country have outgrown a relation so unequal. Nor am I at all afraid that the great Teacher, who, pointing to the multitude for whom he was soon to die, said of them, "Whosoever shall do the will of God, the same is my brother and my sister and my mother," would have objected to any mutual and equal service between man and woman. If we assume that two human beings have immortal souls, there can be no want of dignity to either in serving the other. The greater equality of woman in America seems to be, on this reasoning, a proof of the presence not the absence, of the spirit of Christ; nor does Dr. Christlieb seem quite worthy of the beautiful name he bears, if he feels otherwise.

But if it is really true that a German professor has to cross the Atlantic to witness a phenomenon so very simple as that of a lover-

like husband bringing a shawl for his wife, I
should say, Let the immigration from Germany
be encouraged as much as possible, in order
that even the most learned immigrants may
discover something new.

CHILDLESS   It has not always been regarded
WOMEN   as a thing creditable to woman that
she was the mother of the human race. On
the contrary, the fact was often mentioned, in
the Middle Ages, as a distinct proof of inferiority. The question was discussed in the mediæval Council of Mâcon, and the position taken
that woman was no more entitled to rank as
human, because she brought forth men, than
the garden-earth could take rank with the fruit
and flowers it bore. The same view was revived by a Latin writer of 1595, on the thesis
" *Mulieres non homines esse*," a French translation of which essay was printed under the title
of " *Paradoxe sur les femmes*," in 1766. Napoleon Bonaparte used the same image, carry-
ing it almost as far : —

"Woman is given to man that she may bear
children. Woman is our property; we are not
hers : because she produces children for us ; we
do not yield any to her : she is therefore our
possession, as the fruit-tree is that of the gardener."

Even the fact of parentage, therefore, has been adroitly converted into a ground of inferiority for women; and this is ostensibly the reason why lineage has been reckoned, almost everywhere, through the male line only, ignoring the female; just as, in tracing the seed of some rare fruit, the gardener takes no genealogical account of the garden where it grew. This view is now seldom expressed in full force: but one remnant of it is to be found in the lingering impression, that, at any rate, a woman who is not a mother is of no account; as worthless as a fruitless garden or a barren fruit-tree. Created only for a certain object, she is of course valueless unless that object be fulfilled.

But the race must have fathers as well as mothers; and if we look for evidence of public service in great men, it certainly does not always lie in leaving children to the republic. On the contrary, the rule has rather seemed to be, that the most eminent men have left their bequest of service in any form rather than in that of a great family. Recent inquiries into the matter have brought out some remarkable facts in this regard.

As a rule, there exist no living descendants in the male line from the great authors, artists, statesmen, soldiers, of England. It is stated that there is not one such descendant of Chaucer, Shakespeare, Spenser, Butler, Dryden, Pope, Cowper, Goldsmith, Scott, Byron, or Moore; not one of Drake, Cromwell, Monk, Marlborough, Peterborough, or Nelson ; not one of Strafford, Ormond, or Clarendon; not one of Addison, Swift, or Johnson ; not one of Walpole, Bolingbroke, Chatham, Pitt, Fox, Burke, Grattan, or Canning ; not one of Bacon, Locke, Newton, or Davy; not one of Hume, Gibbon, or Macaulay ; not one of Hogarth or Reynolds ; not one of Garrick, John Kemble, or Edmund Kean. It would be easy to make a similar American list, beginning with Washington, of whom it was said that "Providence made him childless that his country might call him Father."

Now, however we may regret that these great men have left little or no posterity, it does not occur to any one as affording any serious drawback upon their service to their nation. Certainly it does not occur to us that they would have been more useful had they left children to the world, but rendered it no other service. Lord Bacon says that "he that hath wife and children hath given hostages to fortune ; for they are impediments to great enterprises, either of virtue or mischief. Certainly the best works, and of greatest merit for the public, have proceeded from the unmarried or childless men ;

which, both in affection and means, have married and endowed the public." And this is the view generally accepted, — that the public is in such cases rather the gainer than the loser, and has no right to complain.

Since, therefore, every child must have a father and a mother both, and neither will alone suffice, why should we thus heap gratitude on men who from preference or from necessity have remained childless, and yet habitually treat women as if they could render no service to their country except by giving it children? If it be folly and shame, as I think, to belittle and decry the dignity and worth of motherhood, as some are said to do, it is no less folly, and shame quite as great, to deny the grand and patriotic service of many women who have died and left no children among their mourners. Plato puts into the mouth of a woman, — the eloquent Diotima, in the "Banquet," — that, after all, we are more grateful to Homer and Hesiod for the children of their brain than if they had left human offspring.

THE PRE-VENTION OF CRUEL-TY TO MO-THERS   From the Society for the Prevention of Cruelty to Animals we have now advanced to a similar society for the benefit of children. When shall we have a movement for the prevention of cruelty to mothers?

A Rhode Island lady, who had never taken any interest in the woman-suffrage movement, came to me in great indignation the other day, asking if it was true that under Rhode Island laws a husband might, by his last will, bequeath his child away from its mother, so that she might, if the guardian chose, never see it again. I said that it was undoubtedly true, and that such were still the laws in many States of the Union.

"But," she said, "it is an outrage. The husband may have been one of the weakest or worst men in the world; he may have persecuted his wife and children; he may have made the will in a moment of anger, and have neglected to alter it. At any rate, he is dead, and the mother is living. The guardian whom he appoints may turn out a very malicious man, and may take pleasure in torturing the mother ; or he may bring up the children in a way their mother thinks ruinous for them. Why do not all the mothers cry out against such a law?"

"I wish they would," I said. "I have been trying a good many years to make them understand what the law is ; but they do not. People who do not vote pay no attention to the laws until they suffer from them."

She went away protesting that she, at least, would not hold her tongue on the subject, and

I hope she will not. The actual text of the law to which she objected is as follows : —

" Every person authorized by law to make a will, except married women, shall have a right to appoint by his will a guardian or guardians for his children during their minority." [1]

There is not associated with this, in the statute, the slightest clause in favor of the mother ; nor anything which could limit the power of the guardian by requiring deference to her wishes, although he could, in case of gross neglect or abuse, be removed by the court, and another guardian appointed. There is not a line of positive law to protect the mother. Now, in a case of absolute wrong, a single sentence of law is worth all the chivalrous courtesy this side of the Middle Ages.

It is idle to say that such laws are not executed. They are executed. I have had letters, too agonizing to print, expressing the sufferings of mothers under laws like these. There lies before me a letter, — not from Rhode Island, — written by a widowed mother who suffers daily tortures, even while in possession of her child, at the knowledge that it is not legally hers, but held only by the temporary permission of the guardian appointed under her husband's will. " I beg you," she says, "to take this will to the

[1] Gen. Statutes R. I., chap. 154, sect. 1.

hilltop, and urge law-makers in our next legislature to free the State record from the shame-
ful story that no mother can control her child
unless it is born out of wedlock."

"From the moment," she says, "when the
will was read to me, I have made no effort to
set it aside. I wait till God reveals his plans,
so far as my own condition is concerned. But
out of my keen comprehension of this great
wrong, notwithstanding my submission for myself, my whole soul is stirred, — for my child,
who is a little woman; for all women, that the
laws may be changed which subject a true woman, a devoted wife, a faithful mother, to such
mental agonies as I have endured, and shall
endure till I die."

In a later letter she says, "I now have his
[the guardian's] solemn promise that he will
not remove her from my control. To some extent my sufferings are allayed; and yet never,
till she arrives at the age of twenty-one, shall I
fully trust." I wish that mothers who dwell in
sheltered and happy homes would try to bring
to their minds the condition of a mother whose
possession of her only child rests upon the
"promise" of a comparative stranger. We
should get beyond the meaningless cry, "I have
all the rights I want," if mothers could only
remember that among these rights, in most

States of the Union, the right of a widowed
mother to her child is not included.

By strenuous effort, the law on this point
has in Massachusetts been gradually amended,
till it now stands thus : The father is authorized
to appoint a guardian by will ; but the powers
of this guardian do not entitle him to take the
child from the mother.

"The guardian of a minor . . . shall have the
custody and tuition of his ward ; and the care and
management of all his estate, except that the father
of the minor, if living, and in case of his death the
mother, they being respectively competent to trans-
act their own business, shall be entitled to the custody of the person of the minor and the care of his
education." [1]

Down to 1870 the cruel words "while she
remains unmarried" followed the word "mother" in the above law.   Until that time, the
mother if remarried had no claim to the custody
of her child, in case the guardian wished otherwise ; and a very painful scene once took place
in a Boston court-room, where children were
forced away from their mother by the officers,
under this statute, in spite of her tears and
theirs ; and this when no sort of personal charge
had been made against her.   This could not
now happen in Massachusetts, but it might still

[1] Public Statutes, chap. 139, sect. 4.

happen in some other States. It is true that men are almost always better than their laws; but while a bad law remains on the statute-book it gives to any unscrupulous man the power to be as bad as the law.

V

SOCIETY

" Place the sexes in right relations of mutual respect, and a severe morality gives that essential charm to woman which educates all that is delicate, poetic, and self-sacrificing, breeds courtesy and learning, conversation and wit, in her rough mate; so that I have thought a sufficient measure of civilization is the influence of good women." — EMERSON, Society and Solitude, p. 21.

FOAM AND CURRENT   Sometimes, on the beach at Newport, I look at the gayly dressed ladies in their phaetons, and then at the foam which trembles on the breaking wave, or lies palpitating in creamy masses on the beach.   It is as pretty as they, as light, as fresh, as delicate, as changing; and no doubt the graceful foam, if it thinks at all, fancies that it is the chief consummate product of the ocean, and that the main end of the vast currents of the mighty deep is to yield a few glittering bubbles like those.   At least, this seems to me what many of the fair ladies think, as to themselves.

Here is a nation in which the most momentous social and political experiment ever tried by man is being worked out, day by day. There is something ocean-like in the way in which the great currents of life, race, religion, temperament are here chafing with each other, safe from the storms through which all monarchical countries may yet have to pass. As these great currents heave, there are tossed up in every watering-place and every city in America, as on an ocean beach, certain pretty bubbles of foam; and each spot, we may suppose, counts its own bubbles brighter than those of its neighbors, and christens them "society."

It is an unceasing wonder to a thoughtful person, at any such resort, to see the unconscious way in which fashionable society accepts the foam, and ignores the currents. You hear people talk of "a position in society," "the influential circles in society," as if the position they mean were not liable to be shifted in a day; as if the essential influences in America were not mainly to be sought outside the world of fashion. In other countries it is very different. The circle of social caste, whose centre you touch in London, radiates to the farthest shores of the British empire; the upper class controls, not merely fashion, but government; it rules in country as well as city; genius and wealth are but its tributaries. Wherever it is not so, it is because England is so far Ameri-

canized. But in America the social prestige
of the cities is nothing in the country; it is a
matter of the pavement, of a three-mile radius.

Go to the farthest borders of England : there
are still the "county families," and you meet
servants in livery. On the other hand, in a
little village in northern New Hampshire, my
friend was visited in the evening by the land-
lady, who said that several of their "most fashionable ladies" had happened in, and she would
like to show them her guest's bonnet. Then
the different cities ignore each other : the rulers
of select circles in New York may find themselves nobodies in Washington, while a Washington social passport counts for as little in
New York. Boston and Philadelphia affect to
ignore both ; and St. Louis and San Francisco
have their own standards. The utmost social
prestige in America is local, provincial, a matter
of the square inch : it is as if the foam of each
particular beach along the seacoast were to call
itself "society."

There is something pathetic, therefore, in
the unwearied pains taken by ambitious women
to establish a place in some little, local, transi-
tory domain, to "bring out" their daughters
for exhibition on a given evening, to form a
circle for them, to marry them well. A dozen
years hence the millionaires whose notice they

seek may be paupers, or these ladies may be dwelling in some other city, where the visiting cards will bear wholly different names. How idle to attempt to transport into American life the social traditions and delusions which require monarchy and primogeniture, and a standing army, to keep them up — and which cannot always hold their own in England, even with the aid of these!

Every woman, like every man, has a natural desire for influence; and if this instinct yearns, as it often should yearn, to take in more than her own family, she must seek it somewhere outside. I know women who bring to bear on the building-up of a frivolous social circle — frivolous, because it is not really brilliant, but only showy; not really gay, but only bored — talent and energy enough to influence the mind and thought of the nation, if only employed in some effective way. Who are the women of real influence in America? They are the school-teachers, through whose hands each successive American generation has to pass; they are those wives of public men who share their husbands' labor, and help mould their work; they are those women who, through their personal eloquence or through the press, are distinctly influencing the American people in its growth. The influence of such women is felt for good

or for evil in every page they print, every newspaper column they fill: the individual women
may be unworthy their posts, but it is they
who have got hold of the lever, and gone the
right way to work. As American society is
constituted, the largest "social success" that
can be attained here is trivial and local; and
you have to "make believe very hard," like
that other imaginary Marchioness, to find in it
any career worth mentioning. That is the
foam, but these other women are dealing with
the main currents.

IN SOCI-   One sometimes hears from some
ETY   lady the remark that very few people "in society" believe in any movement to
enlarge the rights or duties of women. In a
community of more marked social gradations
than our own, this assertion, if true, might be
very important; and even here it is worth considering, because it leads the way to a little
social philosophy. Let us, for the sake of argument, begin by accepting the assumption that
there is an inner circle, at least in our large
cities, which claims to be "society," *par excellence*. What relation has this favored circle, if
favored it be, to any movement relating to
women?

It has, to begin with, the same relation that

"society" has to every movement of reform. The proportion of smiles and frowns bestowed from this quarter upon the woman - suffrage movement, for instance, is about that formerly bestowed upon the anti-slavery agitation : I see no great difference. In Boston, for example, the names contributed by "society" to the woman-suffrage festivals are about as numerous as those which used to be contributed to the anti-slavery bazaars; no more, no less. Indeed, they are very often the same names; and it has been curious to see, for nearly fifty years, how radical tendencies have predominated in some of the well-known Boston families, and conservative tendencies in others. The traits of blood seem to outlast successive series of special reforms. Be this as it may, it is safe to assume, that, as the anti-slavery movement prevailed with only a moderate amount of sanction from "our best society," the woman - suffrage agitation, which has at least an equal amount, has no reason to be discouraged.

On looking farther, we find that not reforms alone, but often most important and established institutions, exist and flourish with only incidental aid from those "in society." Take, for instance, the whole public school system of our larger cities. Grant that out of twenty ladies "in society," taken at random, not more than one would personally approve of women's voting: it is doubtful whether even that proportion of them would personally favor the public school system so far as to submit their children, or at least their girls, to it. Yet the public schools flourish, and give a better training than most private schools, in spite of this inert practical resistance from those "in society." The natural inference would seem to be, that if an institution so well established as the public schools, and so generally recognized, can afford to be ignored by "society," then certainly a wholly new reform must expect no better fate.

As a matter of fact, I apprehend that what is called "society," in the sense of the more fastidious or exclusive social circle in any community, exists for one sole object,—the preservation of good manners and social refinements. For this purpose it is put very largely under the sway of women, who have, all the world over, a better instinct for these important things. It is true that "society" is apt to do even this duty very imperfectly, and often tolerates, and sometimes even cultivates, just the rudeness and discourtesy that it is set to cure. Nevertheless, this is its mission; but so soon as it steps beyond this, and attempts to claim any special weight outside the sphere of good

manners, it shows its weakness, and must yield
to stronger forces.

One of these stronger forces is religion, which
should train men and women to a far higher
standard than "society" alone can teach. This
standard should be embodied, theoretically, in
the Christian Church; but unhappily "society"
is too often stronger than this embodiment, and
turns the church itself into a mere temple of
fashion. Other opposing forces are known as
science and common-sense, which is only science written in shorthand. On some of these
various forces all reforms are based, the woman-
suffrage reform among them. If it could really
be shown that some limited social circle was opposed to this, then the moral would seem to be,
"So much the worse for the social circle." It
used to be thought in anti-slavery days that one
of the most blessed results of that agitation was
the education it gave to young men and women
who would otherwise have merely grown up "in
society," but were happily taken in hand by a
stronger influence. It is Goethe who suggests,
when discussing Hamlet in "Wilhelm Meister,"
that, if an oak be planted in a flower-pot, it will
be worse in the end for the flower-pot than for
the tree. And to those who watch, year after
year, the young human seedlings planted "in
society," the main point of interest lies in the

discovery which of these are likely to grow into oaks.

But the truth is that the very use of the word " society " in this sense is narrow and misleading. We Americans are fortunate enough to live in a larger society, where no conventional position or family traditions exert an influence that is to be in the least degree compared with the influence secured by education, energy, and character. No matter how fastidious the social circle, one is constantly struck with the limitations of its influence, and with the little power exerted by its members as compared with that which may easily be wielded by tongue and pen. No merely fashionable woman in New York, for instance, has a position sufficiently important to be called influential compared with that of a woman who can speak in public so as to command hearers, or can write so as to secure readers. To be at the head of a normal school, or to be a professor in a college where co-education prevails, is to have a sway over the destinies of America which reduces all mere " social position " to a matter of cards and compliments and page's buttons.

THE
BATTLE
OF THE
CARDS

The great winter's contest of the visiting-cards recommences at the end of every autumn. Suspended during the summer, or only renewed at Newport and such thoroughbred and thoroughly sophisticated haunts, it will set in with fury in the habitable regions of our cities before the snow falls. Now will the atmosphere of certain streets and squares be darkened — or whitened — at the appointed hour by the shower of pasteboard transmitted from dainty kid-gloved hands to the cotton-gloved hands of " John," and destined through him to reach the possibly gloveless hands of some other John, who stands obsequious in the doorway. Now will every lady, after John has slammed the door, drive happily on to some other door, rearranging, as she goes, her display of cards, laid as if for a game on the opposite seat of her carriage, and dealt perhaps in four suits, — her own cards, her daughters', her husband's, her " Mr. and Mrs." cards, and who knows how many more? With all this ammunition, what a very *mitrailleuse* of good society she becomes ; what an accumulation of polite attentions she may discharge at any door ! That one well-appointed woman, as she sits in her carriage, represents the total visiting power of self, husband, daughters, and possibly a son or two beside. She has all their counterfeit presentments in her hands. How happy she is! and how happy will the others be on her return, to think that dear mamma has disposed of so many dear, beloved, tiresome, social foes that morning! It will be three months at least, they think, before the A's and the B's and the C's will have to be "done" again.

Ah! but who knows how soon these fatiguing letters of the alphabet, rallying to the defence, will come, pasteboard in hand, to return the onset? In this contest, fair ladies, "there are blows to take as well as blows to give," in the words of the immortal Webster. Some day, on returning, you will find a half-dozen cards on your own table that will undo all this morning's work, and send you forth on the warpath again. Is it not like a campaign? It is from this subtle military analogy, doubtless, that when gentlemen happen to quarrel, in the very best society, they exchange cards as preliminary to a duel; and that, when French journalists fight, all other French journalists show their sympathy for the survivor by sending him their cards. When we see, therefore, these heroic ladies riding forth in the social battle's magnificently stern array, our hearts render them the homage due to the brave. When we consider how complex their military equipment has grown, we fancy each of these self-devoted mothers to be an Arnold Winkelried, receiving in her martyr-breast the points of a dozen different cards, and shouting, "Make way for liberty!" For is it not securing liberty to have cleared off a dozen calls from your list, and found nobody at home?

If this sort of thing goes on, who can tell where the paper warfare shall end? If ladies may leave cards for their husbands, who are never seen out of Wall Street, except when they are seen at their clubs ; or for their sons, who never forsake their billiards or their books, — why can they not also leave them for their ancestors, or for their remotest posterity? Who knows but people may yet drop cards in the names of the grandchildren whom they only wish for, or may reconcile hereditary feuds by interchanging pasteboard in behalf of two hostile grandparents who died half a century ago?

And there is another social observance in which the introduction of the card system may yet be destined to save much labor, — the attendance on fashionable churches. Already, it is said, a family may sometimes reconcile devout observance with a late breakfast, by stationing the family carriage near the church-door — empty. Really, it would not be a much emptier observance to send the cards alone by the footman ; and doubtless in the progress of civilization we shall yet reach that point. It will have many advantages. The *effete* of society, as some cruel satirist has called them, may then send their orisons on pasteboard to as many different shrines as they approve ; thus insuring their souls, as it were, at several different offices. Church architecture may be simplified, for it will require nothing but a card-basket. The clergyman will celebrate his solemn ritual, and will then look in that convenient receptacle for the names of his fellow-worshippers, as a fine lady, after her "reception," looks over the cards her footman hands her, to know which of her dear friends she has been welcoming. Religion, as well as social proprieties, will glide smoothly over a surface of glazed pasteboard ; and it will be only very humble Christians, indeed, who will do their worshipping in person, and will hold to the worn-out and obsolete practice of " No Cards."

SOME WORKING-WOMEN   It is almost a stereotyped remark, that the women of the more fashionable and worldly class, in America, are indolent, idle, incapable, and live feeble and lazy lives. It has always seemed to me that, on the contrary, they are compelled, by the very circumstances of their situation, to lead very laborious lives, requiring great strength and energy. Whether many of their pursuits are frivolous, is a different question ; but that they are arduous, I do not see how any one can doubt. I think it can be easily shown that the common charges against American fashionable women do not hold against the class I describe.

There is, for instance, the charge of evading the cares of housekeeping, and of preferring a boarding-house or hotel. But no woman with high aims in the world of fashion can afford to relieve herself from household cares in this way, except as an exceptional or occasional thing. She must keep house in order to have entertainments, to form a circle, to secure a position. The law of give and take is as absolute in society as in business ; and the very first essential to social position in our larger cities is a household and a hospitality of one's own. It is far more practicable for a family of high rank in England to live temporarily in lodgings in London, than for any family with social aspirations to do the same in New York. The married woman who seeks a position in the world of society must, therefore, keep house.

And, with housekeeping, there comes at once to the American woman a world of care far beyond that of her European sisters.

Abroad, everything in domestic life is systematized; and services of any grade, up to that of housekeeper or steward, can be secured for money, and for a moderate amount of that. The mere amount of money might not trouble the American woman; but where to get the service? Such a thing as a trained housekeeper, who can undertake, at any salary, to take the work off the shoulders of the lady of the house, — such a thing America hardly affords. Without this, the multiplication of servants only increaseth sorrow; the servants themselves are often but an undisciplined mob, and the lady of the house is like a general attempting to drill his whole command personally, without the aid of a staff-officer or so much as a sergeant. For an occasional grand entertainment, she can, perhaps, import a special force; some fashionable sexton can arrange her invitations, and some genteel caterer her supper. But for the daily routine of the household — guests, children, door-bell, equipage — there is one vast, constant toil every day; and the woman who would have these things done well must give her own orders, and discipline her own retinue. The husband may have no "business," his wealth may supersede the necessity of all toil beyond daily billiards; but for the wife wealth means business, and the more complete the social triumph, the more overwhelming the daily toil.

For instance, I know a fair woman in an Atlantic city who is at the head of a household including six children and nine servants. The whole domestic management is placed absolutely in her hands : she engages or dismisses every person employed, incurs every expense, makes every purchase, and keeps all the accounts ; her husband only ordering the fuel, directing the affairs of the stable, and drawing checks for the bills. Every hour of her morning is systematically appropriated to these things. Among other things, she has to provide for nine meals a day; in dining-room, kitchen, and nursery, three each. Then she has to plan her social duties, and to drive out, exquisitely dressed, to make her calls. Then there are constantly dinner-parties and evening entertainments ; she reads a little, and takes lessons in one or two languages. Meanwhile her husband has for daily occupation his books, his club, and the above-mentioned light and easy share in the cares of the household. Many men in his position do not even keep an account of personal expenditures.

There is nothing exceptional in this lady's case, except that the work may be better done than usual : the husband could not well contribute more than his present share without hurting domestic discipline ; nor does the wife do all this from pleasure, but in a manner from necessity. It is the condition of her social position : to change it, she must withdraw herself from her social world. A few improvements, such as "family hotels," are doing something to relieve this class to whom luxury means labor. The great undercurrent which is sweeping us all toward some form of associated life is as obvious in this new improvement in housekeeping, as in coöperative stores or trades-unions ; but it will nevertheless be long before the " women of society " in America can be anything but a hard-working class.

The question is not whether such a life as I have described is the ideal life. My point is that it is, at any rate, a life demanding far more of energy and toil, at least in America, than the men of the same class are called upon to exhibit. There is growing up a class of men of leisure in America ; but there are no women of leisure in the same circle. They hold their social position on condition of " an establishment," and an establishment makes them working-women. One result is the constant exodus of this class to Europe, where domestic life is just now easier. Another consequence is that you hear woman suffrage denounced by women of this class, not on the ground that it involves any harder work than they already do, but on the ground that they have work enough already, and will not bear the suggestion of any more.

THE EM-PIRE OF MANNERS   I was present at a lively discourse, administered by a young lady just from Europe to a veteran politician. "It is of very little consequence," she said, "what kind of men you send out as foreign ministers. The thing of real importance is that they should have the right kind of wives. Any man can sign a treaty, I suppose, if you tell him what kind of treaty it must be. But all his social relations with the nations to which you send him will depend on his wife." There was some truth, certainly, in this audacious conclusion. It reminded me of the saying of a modern thinker, "The only empire freely conceded to women is that of manners, — but it is worth all the rest put together."

Every one instinctively feels that the graces and amenities of life must be largely under the direction of women. The fact that this feeling has been carried too far, and has led to the dwarfing of women's intellect, must not lead to a rejection of this important social sphere. It is too strong a power to be ignored. George

Eliot says well that "the commonest man, who has his ounce of sense and feeling, is conscious of the difference between a lovely, delicate woman, and a coarse one. Even a dog feels a difference in their presence." At a summer resort, for instance, one sees women who may be intellectually very ignorant and narrow, yet whose mere manners give them a social power which the highest intellects might envy. To lend joy and grace to all one's little world of friendship ; to make one's house a place which every guest enters with eagerness, and leaves with reluctance ; to lend encouragement to the timid, and ease to the awkward ; to repress violence, restrain egotism, and make even controversy courteous, — these belong to the empire of woman. It is a sphere so important and so beautiful, that even courage and self-devotion seem not quite enough, without the addition of this supremest charm.

This courtesy is so far from implying falsehood, that its very best basis is perfect simplicity. Given a naturally sensitive organization, a loving spirit, and the early influence of a refined home, and the foundation of fine manners is secured. A person so favored may be reared in a log hut, and may pass easily into a palace ; the few needful conventionalities are so readily acquired. But I think it is a mistake to tell

children, as we sometimes do, that simplicity
and a kind heart are absolutely all that are
needful in the way of manners. There are
persons in whom simplicity and kindness are
inborn. and who yet never attain to good manners for want of refined perceptions. And it
is astonishing how much refinement alone can
do, even if it be not very genuine or very full
of heart, to smooth the paths and make social
life attractive.

All the acute observers have recognized the
difference between the highest standard, which
is nature's, and that next to the highest, which
is art's. George Eliot speaks of that fine polish which is " the expensive substitute for simplicity," and Tennyson says of manners, —

> " Kind nature's are the best : those next to best
> That fit us like a nature second-hand ;
> Which are indeed the manners of the great."

In our own national history we have learned
to recognize that the personal demeanor of women may be a social and political force. The
slave-power owed much of its prolonged control
at Washington, and the larger part of its favor
in Europe, to the fact that the manners of
Southern women had been more sedulously
trained than those of Northern women. Even
at this moment, one may see at any watering-
place that the relative social influence of differ-

ent cities does not depend upon the intellectual training of their women, so much as on the manners. And, even if this is very unreasonable, the remedy would seem to be, not to go about lecturing on the intrinsic superiority of the Muses to the Graces, but to pay due homage at all the shrines.

It is a great deal to ask of reformers, especially, that they should be ornamental as well as useful ; and I would by no means indorse the views of a lady who once told me that she was ready to adopt the most radical views of the women-reformers if she could see one well-dressed woman who accepted them. The place where we should draw the line between independence and deference, between essentials and non-essentials, between great ideas and little courtesies, will probably never be determined — except by actual examples. Yet it is safe to fall back on Miss Edgeworth's maxim in " Helen," that " Every one who makes goodness disagreeable commits high treason against virtue." And it is not a pleasant result of our good deeds, that others should be immediately driven into bad deeds by the burning desire to be unlike us.

GIRLSTER-
OUSNESS
They tell the story of a little boy, a young scion of the house of Beecher, that, on being rebuked for some noisy proceeding, in which his little sister had also shared, he claimed that she also should be included in the indictment. "If a boy makes too much noise," he said, "you tell him he must n't be boisterous. Well, then, when a girl makes just as much noise, you ought to tell her not to be so *girlsterous*."

I think that we should accept, with a sense of gratitude, this addition to the language. It supplies a name for a special phase of feminine demeanor, inevitably brought out of modern womanhood. Any transitional state of society develops some evil with the good. Good results are unquestionably proceeding from the greater freedom now allowed to women. The drawback is that we are developing, here and now, more of "girlsterousness" than is apt to be seen in less enlightened countries.

The more complete the subjection of woman, the more "subdued" in every sense she is. The typical woman of savage life is, at least in youth, gentle, shy, retiring, timid. A Bedouin woman is modest and humble ; an Indian girl has a voice "gentle and low." The utmost stretch of the imagination cannot picture either of them as "girlsterous." That perilous qual-

ity can only come as woman is educated, self-
respecting, emancipated. " Girlsterousness "
is the excess attendant on that virtue, the
shadow which accompanies that light. It is
more visible in England than in France, in
America than in England.

It is to be observed, that, if a girl wishes to
be noisy, she can be as noisy as anybody. Her
noise, if less clamorous, is more shrill and pene-
trating. The shrieks of schoolgirls, playing in
the yard at recess-time, seem to drown the
voices of the boys. As you enter an evening
party, it is the women's tones you hear most
conspicuously. There is no defect in the organ,
but at least an adequate vigor. In travelling
by rail, when sitting near some rather under-
bred party of youths and damsels, I have commonly noticed that the girls were the noisiest.
The young men appeared more regardful of
public opinion, and looked round with solicitude,
lest they should attract too much attention. It
is "girlsterousness" that dashes straight on,
regardless of all observers.

Of course reformers exhibit their full share
of this undesirable quality. Where the emancipation of women is much discussed in any
circle, some young girls will put it in practice
gracefully and with dignity, others rudely. Yet
even the rudeness may be but a temporary

phase, and at last end well. When women were being first trained as physicians, years ago, I remember a young girl who came from a Southern State to a Northern city, and attended the medical lectures. Having secured her lecture-tickets, she also bought season-tickets to the theatre and to the pistol-gallery, laid in a box of cigars, and began her professional training. If she meant it as a satire on the pursuits of the young gentlemen around her, it was not without point. But it was, I suppose, a clear case of "girlsterousness;" and I dare say that she sowed her wild oats much more innocently than many of her male contemporaries, and that she has long since become a sedate matron. But I certainly cannot commend her as a model.

Yet I must resolutely deny that any sort of hoydenishness or indecorum is an especial characteristic of radicals, or even "provincials," as a class. Some of the fine ladies who would be most horrified at the "girlsterousness" of this young maiden would themselves smoke their cigarettes in much worse company, morally speaking, than she ever tolerated. And, so far as manners are concerned, I am bound to say that the worst cases of rudeness and ill-breeding that have ever come to my knowledge have not occurred in the "rural districts," or among the lower ten thousand, but in those

circles of America where the whole aim in life
might seem to be the cultivation of its ele-
gances.

And what confirms me in the fear that the
most profound and serious types of this disease
are not to be found in the wildcat regions is
the fact that so much of it is transplanted to
Europe, among those who have the money to
travel. It is there described broadly as " Ameri-
canism ; " and, so surely as any peculiarly shrill
group is heard coming through a European pic-
ture-gallery, it is straightway classed by all
observers as belonging to the great Republic.
If the observers are enamoured at sight with
the beauty of the young ladies of the party,
they excuse the voices ;

> " Strange or wild, or madly gay,
> They call it only pretty Fanny's way."

But other observers are more apt to call it
only Columbia's way ; and if they had ever
heard the word " girlsterousness," they would
use that too.

Emerson says, " A gentleman makes no
noise ; a lady is serene." If we Americans
often violate this perfect maxim of good manners, it is something that America has, at least,
furnished the maxim. And, between Emerson
and " girlsterousness," our courteous philosopher may yet carry the day.

ARE
WOMEN
NATURAL
ARISTO-
CRATS?

A clergyman's wife in England has lately set on foot a reform movement in respect to dress ; and, like many English reformers, she aims chiefly to elevate the morals and manners of the lower classes, without much reference to her own social equals. She proposes that "no servant, under pain of dismissal, shall wear flowers, feathers, brooches, buckles or clasps, earrings, lockets, neck - ribbons, velvets, kid gloves, parasols, sashes, jackets, or trimming of any kind on dresses, and, above all, no crinoline ; no pads to be worn, or frisettes, or *chignons*, or hair-ribbons. The dress is to be gored and made just to touch the ground, and the hair to be drawn closely to the head, under a round white cap, without trimming of any kind. The same system of dress is recommended for Sunday-school girls, schoolmistresses, church-singers, and the lower orders generally."

The remark is obvious, that in this country such a course of discipline would involve the mistress, not the maid, in the "pain of dismissal." The American clergyman and clergyman's wife who should even "recommend" such a costume to a schoolmistress, church-singer, or Sunday-school girl, — to say nothing of the rest of the "lower orders," — would soon find themselves without teachers, without pupils, without a choir, and probably without a parish. It is a comfort to think that even in older countries there is less and less of this impertinent interference : the costume of different ranks is being more and more assimilated ; and the incidental episode of a few liveries in our cities is not enough to interfere with the general current. Never yet, to my knowledge, have I seen even a livery worn by a white native American ; and to restrain the Sunday bonnets of her handmaidens, what lady has attempted?

This is as it should be. The Sunday bonnet of the Irish damsel is only the symbol of a very proper effort to obtain her share of all social advantages. Long may those ribbons wave! Meanwhile I think the fact that it is easier for the gentleman of the house to control the dress of his groom than for the lady to dictate that of her waiting-maid, — this must count against the theory that it is women who are the natural aristocrats.

Women are no doubt more sensitive than men upon matters of taste and breeding. This is partly from a greater average fineness of natural perception, and partly because their more secluded lives give them less of miscellaneous contact with the world. If Maud Muller and her husband had gone to board at the

same boarding-house with the Judge and his
wife, that lady might have held aloof from the
rustic bride, simply from inexperience in life,
and not knowing just how to approach her.
But the Judge, who might have been talking
politics or real estate with the young farmer on
the doorsteps that morning, would certainly
find it easier to deal with him as a man and a
brother at the dinner-table. From these different causes women get the credit or discredit
of being more aristocratic than men are; so
that in England the Tory supporters of female
suffrage base it on the ground that these new
voters at least will be conservative.

But, on the other hand, it is women, even
more than men, who are attracted by those
strong qualities of personal character which are
always the antidote to aristocracy. No bold
revolutionist ever defied the established con-
ventionalisms of his times without drawing his
strongest support from women. Poet and novelist love to depict the princess as won by the
outlaw, the gypsy, the peasant. Women have
a way of turning from the insipidities and proprieties of life to the wooer who has the
stronger hand; from the silken Darnley to the
rude Bothwell. This impulse is the natural
corrective to the aristocratic instincts of womanhood; and though men feel it less, it is

still, even among them, one of the supports of
republican institutions. We need to keep always balanced between the two influences of
refined culture and of native force. The patrician class, wherever there is one, is pretty sure
to be the more refined ; the plebeian class, the
more energetic. That woman is able to appre-
ciate both elements is proof that she is quite
capable of doing her share in social and political life. This English clergyman's wife, who
devotes her soul to the trimmings and gored
skirts of the lower orders, is no more entitled
to represent her sex than are those ladies who
give their whole attention to the "novel and
intricate bonnets" advertised this season on
Broadway.

MRS.
BLANK'S
DAUGH-
TERS

Mrs. Blank, of Far West — let us
not draw her from the "sacred pri-
vacy of woman" by giving the name
or place too precisely — has an insurmountable objection to woman's voting. So
the newspapers say ; and this objection is that
she does not wish her daughters to encounter
disreputable characters at the polls.

It is a laudable desire, to keep one's daughters from the slightest contact with such persons. But how does Mrs. Blank precisely
mean to accomplish this ? Will she shut up

the maidens in a harem? When they go out, will she send messengers through the streets to bid people hide their faces, as when an Oriental queen is passing? Will she send them travelling on camels, veiled by *yashmaks*? Will she prohibit them from being so much as seen by a man, except when a physician must be called for their ailments, and Miss Blank puts her arm through a curtain, in order that he may feel her pulse and know no more?

Who is Mrs. Blank, and how does she bring up her daughters? Does she send them to the post-office? If so, they may wait a half-hour at a time for the mail to open, and be elbowed by the most disreputable characters, waiting at their side. If it does the young ladies no harm to encounter this for the sake of getting their letters out, will it harm them to do it in order to get their ballots in? If they go to hear a concert they may be kept half an hour at the door, elbowed by saint and sinner indiscriminately. If they go to Washington to the President's inauguration, they may stand two hours with Mary Magdalen on one side of them and Judas Iscariot on the other. If this contact is rendered harmless by the fact that they are receiving political information, will it hurt them to stay five minutes longer in order to act upon the knowledge they have received?

This is on the supposition that the household of Blank are plain, practical women, unversed in the vanities of the world. If they belong to fashionable circles, how much harder to keep them wholly clear of disreputable contact! Should they, for instance, visit Newport, they may possibly be seen at the Casino, looking very happy as they revolve rapidly in the arms of some very disreputable characters; they will be seen in the surf, attired in the most scanty and clinging drapery, and kindly aided to preserve their balance by the devoted attentions of the same companions. Mrs. Blank, meanwhile, will look complacently on, with the other matrons: they are not supposed to know the current reputation of those whom their daughters meet "in society;" and, so long as there is no actual harm done, why should they care? Very well; but why, then, should they care if they encounter those same disreputable characters when they go to drop a ballot in the ballot-box? It will be a more guarded and distant meeting. It is not usual to dance round-dances at the ward-room, so far as I know, or to bathe in clinging drapery at that rather dry and dusty resort. If such very close intimacies are all right under the gas-light or at the beach, why should there be poison in merely passing near a disreputable character at the City Hall?

On the whole, the prospects of Mrs. Blank are not encouraging. Should she consult a physician for her daughters, he may be secretly or openly disreputable; should she call in a clergyman, he may, though a bishop, have carnal rather than spiritual eyes. If Miss Blank be caught in a shower, she may take refuge under the umbrella of an undesirable acquaintance; should she fall on the ice, the woman who helps to raise her may have sinned. There is not a spot in any known land where a woman can live in absolute seclusion from all contact with evil. Should the Misses Blank even turn Roman Catholics, and take to a convent, their very confessor may not be a genuine saint; and they may be glad to flee for refuge to the busy, buying, selling, dancing, voting world outside.

No: Mrs. Blank's prayers for absolute protection will never be answered, in respect to her daughters. Why not, then, find a better model for prayer in that made by Jesus for his disciples: "I pray Thee, not that Thou shouldst take them out of the world, but that Thou shouldst keep them from the evil." A woman was made for something nobler in the world, Mrs. Blank, than to be a fragile toy, to be put behind a glass case, and protected from contact. It is not her mission to be hidden

away from all life's evil, but bravely to work
that the world may be reformed.

THE EURO-   Every mishap among American
PEAN PLAN   women brings out renewed sugges-
tions of what may be called the " European
plan " in the training of young girls, — the
plan, that is, of extreme seclusion and helpless-
ness. It is usually forgotten, in these sugges-
tions, that not much protection is really given
anywhere to this particular class as a whole.
Everywhere in Europe the restrictions are of
caste, not of sex. Even in Turkey, travellers
tell us, women of the humbler vocations are not
much secluded. It is not the object of the
" European plan," in any form, to protect the
virtue of young women, as such, but only of
young ladies ; and the protection is pretty effectually limited to that order. Among the Portuguese in the island of Fayal I found it to be
the ambition of each humble family to bring
up one daughter in a sort of lady-like seclusion : she never went into the street alone, or
without a hood which was equivalent to a veil ;
she was taught indoor industries only ; she was
constantly under the eye of her mother. But
in order that one daughter might be thus protected, all the other daughters were allowed to
go alone, day or evening, bareheaded or bare-

footed, by the loneliest mountain-paths, to bring oranges or firewood or whatever their work may be — heedless of protection. The safeguard was for a class : the average exposure of young womanhood was far greater than with us. So in London, while you rarely see a young lady alone in the streets, the housemaid is sent on errands at any hour of the evening with a freedom at which our city domestics would quite rebel ; and one has to stay but a short time in Paris to see how entirely limited to a class is the alleged restraint under which young French girls are said to be kept.

Again, it is to be remembered that the whole "European plan," so far as it is applied on the continent of Europe, is a plan based upon utter distrust and suspicion, not only as to chastity, but as to all other virtues. It is applied among the higher classes almost as consistently to boys as to girls. In every school under church auspices, it is the French theory that boys are never to be left unwatched for a moment ; and it is as steadily assumed that girls will be untruthful if left to themselves, as that they will do every other wrong. This to the Anglo-Saxon race seems very demoralizing. "Suspicion," said Sir Philip Sidney, "is the way to lose that which we fear to lose." Readers of the Brontë novels will remember the disgust of the English pupils and teachers in French schools at the constant espionage around them; and I have more than once heard young girls who had been trained at such institutions say that it was a wonder if they had any truthfulness left, so invariable was the assumption that it was the nature of young girls to lie. I cannot imagine anything less likely to create upright and noble character, in man or woman, than the systematic application of the " European plan."

And that it produces just the results that might be feared, the whole tone of European literature proves. Foreigners, no doubt, do habitual injustice to the morality of French households; but it is impossible that fiction can utterly misrepresent the community which produces and reads it. When one thinks of the utter lightness of tone with which breaches, both of truth and chastity, are treated even in the better class of French novels and plays, it seems absurd to deny the correctness of the picture. Besides, it is not merely a question of plays and novels. Consider, for instance, the contempt with which Taine treats Thackeray for representing the mother of Pendennis as suffering agonies when she thinks that her son has seduced a young girl, a social inferior. Thackeray is not really considered a model of elevated tone, as to such matters, among English writers ; but the Frenchman is simply amazed that the Englishman should describe even the saintliest of mothers as attaching so much weight to such a small affair.

An able newspaper writer, quoted with apparent approval by the " Boston Daily Advertiser," praises the supposed foreign method for the "habit of dependence and deference" that it produces ; and because it gives to a young man a wife whose "habit of deference is established." But it must be remembered, that, where this theory is established, the habit of deference is logically carried much farther than mere conjugal convenience would take it. Its natural outcome is the authority of the priest, not of the husband. That domination of the women of France by the priesthood which forms even now the chief peril of the republic — which is the strength of legitimism and imperialism and all other conspiracies against the liberty of the French people — is only the visible and inevitable result of this dangerous docility.

One thing is certain, that the best preparation for freedom is freedom; and that no young girls are so poorly prepared for American life as those whose early years are passed in Europe. Some of the worst imprudences, the most unmaidenly and offensive actions, that I have ever heard of in decent society, have been on the

part of young women educated abroad, who
have been launched into American life without its early training, — have been treated as
children until they suddenly awakened to the
freedom of women. On the other hand, I remember with pleasure, that a cultivated French
mother, whose daughter's fine qualities were
the best seal of her motherhood, once told me
that the models she had chosen in her daughter's training were certain families of American
young ladies, of whom she had, through peculiar circumstances, seen much in Paris.

FEA-   One of the most amusing letters
THERSES   ever quoted in any book is that
given in Curzon's " Monasteries of the Levant,"
as the production of a Turkish sultana who had
just learned English.   It is as follows : —

NOTE FROM ADILE SULTANA, THE BETROTHED OF
ABBAS PASHA, TO HER ARMENIAN COMMISSIONER.

CONSTANTINOPLE, 1844.

MY NOBLE FRIEND : — Here are the featherses
sent my soul, my noble friend, are there no other
featherses leaved in the shop besides these featherses ? and these featherses remains, and these
featherses are ukly. They are very dear, who
buyses dheses ? And my noble friend, we want
a noat from yourself; those you brought last tim,
those you sees were very beautiful ; we had searched ;

my soul, I want featherses again, of those featherses. In Kalada there is plenty of feather.
Whatever bees, I only want beautiful featherses ; I
want featherses of every desolation to-morrow.
(Signed)   You Know Who.

The first steps in culture do not, then, it
seems, remove from the feminine soul the love
of pretty things. Nor do the later steps wholly
extinguish it ; for did not Grace Greenwood hear
the learned Mary Somerville conferring with
the wise Harriet Martineau as to whether a
certain dress should be dyed to match a certain shawl ? Well ! why not ? Because women
learn the use of the quill, are they to ignore
"featherses"? Because they learn science,
must they unlearn the arts, and, above all, the
art of being beautiful? If men have lost it,
they have reason to regret the loss. Let women
hold to it, while yet within their reach.

Mrs. Rachel Howland of New Bedford, much
prized and trusted as a public speaker among
Friends, and a model of taste and quiet beauty
in costume, delighted the young girls at a Newport Yearly Meeting, a few years since, by
boldly declaring that she thought God meant
women to make the world beautiful, as much as
flowers and butterflies, and that there was no
sin in tasteful dress, but only in devoting to it
too much money or too much time. It is a

blessed doctrine. The utmost extremes of dress, the love of colors, of fabrics, of jewels, of "featherses," are, after all, but an effort after the beautiful. The reason why the beautiful is not always the result is because so many women are ignorant or merely imitative. They have no sense of fitness : the short wear what belongs to the tall, and brunettes sacrifice their natural beauty to look like blondes. Or they have no adaptation ; and even an emancipated woman may show a disregard for appropriateness, as where a fine lady sweeps the streets, or a fair orator the platform, with a silken or velvet train which accords only with a carpet as luxurious as itself. What is inappropriate is never beautiful. What is merely in the fashion is never beautiful. But who does not know some woman whose taste and training are so perfect that fashion becomes to her a means of grace instead of a despot, and the worst excrescence that can be prescribed — a *chignon*, a hoop, a panier — is softened into something so becoming that even the Parisian bondage seems but a chain of roses ?

In such hands, even "featherses" become a fine art, not a matter of vanity. Are women so much more vain than men? No doubt they talk more about their dress, for there is much more to talk about ; yet did you never hear the

men of fashion discuss boots and hats and the
liveries of grooms? A good friend of mine, a
shoemaker, who supplies very high heels for
a great many pretty feet on Fifth Avenue in
New York, declares that women are not so
vain in that direction as men. "A man who
thinks he has a handsome foot," quoth our fashionable Crispin, "is apt to give us more trouble
than any lady among our customers. I have
noticed this for twenty years." The testimony
is consoling — to women.

And this naturally suggests the question,
What is to be the future of masculine costume? Is the present formlessness and grace-
lessness and monotony of hue to last forever,
as suited to the rough needs of a workaday
world? It is to be remembered that the difference in this respect between the dress of
the sexes is a very recent thing. Till within a
century or so, men dressed as picturesquely as
women, and paid as minute attention to their
costume. Even the fashions in armor varied as
extensively as the fashions in gowns. One of
Henry III.'s courtiers, Sir J. Arundel, had fifty-
two complete suits of cloth of gold. No satin,
no velvet, was too elegant for those who sat to
Copley for their pictures. In Puritan days the
laws could hardly be made severe enough to
prevent men from wearing silver-lace and

"broad bone-lace," and shoulder-bands of undue width, and double ruffs and "immoderate
great breeches." What seemed to the Cava-
liers the extreme of stupid sobriety in dress
would pass now for the most fantastic array.
Fancy Samuel Pepys going to a wedding of
to-day in his "new colored silk suit and coat
trimmed with gold buttons, and gold broad lace
round his hands, very rich and fine." It would
give to the ceremony the aspect of a fancy
ball; yet how much prettier a sight is a fancy
ball than the ordinary entertainment of the
period!

At intervals the rigor of masculine costume
is a little relaxed; velvets resume their pictur-
esque sway: and, instead of the customary suit
of solemn black, gentlemen even appear in blue
and gold editions at evening parties. Let us
hope that good sense and taste may yet meet
each other, for both sexes; that men may bor-
row for their dress some womanly taste, women
some masculine sense; and society may again
witness a graceful and appropriate costume,
without being too much absorbed in "featherses."

VI

STUDY AND WORK

"Movet me ingens scientiarum admiratio, seu legis communis æquitas, ut in nostro sexu, rarum non esse feram, id quod omnium votis dignissimum est. Nam cum sapientia tantum generis humani ornamentum sit, ut ad omnes et singulos (quoad quidem per sortem cujusque liceat) extendi jure debeat, non vidi, cur virgini, in qua excolendi sese ornandique sedulitatem admittimus, non conveniat mundus hic omnium longè pulcherrimus." — ANNÆ MARIÆ À SCHURMAN EPISTOLÆ. (1638.)

"A great reverence for knowledge and the natural sense of justice urge me to encourage in my own sex that which is most worthy the aspirations of all. For, since wisdom is so great an ornament of the human race that it should of right be extended (so far as practicable) to each and every one, I have not perceived why this fairest of ornaments should not be appropriate for the maiden, to whom we permit all diligence in the decoration and adornment of herself."

EXPERI-
MENTS
Why is it, that, whenever anything is done for women in the way of education, it is called "an experiment," — something that is to be long considered, stoutly opposed, grudgingly yielded, and dubiously watched, — while, if the same thing is done for men, its desirableness is assumed as a

matter of course, and the thing is done? Thus, when Harvard College was founded, it was not regarded as an experiment, but as an institution. The "General Court," in 1636, "agreed to give 400*l*. towards a schoale or colledge," and the affair was settled. Every subsequent step in the expanding of educational opportunities for young men has gone in the same way. But when there seems a chance of extending, however irregularly, some of the same collegiate advantages to women, I observe that respectable newspapers, in all good faith, are apt to speak of the measure as an "experiment."

It seems to me no more of an "experiment" than when a boy who has usually eaten up his whole apple becomes a little touched with a sense of justice, and finally decides to offer his sister the smaller half. If he has ever regarded that offer as an experiment, the first actual trial will put the result into the list of certainties ; and it will become an axiom in his mind that girls like apples. Whatever may be said about the position of women in law and society, it is clear that their educational disadvantages have been a prolonged disgrace to the other sex, and one for which women themselves are in no way accountable. When Françoise de Saint-onges, in the sixteenth century, wished to establish girls' schools in France, she was hooted

in the streets, and her father called together
four doctors of law to decide whether she was
possessed of a devil in planning to teach women, — "*pour s'assurer qu'instruire des femmes
n'était pas un œuvre du démon.*" From that
day to this we have seen women almost always
more ready to be taught than was any one else
to teach them. Talk as you please about their
wishing or not wishing to vote : they have certainly wished for instruction, and have had it
doled out to them almost as grudgingly as if it
were the ballot itself.

Consider the educational history of Massachusetts, for instance. The wife of President
John Adams was born in 1744 ; and she says
of her youth that "female education, in the
best families, went no farther than writing and
arithmetic." Barry tells us in his " History of
Massachusetts," that the public education was
first provided for boys only ; "but light soon
broke in, and girls were allowed to attend the
public schools two hours a day." [1] It appears
from President Quincy's " Municipal History
of Boston," [2] that from 1790 girls were there
admitted to such schools, but during the summer months only, when there were not boys
enough to fill them, — from April 20 to Octo-
ber 20 of each year. This lasted until 1822,

---

[1] Vol. iii. 323.   [2] Page 21.

when Boston became a city. Four years after, an attempt was made to establish a high school for girls, which was not, however, to teach Latin and Greek. It had, in the words of the school committee of 1854, "an alarming success;" and the school was abolished after eighteen months' trial, because the girls crowded into it; and as Mr. Quincy, with exquisite simplicity, records, "not one voluntarily quitted it, and there was no reason to suppose that any one admitted to the school would voluntarily quit for the whole three years, except in case of marriage!"

How amusing seems it now to read of such an "experiment" as this, abandoned only because of its overwhelming success! How absurd now seem the discussions of a few years ago! — the doubts whether young women really desired higher education, whether they were capable of it, whether their health would bear it, whether their parents would permit it. An address I gave before the Social Science Association on this subject, at Boston, May 14, 1873, now seems to me such a collection of platitudes that I hardly see how I dared come before an intelligent audience with such needless reasonings. It is as if I had soberly labored to prove that two and two make four, or that ginger is "hot i' the mouth." Yet the subsequent discussion in that meeting showed that around even these harmless and commonplace propositions the battle of debate could rage hot ; and it really seemed as if even to teach women the alphabet ought still to be mentioned as "a promising experiment." Now, with the successes before us of so many colleges ; with the spectacle at Cambridge of young women actually reading Plato "at sight" with Professor Goodwin, — it surely seems as if the higher education of women might be considered quite beyond the stage of experiment, and might henceforth be provided for in the same common-sense and matter-of-course way which we provide for the education of young men.

And, if this point is already reached in education, how long before it will also be reached in political life, and women's voting be viewed as a matter of course, and a thing no longer experimental ?

INTELLEC-
TUAL CIN-
DERELLAS When, some thirty years ago, the extraordinary young mathematician, Truman Henry Safford, first attracted the attention of New England by his rare powers, I well remember the pains that were taken to place him under instruction by the ablest Harvard professors : the greater his abilities, the more needful that he should have

careful and symmetrical training. The men of
science did not say, "Stand off! let him alone!
let him strive patiently until he has achieved
something positively valuable, and he may be
sure of prompt ·and generous recognition —
when he is fifty years old." If such a course
would have been mistaken and ungenerous if
applied to Professor Safford, why is it not something to be regretted that it was applied to Mrs.
Somerville? In her case, the mischief was
done : she was, happily, strong enough to bear
it ; but, as the English critics say, we never
shall know what science has lost by it. We
can do nothing for her now ; but we could do
something for future women like her, by pointing this obvious moral for their benefit, instead
of being content with a mere tardy recognition
of success, after a woman has expended half a
century in struggle.

It is commonly considered to be a step forward in civilization, that whereas ancient and
barbarous nations exposed children to special
hardships, in order to kill off the weak and
toughen the strong, modern nations aim to rear
all alike carefully, without either sacrificing or
enfeebling. If we apply this to muscle, why
not to mind? and if to men's minds, why not
to women's? Why use for men's intellects,
which are claimed to be stronger, the forcing

process, — offering, for instance, many thousand
dollars a year in gratuities at our colleges, that
young men may be induced to come and learn,
— and only withhold assistance from the weaker
minds of women ? A little schoolgirl once told
me that she did not object to her teacher's
showing partiality, but thought she "ought to
show partiality to all alike." If all our university systems are wrong, and the proper diet for
mathematical genius consists of fifty years'
snubbing, let us employ it, by all means ; but
let it be applied to both sexes.

That it is the duty of women, even under
disadvantageous circumstances, to prove their
purpose by labor, to " verify their credentials,"
is true enough ; but this moral is only part of
the moral of Mrs. Somerville's book, and is
cruelly incomplete without the other half. What
a garden of roses was Mrs. Somerville's life,
according to some comfortable critics ! " All
that for which too many women nowadays are
content to sit and whine, or fitfully and care-
lessly struggle, came naturally and quietly to
Mrs. Somerville. And the reason was that she
never asked for anything until she had earned
it ; or, rather, she never asked at all, but was
content to earn." Naturally and quietly ! You
might as well say that Garrison fought slavery
" quietly," or that Frederick Douglass's escape

came to him "naturally." Turn to the book itself, and see with what strong, though never actually bitter, feeling, the author looks back upon her hard struggle.

"I was intensely ambitious to excel in something; for I felt in my own breast that women were capable of taking a higher place in creation than that assigned them in my early days, which was very low" (p. 60). "Nor . . . should I have had courage to ask any of them a question, for I should have been laughed at. I was often very sad and forlorn; not a hand held out to help me" (p. 47). "My father came home for a short time, and, somehow or other finding out what I was about, said to my mother, 'Peg, we must put a stop to this, or we shall have Mary in a strait-jacket one of these days'" (p. 54). "I continued my mathematical and other pursuits, but under great disadvantages; for, although my husband did not prevent me from studying, I met with no sympathy whatever from him, as he had a very low opinion of the capacity of my sex, and had neither knowledge of nor interest in science of any kind" (p. 75). "I was considered eccentric and foolish; and my conduct was highly disapproved of by many, especially by some members of my own family" (p. 80). "A man can always command his time under the plea of business: a woman is not allowed any such excuse" (p. 164). And so on.

At last, in 1831, — Mrs. Somerville being

then fifty-one, — her work on " The Mechanism of the Heavens" appeared. Then came universal recognition, generous if not prompt, a tardy acknowledgment. " Our relations," she says, " and others who had so severely criticised and ridiculed me, astonished at my success, were now loud in my praise." [1] No doubt. So were, probably, Cinderella's sisters loud in her praise, when the prince at last took her from the chimney-corner, and married her. They had kept for themselves, to be sure, as long as they could, the delights and opportunities of life ; while she had taken the place assigned her in her early days, — " which was very low," as Mrs. Somerville says. But, for all that, they were very kind to her in the days of her prosperity ; and no doubt packed their little trunks and came to visit their dear sister at the palace as often as she could wish. And, doubtless, the Fairyland Monthly of that day, when it came to review Cinderella's " Personal Recollections," pointed out that, as soon as that distinguished lady had " achieved something positively valuable," she received " prompt and generous recognition."

[1] Page 176.

CUPID-
AND-PSY-
CHOLOGY
The learned Master of Trinity College, Cambridge, England, is frequently facetious ; and his jokes are quoted with the deference due to the chief officer of the chief college of that great university. Now it is known that the Cambridge colleges, and Trinity College in particular, are doing a great deal for the instruction of women. The young women of Girton College and Newnham College — both of these being institutions for their benefit, in or near Cambridge — not only enjoy the instruction of the university, but they share it under a guaranty that it shall be of the best quality ; because they attend, in many cases, the very same lectures with the young men. Where this is not done, they sometimes use the vacant lecture-rooms of the college; and it was in connection with an application for this privilege that the Master of Trinity College made a celebrated joke. When told that the lecture-room was needed for a class of young women in psychology, he said, " Psychology ? What kind of psychology ? Cupid-and-Psychology, I suppose."

Cupid-and-Psychology is, after all, not so bad a department of instruction. It may be taken as a good enough symbol of that mingling of head and heart which is the best result of all training. One of the worst evils of the sepa-

rate education of the sexes has been the easy
assumption that men were to become all head,
and women all heart. It was to correct the
evils of this that Ben Jonson proposed for his
ideal woman

"a learned and a manly soul."

It was an implied recognition of it from the
other side when the great masculine intellect,
Goethe, held up as a guiding force in his Faust
"the eternal womanly" (*das ewige weibliche*).
After all, each sex must teach the other, and
impart to the other. It will never do to have
all the brains poured into one human being,
and christened "man;" and all the affections
decanted into another, and labelled "woman."
Nature herself rejects this theory. Darwin
himself, the interpreter of nature, shows that
there is a perpetual effort going on, by unseen
forces, to equalize the sexes, since sons often
inherit from the mother, and daughters from
the father. And we all take pleasure in discovering in the noblest of each sex something
of the qualities of the other, — the tender affections in great men, the imperial intellect in
great women.

On the whole, there is no harm, but rather
good, in the new science of Cupid-and-Psychology. There are combinations for which no
single word can suffice. The phrase belongs

to the same class with Lowell's witty denunciation of a certain tiresome letter-writer, as being,
not his incubus, but his "pen-and-inkubus."
It is as well to admit it first as last : Cupid-and-
Psychology will be taught wherever young men
and women study together. Not in the direct
and simple form of mutual love-making, perhaps ; for they tell the visitor, at universities
which admit both sexes, that the young men
and maidens do not fall in love with each other,
but are apt to seek their mates elsewhere. The
new science has a wider bearing, and suggests
that the brain is incomplete, after all, without
the affections ; and so are the affections without the brain. A certain professorship at Harvard University which the Rev. Dr. Francis G.
Peabody now fills, and which Phillips Brooks
was once invited to fill, was founded by a woman, Miss Plummer; and the name proposed
by her for it was "a professorship of the heart,"
though they after all called it only a professorship of "Christian morals." We need the heart
in our colleges, it seems, even if we only get it
under the ingenious title of Cupid-and-Psychology.

SELF-SUP-   For one, I have never been fasci-
PORTING   nated by the style of domestic para-
WIVES
               dise that English novels depict, —
half a dozen unmarried daughters round the
family hearth, all assiduously doing worsted-
work and petting their papa. I believe a suffi-
ciency of employment to be the only normal
and healthy condition for a human being; and
where there is not work enough to employ the
full energies of all at home, it seems as proper
for young women as for young birds to leave
the parental nest. If this additional work is
done for money, very well. It is the conscious
dignity of self-support that removes the traditional curse from labor, and woman has a right
to claim her share in that dignified position.

Yet I cannot agree, on the other hand, with
those who maintain that the true woman should
be self-supporting, even in marriage. Woman's
part of the family task — the care of home and
children — is just as essential to building up the
family fortunes as the very different toil of the
out-door partner. For young married women
to undertake any more direct aid to the family
income is in most cases utterly undesirable, and
is asking of themselves a great deal too much.
And this is not because they are to be encouraged in indolence, but because they already, in
a normal condition of things, have their hands

full.   As, on this point, I may differ from some
of my readers, let me explain precisely what I
mean.

As I write, there are at work, in another part
of the house, two paper-hangers, a man and his
wife, each forty-five or fifty years of age.   Their
children are grown up, and some of them married: they have a daughter at home, who is old
enough to do the housework, and leave the
mother free.   There is no way of organizing
the labors of this household better than this:
the married pair toil together during the day,
and go home together to their evening rest.   A
happier couple I never saw; it is a delight to
see them cheerily at work together, cutting,
pasting, hanging : their life seems like a prolonged industrial picnic ; and if I had the ill-
luck to own as many palaces as an English
duke I should keep them permanently occupied
in putting fresh papers on the walls.

But the merit of this employment for the
woman is that it interferes with no other duty.
Were she a young mother with little children,
and obliged by her paper-hanging to neglect
them, or to leave them at a " day-nursery," or
to overwork herself by combining too many
cares, then the sight of her would be very
sad.   So sacred a thing is motherhood, so para-
mount and absorbing the duty of a mother to

her child, that in a true state of society I think
she should be utterly free from all other duties,
— even, if possible, from the ordinary cares
of housekeeping. If she has spare health and
strength to do these other things as pleasures,
very well; but she should be relieved from them
as duties. And as to the need of self-support,
I can hardly conceive of an instance where it
can be to the mother of young children anything but a disaster. As we all know, this
calamity often occurs ; I have seen it among
the factory operatives at the North, and among
the negro women in the cotton-fields at the
South : in both cases it is a tragedy, and the
bodies and brains of mother and children alike
suffer. That the mother should bear and tend
and nurture, while the father supports and protects, — this is the true division.

Does this bear in any way upon suffrage ?
Not at all. The mother can inform herself
upon public questions in the intervals of her
cares, as the father among his ; and the baby
in the cradle is a perpetual appeal to her, as
to him, that the institutions under which that
baby dwells may be kept pure. One of the
most devoted young mothers I ever knew —
the younger sister of Margaret Fuller Ossoli —
made it a rule, no matter how much her children absorbed her, to read books or newspapers

for an hour every day; in order, she said, that she should be more to them than a mere source of physical nurture, and that her mind should be kept fresh and alive for them. But to demand in addition that such a mother should earn money for them is to ask too much; and there is many a tombstone in New England, which, if it told the truth, would tell what comes of such an effort.

THOROUGH   "The hopeless defect of women in all practical matters," said a shrewd merchant the other day, "is that it is impossible to make them thorough." It was a shallow remark, and so I told him. Women are thorough in the things which they have been expected to regard as their sphere, — in their housekeeping and their dress and their social observances. There is nothing more thorough on earth than the way housework is done in a genuine New England household. There is an exquisite thoroughness in the way a milliner's or a dressmaker's work is done, — a work such as clumsy man cannot rival, and can hardly estimate. No general plans his campaigns or marshals his armies better than some women of society — the late Mrs. Paran Stevens, for instance — manage the circles of which they are the centre. Day and night, winter and sum-

mer, at city or watering-place, year in and year
out, such a woman keeps open house for her gay
world.   She has a perpetual series of guests
who must be fed luxuriously, and amused pro-
fusely; she talks to them in three or four languages; at her entertainments she notes who
is present and who absent, as carefully as Napoleon watched his soldiers; her interchange of
cards, alone, is a thing as complex as the army
muster-rolls : thus she plans, organizes, con-
quers, and governs.   People speak of her existence as that of a doll or a toy, when she is the
most untiring of campaigners.   Grant that her
aim is, after all, unworthy, and that you pity
the worn face which has to force so many
smiles.   No matter : the smiles are there, and
so is the success.   I often wish that the reformers would do their work as thoroughly as
the women of society do theirs.

No, there is no constitutional want of thoroughness in women.   The trouble is that into
the new work upon which they are just enter-
ing they have not yet brought their thoroughness to bear.   They suffer and are defrauded
and are reproached, simply because they have
not yet nerved themselves to do well the things
which they have asserted their right to do.   A
distinguished woman, who earns one of the largest incomes ever honestly earned by any one

of her sex, off the stage, told me the other day
that she left all her business affairs to the
management of others, and did not even know
how to draw a check on a bank. What a
melancholy self-exhibition was that of a clever
American woman, whom I knew, the author
of half a dozen successful books, refusing to
look her own accounts in the face until they
had got into such a tangle that not even her
own referees could disentangle them to suit
her! These things show, not that women are
constitutionally wanting in thoroughness, but
that it is hard to make them carry this quality
into new fields.

I wish I could possibly convey to the young
women who write for advice on literary projects
something of the meaning of this word "thorough" as applied to literary work. Scarcely
any of them seem to have a conception of it.
Dash, cleverness, recklessness, impatience of
revision or of patient investigation, these are
the common traits. To a person of experience, no stupidity is so discouraging as a brilliancy that has no roots. It brings nothing to
pass ; whereas a slow stupidity, if it takes time
enough, may conquer the world. Consider that
for more than twenty years the path of literature has been quite as fully open for women as
for men, in America, — the payment the same,

the honor the same, the obstacles no greater. Collegiate education has until quite recently been denied them, but how many men succeed as writers without that advantage! Yet how little, how very little, of permanent literary work has yet been done by American women! Young girls appear one after another: each writes a single clever story or a single sweet poem, and then disappears forever. Look at Griswold's "Female Poets of America," and you are disposed to turn back to the title-page, and see if these utterly forgotten names do not really represent the "female poets" of some other nation. They are forgotten, as most of the more numerous "female prose writers" are forgotten, because they had no root. Nobody doubts that women have cleverness enough, and enough of power of expression. If you could open the mails, and take out the women's letters, as somebody says, they would prove far more graphic and entertaining than those of the men. They would be written, too, in what Macaulay calls — speaking of Madame d'Arblay's early style — "true woman's English, clear, natural, and lively." What they need, in order to convert this epistolary brilliancy into literature, is to be thorough.

You cannot separate woman's rights and her responsibilities. In all ages of the world she has had a certain limited work to do, and has done that well. All that is needed, when new spheres are open, is that she should carry the same fidelity into those. If she will work as hard to shape the children of her brain as to rear her bodily offspring, will do intellectual work as well as she does housework, and will meet her moral responsibilities as she meets her social engagements, then opposition will soon disappear. The habit of thoroughness is the key to all high success. Whatever is worth doing is worth doing well. Only those who are faithful in a few things will rightfully be made rulers over many.

LITERARY ASPIRANTS   The brilliant Lady Ashburton used to say of herself that she had never written a book, and knew nobody whose books she would like to have written. This does not seem to be the ordinary state of mind among those who write letters of inquiry to authors. If I may judge from these letters, the yearning for a literary career is now almost greater among women than among men. Perhaps this is because of some literary successes lately achieved by women. Perhaps it is because they have fewer outlets for their energies. Perhaps they find more obstacles in literature than young men find, and have, therefore, more need to write letters of inquiry about it. It is certain that they write such letters quite often; and ask questions that test severely the supposed omniscience of the author's brain, — questions bearing on logic, rhetoric, grammar, and orthography; where to find a publisher, and how to obtain a well-disciplined mind.

These letters may sometimes be too long or come too often for convenience, nor is the consoling postage-stamp always remembered. But they are of great value as giving real glimpses of American social life, and of the present tendencies of American women. They sometimes reveal such intellectual ardor and imagination, such modesty, and such patience under difficulties, as to do good to the reader, whatever they may do to the writer. They certainly suggest a few thoughts, which may as well be expressed, once for all, in print.

Behind almost all these letters there lies a laudable desire to achieve success. "Would you have the goodness to tell us how success can be obtained?" How can this be answered, my dear young lady, when you leave it to the reader to guess what your definition of success may be? For instance, here is Mr. Mansfield Tracy Walworth, who was murdered the other day in New York. He was at once mentioned

in the newspapers as a "celebrated author."
Never in my life having heard of him, I looked
in a "Manual of American Literature," and
there found that Mr. Walworth's novel of
"Warwick" had a sale of seventy-five thousand
copies, and his "Delaplaine" of forty-five thousand. Is it a success to have secured a sale
like that for your books, and then to die, and
have your brother penmen ask, "Who was he?"
Yet, certainly, a sale of seventy-five thousand
copies is not to be despised; and I fear I know
many youths and maidens who would willingly
write novels much poorer than "Warwick" for
the sake of a circulation like that. I do not
think that Hawthorne, however, would have accepted these conditions; and he certainly did
not have this style of success.

Nor do I think he had any right to expect it.
He had made his choice, and had reason to be
satisfied. The very first essential for literary
success is to decide what success means. If
a young girl pines after the success of Marion
Harland and Mrs. Southworth, let her seek it.
It is possible that she may obtain it, or surpass
it; and though she might do better, she might
do far worse. It is, at any rate, a laudable aim
to be popular: popularity may be a very creditable thing, unless you pay too high a price for it.
It is a pleasant thing, and has many contingent

advantages, — balanced by this great danger,
that one is apt to mistake it for real success.

"Learning hath made the most," said old
Fuller, "by those books on which the booksell-
ers have lost." If this be true of learning, it is
quite as true of genius and originality. A book
may be immediately popular and also immortal,
but the chances are the other way. It is more
often the case that a great writer gradually creates the taste by which he is enjoyed. Wordsworth in England and Emerson in America were
striking instances of this; and authors of far
less fame have yet the same choice which they
had. You can take the standard which the book
market offers, and train yourself for that. This
will, in the present age, be sure to educate certain qualities in you,—directness, vividness, animation, dash, — even if it leaves other qualities
untrained. Or you can make a standard of your
own, and aim at that, taking your chance of
seeing the public agree with you. Very likely
you may fail; perhaps you may be wrong in
your fancy, after all, and the public may be
right : if you fail, you may find it hard to bear;
but, on the other hand, you may have the
inward "glory and joy" which nothing but
fidelity to an ideal standard can give. All this
applies to all forms of work, but it applies conspicuously to literature.

Instead, therefore, of offering to young writers the usual comforting assurance, that, if they produce anything of real merit, it will be sure to succeed, I should caution them first to make their own definition of success, and then act accordingly. Hawthorne succeeded in his way, and Mr. M. T. Walworth in his way; and each of these would have been very unreasonable if he had expected to succeed in both ways. There is always an opening for careful and conscientious literary work; and by such work many persons obtain a modest support. There are also some great prizes to be won; but these are commonly, though not always, won by work of a more temporary and sensational kind. Make your choice; and, when you have got precisely what you asked for, do not complain because you have missed what you would not take.

THE CA-
REER OF
LETTERS
A young girl of some talent once told me that she had devoted herself to "the career of letters." I found, on inquiry, that she had obtained a situation as writer of society gossip for a New York newspaper. I can hardly imagine any life that leads more directly away from any really literary career, or any life about which it is harder to give counsel. The work of a newspaper correspondent, especially in the "society" direc-

tion, is so full of trials and temptations, for one
of either sex, in our dear, inquisitive, gossip-
ing America, that one cannot help watching
with especial solicitude all women who enter it.
Their special gifts as women are a source of
danger : they are keener of observation from
the very fact of their sex, more active in curios-
ity, more skilful in achieving their ends ; in a
world of gossip they are the queens, and men
but their subjects, hence their greater danger.

In Newport, New York, Washington, it is
the same thing. The unbounded appetite for
private information about public or semi-public
people creates its own purveyors ; and these,
again, learn to believe with unflinching heartiness in the work they do. I have rarely encountered a successful correspondent of this
description who had not become thoroughly
convinced that the highest desire of every
human being is to see his name in print, no
matter how. Unhappily, there is a great deal
to encourage this belief : I have known men to
express great indignation at an unexpected
newspaper-puff, and then to send ten dollars
privately to the author. This is just the calamity of the profession, that it brings one in contact with this class of social hypocrites ; and
the " personal " correspondent gradually loses
faith that there is any other class to be found.

Then there is the perilous temptation to pay off grudges in this way, to revenge slights, by the use of a power with which few people are safely to be trusted. In many cases, such a correspondent is simply a child playing with poisoned arrows : he poisons others ; and it is no satisfaction to know that in time he may also poison himself, and paralyze his own power for mischief.

There lies before me a letter written some years ago to a young lady anxious to enter on this particular "career of letters," — a letter from an experienced New York journalist. He has employed, he says, hundreds of lady correspondents, for little or no compensation ; and one of his few successful writers he thus describes : " She succeeds by pushing her way into society, and extracting information from fashionable people and officials and their wives. . . . She flatters the vain, and overawes the weak, and gets by sheer impudence what other writers cannot. . . . I would not wish you to be like her, or reduced to the necessity of doing what she does, for any success journalism can possibly give." And who can help echoing this opinion ? If this is one of the successful laborers, where shall we place the unsuccessful ; or, rather, is success, or failure, the greater honor ?

Personal journalism has a prominence in this country with which nothing in any other coun-

try can be compared.   What is called publicity
in England or France means the most peaceful
seclusion, compared with the glare of notoriety
which an enterprising correspondent can flash
out at any time — as if by opening the bull's-
eye of a dark lantern — upon the quietest of
his contemporaries.   It is essentially an American institution, and not one of those in which
we have reason to feel most pride.   It is to be
observed, however, that foreigners, if in office,
take to it very readily; and it is said that no
people cultivate the reporters at Washington
more assiduously than the diplomatic corps, who
like to send home the personal notices of themselves, in order to prove to their governments
that they are highly esteemed in the land to
which they are appointed.   But however it may
be with them, it is certain that many people
still like to keep their public and private lives
apart, and shrink from even the inevitable eminence of fame.   One of the very most popular
of American authors has said that he never, to
this day, has overcome a slight feeling of repugnance on seeing his own name in print.

TALKING   Every time a woman does any-
AND TAK-   thing original or remarkable, — in-
ING   venting a rat-trap, let us say, or
carving thirty-six heads on a walnut-shell, — all

observers shout applause. "There's a woman for you, indeed! Instead of talking about her rights, she takes them. That's the way to do it. What a lesson to these declaimers upon the platform!"

It does not seem to occur to these wise people that the right to talk is itself one of the chief rights in America, and the way to reach all the others. To talk is to make a beginning, at any rate. To catch people with your ideas is more than to contrive a rat-trap ; and Isotta Nogarola, carving thirty-six empty heads, was not working in so practical a fashion as Mary Livermore when she instructs thirty-six hundred full ones.

It shows the good sense of the woman-suffrage agitators, that they have decided to begin with talk. In the first place, talking is the most lucrative of all professions in America ; and therefore it is the duty of American women to secure their share of it. Mrs. Frances Anne Kemble used to say that she read Shakespeare in public "for her bread ; " and when, after melting all hearts by a course of farewell readings, she decided to begin reading again, she said she was doing it "for her butter." So long as women are often obliged to support themselves and their children, and perhaps their husbands, by their own labor, they have no right to work cheaply, unless driven to it. Anna Dickinson had no right to make fifteen dollars a week by sewing, if, by stepping out of the ranks of needle-women into the ranks of the talkers, she could make a hundred dollars a day. Theorize as we may, the fact is that there is no kind of work in America which brings such sure profits as public speaking. If women are unfitted for it, or if they "know the value of peace and quietness," as the hand-organ man says, and can afford to hold their tongues, let them do so. But if they have tongues, and like to use them, they certainly ought to make some money by the performance.

This is the utilitarian view. And when we bring in higher objects, it is plain that the way to get anything in America is to talk about it. Silence is golden, no doubt, and like other gold remains in the bank-vaults, and does not just now circulate very freely as currency. Even literature in America is utterly second to oratory as a means of immediate influence. Of all sway, that of the orator is the most potent and most perishable; and the student and the artist are apt to hold themselves aloof from it, for this reason. But it is the one means in America to accomplish immediate results, and women who would take their rights must take them through talking. It is the appointed way.

Under a good old-fashioned monarchy, if a woman wished to secure anything for her sex, she must cajole a court, or become the mistress of a monarch. That epoch ended with the French Revolution. When Bonaparte wished to silence Madame de Staël, he said, "What does that woman want? Does she want the money the government owes to her father?" When Madame de Staël heard of it, she said, "The question is not what I want, but what I think." Henceforth women, like men, are to say what they think. For all that flattery and seduction and sin, we have substituted the simple weapon of talk. If women wish education, they must talk; if better laws, they must talk. The one chief argument against woman suffrage, with men, is that so few women even talk about it.

As long as the human voice can effect anything, it is the duty of women to use it; and in America, where it effects everything, they should talk all the time. When they have obtained, as a class, absolute equality of rights with men, their appeals on this subject may cease, and they may accept, if they please, that naughty masculine definition of a happy marriage, — the union of a deaf man with a dumb woman.

HOW TO SPEAK IN PUBLIC   There are other things that women wish to do, it seems, beside studying and voting. There are a good many — if I may judge from letters that occasionally come to me — who are taking, or wish to take, their first lessons in public speaking. Not necessarily very much in public, or before mixed audiences, but perhaps merely to say to a roomful of ladies, or before the committee of a Christian Union, what they desire to say. " How shall I make myself heard? How shall I learn to express myself? How shall I keep my head clear? Is there any school for debate?" And so on. My dear young lady, it does not take much wisdom, but only a little experience, to answer some of these questions. So I am not afraid to try.

The best school for debate is debating. So far as mere confidence and comfort are concerned, the great thing is to gain the habit of speech, even if one speaks badly. And the practice of an ordinary debating society has also this advantage, that it teaches you to talk sense (lest you be laughed at), to speak with some animation (lest your hearers go to sleep), to think out some good arguments (because you are trying to convince somebody), and to guard against weak reasoning or unfounded assertion (lest your opponent trip you up). Speaking in a debating society thus gives you the same advantage that a lawyer derives from the presence of an opposing counsel : you learn to guard yourself at all points. It is the absence of this check which is the great intellectual disadvantage of the pulpit. When a lawyer says a foolish thing in an argument, he is pretty sure to find it out ; but a clergyman may go on repeating his foolish thing for fifty years without discovering it, for want of an opponent.

For the art of making your voice heard, I must refer you to an elocutionist. Yet one thing at least you might acquire for yourself, — a thing that lies at the foundation of all good speaking, — the complete and thorough enunciation of every syllable. So great is the delight, to my ear at least, of a perfectly distinct and clear-cut utterance, that I fear I should rather listen for an hour to the merest nonsense, so uttered, than to the very wisdom of angels if given in a confused or nasal or slovenly way. If you wish to know what I mean by a clear and satisfactory utterance, go to a woman-suffrage convention, and hear Miss Mary F. Eastman.

As to your employment of language, the great aim is to be simple, and, in a measure, conversational ; and then let eloquence come of itself. If most people talked as well in public as in private, public meetings would be more interesting. To acquire a conversational tone, there is good sense in Edward Everett Hale's suggestion, that every person who is called on to speak, — let us say, at a public dinner, — instead of standing up and talking about his surprise at being called on, should simply make his last remark to his neighbor at the table the starting-point for what he says to the whole company. He will thus make sure of a perfectly natural key, to begin with ; and can go on from this quiet " As I was just saying to Mr. Smith," to discuss the gravest question of Church or State. It breaks the ice for him, like the remark upon the weather by which we open our interview with the person whom we have longed for years to meet. Beginning in this way at the level of the earth's surface, we can join hands and rise to the clouds. Begin in the clouds, — as some of my most esteemed friends are wont to do, — and you have to sit down before reaching the earth.

And, to come last to what is first in importance, I am taking it for granted that you have something to say, and a strong desire to say it. Perhaps you can say it better for writing it out in full beforehand. But whether you do this or not, remember that the more simple and consecutive your thought, the easier it will be both to keep it in mind and to utter it. The more orderly your plan, the less likely you will be to " get bewildered," or to " lose the thread." Think it out so clearly that the successive parts lead to one another, and then there will be little strain upon your memory. For each point you make, provide at least one good argument and one good illustration, and you can, after a little practice, safely leave the rest to the suggestion of the moment. But so much as this you must have, to be secure. Methods of preparation of course vary extremely ; yet I suppose the secret of the composure of an experienced speaker to lie usually in this, that he has made sure before-hand of a sufficient number of good points to carry him through, even if nothing good should occur to him on the spot. Thus wise people, in going on a fishing excursion, take with them not merely their fishing tackle, but a few fish ; and then, if they are not sure of their luck, they will be sure of their chowder.

These are some of the simple hints that might be given, in answer to inquiring friends. I can remember when they would have saved me some anguish of spirit ; and they may be of some use to others now. I write, then, not to induce any one to talk for the sake of talking, — Heaven forbid ! — but that those who are longing to say something should not fancy the obstacles insurmountable, when they are really slight.

VII

PRINCIPLES OF GOVERNMENT

" That liberty, or freedom, consists in having an actual
share in the appointment of those who frame the laws, and
who are to be the guardians of every man's life, property, and
peace ; for the all of one man is as dear to him as the all of
another, and the poor man has an equal right, but more need,
to have representatives in the legislature than the rich one.
That they who have no voice nor vote in the electing of representatives do not enjoy liberty, but are absolutely enslaved
to those who have votes, and to their representatives ; for to
be enslaved is to have governors whom other men have set
over us, and be subject to laws made by the representatives
of others, without having had representatives of our own to
give consent in our behalf." — BENJAMIN FRANKLIN, in
Sparks's Franklin, ii. 372.

WE THE
PEOPLE
I remember that when I went to
school I used to look with wonder
on the title of a now forgotten newspaper of
those days which was then often in the hands
of one of the older scholars. I remember nothing else about the newspaper, or about the
boy, except that the title of the sheet he used
to unfold was " We the People ; " and that he
derived from it his school nickname, by a char-

acteristic boyish parody, and was usually mentioned as " Us the Folks."

Probably all that was taught in that school, in regard to American history, was not of so much value as the permanent fixing of this phrase in our memories. It seemed very natural, in later years, to come upon my old friend "Us the Folks," reproduced in almost every charter of our national government, as thus : —

"WE THE PEOPLE of the United States, in order to form a more perfect union, establish justice, insure domestic tranquillity, provide for the common defence, promote the general welfare, and secure the blessings of liberty to ourselves and our posterity, do ordain and establish this Constitution for the United States of America." — *United States Constitution, Preamble.*

"WE THE PEOPLE of Maine do agree," etc. — *Constitution of Maine.*

"All government of right originates from THE PEOPLE, is founded in their consent, and instituted for the general good." — *Constitution of New Hampshire.*

"The body politic is formed by a voluntary association of individuals ; it is a social compact, by which THE WHOLE PEOPLE covenants with each citizen, and each citizen with the whole people, that all shall be governed by certain laws for the common good." — *Constitution of Massachusetts.*

"WE THE PEOPLE of the State of Rhode Island

and Providence Plantations . . . do ordain and establish this constitution of government." — *Constitution of Rhode Island.*

"THE PEOPLE of Connecticut do, in order more effectually to define, secure, and perpetuate the liberties, rights, and privileges which they have derived from their ancestors, hereby ordain and establish the following constitution and form of civil government." — *Constitution of Connecticut.*

And so on through the constitutions of almost every State in the Union. Our government is, as Lincoln said, "a government of the people, by the people, and for the people." There is no escaping it. To question this is to deny the foundations of the American government. Granted that those who framed these provisions may not have understood the full extent of the principles they announced. No matter : they gave us those principles ; and, having them, we must apply them.

Now, women may be voters or not, citizens or not ; but that they are a part of the people, no one has denied in Christendom — however it may be in Japan, where, as Mrs. Leonowens tells us, the census of population takes in only men, and the women and children are left to be inferred. "WE THE PEOPLE," then, includes women. Be the superstructure what it may, the foundation of the government clearly provides a place for them : it is impossible to state the national theory in such a way that it shall not include them.   It is impossible to deny the natural right of women to vote, except on grounds which exclude all natural right. The fundamental charters are on our side. There are certain statute limitations which may prove greater or less.   But these are temporary and trivial things, always to be interpreted, often to be modified, by reference to the principles of the Constitution.   For instance, when a constitutional convention is to be held, or new conditions of suffrage to be created, the whole people should vote upon the matter, including those not hitherto enfranchised.   This is the view insisted on, many years since, by that eminent jurist, William Beach Lawrence.   He maintained, in a letter to Charles Sumner and in opposition to his own party, that if the question of " negro suffrage " in the Southern States of the Union were put to vote, the colored people themselves had a natural right to vote on the question.   The same is true of women. It should never be forgotten by advocates of woman suffrage, that the deeper their reasonings go, the stronger foundation they find ; and that we have always a solid fulcrum for our lever in that phrase of our charters, " We the people."

THE USE OF THE DECLARATION OF INDEPENDENCE   When young people begin to study geometry, they expect to begin with hard reasoning on the very first page. To their surprise, they find that the early pages are not occupied by reasoning, but by a few simple, easy, and rather commonplace sentences, called " axioms," which are really a set of pegs on which all the reasoning is hung. Pupils are not expected to go back in every demonstration and prove the axioms. If Almira Jones happens to be doing a problem at the blackboard on examination day, at the high school, and remarks in the course of her demonstration that " things which are equal to the same thing are equal to one another," and if a sharp questioner jumps up, and says, "How do you know it ? " she simply lays down her bit of chalk, and says fearlessly, " That is an axiom," and the teacher sustains her. Some things must be taken for granted.

The same service rendered by axioms in the geometry is supplied in America, as to government, by the simple principles of the Declaration of Independence. Right or wrong, they are taken for granted. Inasmuch as all the legislation of the country is supposed to be based in them, — they stating the theory of our government, while the Constitution itself only puts into organic shape the application, —

we must all begin with them. It is a great
advantage, and saves great trouble in all reforms. To the Abolitionists, for instance, what
an inestimable labor-saving machine was the
Declaration of Independence! Let them have
that, and they asked no more. Even the brilliant lawyer Rufus Choate, when confronted
with its plain provisions, could only sneer at
them as "glittering generalities," which was
equivalent to throwing down his brief, and
throwing up his case. It was an admission that,
if you were so foolish as to insist on applying
the first principles of the government, it was
all over with him.

Now, the whole doctrine of woman suffrage
follows so directly from these same political
axioms, that they are especially convenient for
women to have in the house. When the Declaration of Independence enumerates as among
"self-evident" truths the fact of governments
"deriving their just powers from the consent of
the governed," then that point may be considered as settled. In this school-examination of
maturer life, in this grown-up geometry class,
the student is not to be called upon by the committee to prove that. She may rightfully lay
down her demonstrating chalk, and say, "That
is an axiom. You admit that yourselves."

It is a great convenience. We cannot al-

ways be going back, like a Hindoo history, to
the foundations of the world. Some things may
be taken for granted. How this simple axiom
sweeps away, for instance, the cobweb specula-
tions as to whether voting is a natural right, or
a privilege delegated by society! No matter
which. Take it which way you please. That
is an abstract question ; but the practical question is a very simple one. "Governments owe
their just powers to the consent of the governed." Either that axiom is false, or, whenever women as a class refuse their consent to
the present exclusively masculine government,
it can no longer claim just powers. The remedy then may be rightly demanded, which the
Declaration of Independence goes on to state :
"Whenever any form of government becomes
destructive of these ends, it is the right of the
people to alter or to abolish it, and to institute
a new government, laying its foundation on
such principles, and organizing its powers in
such form, as to them shall seem most likely to
effect their safety and happiness."

This is the use of the Declaration of Independence. Women, as a class, may not be
quite ready to use it. It is the business of this
book to help make them ready. But so far as
they are ready these plain provisions are the
axioms of their political faith. If the axioms

mean anything for men, they mean something for women. If men deride the axioms, it is a concession, like that of Rufus Choate, that these fundamental principles are very much in their way. But so long as the sentences stand in that document they can be made useful. If men try to get away from the arguments of women by saying, " But suppose we have nothing in our theory of government which requires us to grant your demand?" then women can answer, as the straightforward Traddles answered Uriah Heep, "But you have, you know : therefore, if you please, we won't suppose any such thing."

SOME OLD-FASHIONED PRINCIPLES   There has been an effort, lately, to show that when our fathers said, "Taxation without representation is tyranny," they referred not to personal liberties, but to the freedom of a state from foreign power. It is fortunate that this criticism has been made, for it has led to a more careful examination of passages ; and this has made it clear, beyond dispute, that the Revolutionary patriots carried their statements more into detail than is generally supposed, and affirmed their principles for individuals, not merely for the state as a whole.

In that celebrated pamphlet by James Otis,

for instance, published as early as 1764, "The Rights of the Colonies Vindicated," he thus clearly lays down the rights of the individual as to taxation : —

"The very act of taxing, exercised over those who are not represented, appears to me to be depriving them of one of their most essential rights as freemen ; and, if continued, seems to be, in effect, an entire disfranchisement of every civil right. For what one civil right is worth a rush, after a man's property is subject to be taken from him at pleasure, without his consent ? If a man is not his own assessor, in person or by deputy, his liberty is gone, or he is entirely at the mercy of others." [1]

This fine statement has already done duty for liberty, in another contest ; for it was quoted by Mr. Sumner in his speech of March 7, 1866, with this commentary : —

"Stronger words for universal suffrage could not be employed. His argument is that if men are taxed without being represented, they are deprived of essential rights ; and the continuance of this deprivation despoils them of every civil right, thus making the latter depend upon the right of suffrage, which by a neologism of our day is known as a political right instead of a civil right. Then, to give point to this argument, the patriot insists

1 Otis, *Rights of the Colonies*, p. 58.

that in determining taxation, 'every man must be his own assessor, in person or by deputy,' without which his liberty is entirely at the mercy of others. Here, again, in a different form, is the original thunderbolt, 'Taxation without representation is tyranny;' and the claim is made not merely for communities, but for 'every man.'"

In a similar way wrote Benjamin Franklin, some six years after, in that remarkable sheet found among his papers, and called "Declaration of those Rights of the Commonalty of Great Britain, without which they cannot be free." The leading propositions were these three : —

"That every man of the commonalty (excepting infants, insane persons, and criminals) is of common right and by the laws of God a freeman, and entitled to the free enjoyment of liberty. That liberty, or freedom, consists in having an actual share in the appointment of those who frame the laws, and who are to be the guardians of every man's life, property, and peace; for the all of one man is as dear to him as the all of another; and the poor man has an equal right, but more need, to have representatives in the legislature than the rich one. That they who have no voice nor vote in the electing of representatives do not enjoy liberty, but are absolutely enslaved to those who have votes, and to their representatives; for to be enslaved is to have governors whom other men have set over us, and be subject to laws made by the representatives of others, without having had representatives of our own to give consent in our behalf." [1]

In quoting these words of Dr. Franklin, one of his biographers feels moved to add, " These principles, so familiar to us now and so obviously just, were startling and incredible novelties in 1770, abhorrent to nearly all Englishmen, and to great numbers of Americans." Their fair application is still abhorrent to a great many ; or else, not willing quite to deny the theory, they limit the application by some such device as "virtual representation." Here, again, James Otis is ready for them ; and Charles Sumner is ready to quote Otis, as thus : —

" No such phrase as virtual representation was ever known in law or constitution. It is altogether a subtlety and illusion, wholly unfounded and absurd. We must not be cheated by any such phantom, or any other fiction of law or politics, or any monkish trick of deceit or blasphemy."

These are the sharp words used by the patriot Otis, speaking of those who were trying to convince American citizens that they were virtually represented in Parliament. Sumner applied the same principle to the freedmen : it is now applied to women. " Taxation without represen-

1 Sparks's *Franklin*, ii. 372.

tation is tyranny." "Virtual representation is altogether a subtlety and illusion, wholly unfounded and absurd." No ingenuity, no evasion, can give any escape from these plain principles. Either you must revoke the maxims of the American Revolution, or you must enfranchise woman. Stuart Mill well says in his autobiography, "The interest of woman is included in that of man exactly as much (and no more) as that of subjects in that of kings."

FOUNDED   If there is any one who is re-
ON A ROCK cognized as a fair exponent of our national principles, it is our martyr-president Abraham Lincoln ; whom Lowell calls, in his noble Commemoration Ode at Cambridge, —

"New birth of our new soil, the first American."

What President Lincoln's political principle was, we know. On his journey to Washington for his first inauguration he said, " I have never had a feeling that did not spring from the sentiments embodied in the Declaration of Independence." To find out what was his view of those sentiments, we must go back several years earlier, and consider that remarkable letter of his to the Boston Republicans who had invited him to join them in celebrating Jefferson's birthday, in April, 1859. It was well called by Charles

Sumner "a gem in political literature ; " and it seems to me almost as admirable, in its way, as the Gettysburg address.

" The principles of Jefferson are the definitions and axioms of free society. And yet they are denied and evaded with no small show of success. One dashingly calls them ' glittering generalities.' Another bluntly styles them ' self-evident lies.' And others insidiously argue that they apply only to ' superior races.' "

" These expressions, differing in form, are identical in object and effect, — the subverting the principles of free government, and restoring those of classification, caste, and legitimacy. They would delight a convocation of crowned heads plotting against the people. They are the vanguard, the sappers and miners of returning despotism. We must repulse them, or they will subjugate us."

" All honor to Jefferson ! — the man who, in the concrete pressure of a struggle for national independence by a single people, had the coolness, forecast, and capacity to introduce into a merely revolutionary document *an abstract truth applicable to all men and all times*, and so to embalm it there that to-day and in all coming days it shall be a rebuke and a stumbling-block to the harbingers of reappearing tyranny and oppression."

The special "abstract truth " to which President Lincoln thus attaches a value so great, and which he pronounces "applicable to all

men and all times," is evidently the assertion
of the Declaration that governments derive
their just powers from the consent of the governed, following the assertion that all men are
born free and equal ; that is, as some one has
well interpreted it, equally men. I do not see
how any person but a dreamy recluse can deny
that the strength of our republic rests on these
principles ; which are so thoroughly embedded
in the average American mind that they take
in it, to some extent, the place occupied in the
average English mind by the emotion of personal loyalty to a certain reigning family. But
it is impossible to defend these principles logically, as Senator Hoar has well pointed out,
without recognizing that they are as applicable
to women as to men. If this is the case, the
claim of women rests on a right, — indeed,
upon the same right which is the foundation of
all our institutions.

The encouraging fact in the present condition of the whole matter is not that we get
more votes here or there for this or that form
of woman suffrage — for experience has shown
that there are great ups and downs in that respect; and States that at one time seemed nearest to woman suffrage, as Maine and Kansas,
now seem quite apathetic. But the real encouragement is that the logical ground is more and

more conceded ; and the point now usually
made is not that the Jeffersonian maxim ex-
cludes women, but that " the consent of the
governed" is substantially given by the general
consent of women. That this argument has
a certain plausibility may be conceded ; but
it is equally clear that the minority of women,
those who do wish to vote, includes on the
whole the natural leaders, — those who are foremost in activity of mind, in literature, in art, in
good works of charity. It is, therefore, pretty
sure that they only predict the opinions of the
rest, who will follow them in time. And even
while waiting it is a fair question whether the
" governed " have not the right to give their
votes when they wish, even if the majority of
them prefer to stay away from the polls. We
do not repeal our naturalization laws, although
only the minority of our foreign-born inhabitants as yet take the pains to become natural-
ized.

THE GOOD   In Paris, some years ago, I was
OF THE   for a time a resident in a cultivated
GOVERNED
            French family, where the father was
non-committal in politics, the mother and son
were republicans, and the daughter was a Bona-
partist. Asking the mother why the young
lady thus held to a different creed from the

rest, I was told that she had made up her mind that the streets of Paris were kept cleaner under the empire than since its disappearance : hence her imperialism.

I have heard American men advocate the French empire at home and abroad, without offering reasons so good as those of the lively French maiden. But I always think of her remark when the question is seriously asked, as Mr. Parkman, for instance, once gravely put it in "The North American Review," — "The real issue is this : Is the object of government the good of the governed, or is it not?" Taken in a general sense, there is probably no disposition to discuss this conundrum, for the simple reason that nobody dissents from it. But the important point is : What does "the good of the governed" mean? Does it merely mean better street cleaning, or something more essential?

There is nothing new in the distinction. Ever since De Tocqueville wrote his "Democracy in America," forty years ago, this precise point has been under active discussion. That acute writer himself recurs to it again and again. Every government, he points out, nominally seeks the good of the people, and rests on their will at last. But there is this difference : A monarchy organizes better, does its work better, cleans the streets better. Nevertheless De Tocqueville, a monarchist, sees this advantage in a republic, that when all this is done by the people for themselves, although the work done may be less perfect, yet the people themselves are more enlightened, better satisfied, and, in the end, their good is better served. Thus in one place he quotes "a writer of talent" who complains of the want of administrative perfection in the United States, and says, "We are indebted to centralization, that admirable invention of a great man, for the uniform order and method which prevails alike in all the municipal budgets (of France) from the largest town to the humblest commune." But, says De Tocqueville, —

"Whatever may be my admiration of this result, when I see the communes (municipalities) of France, with their excellent system of accounts, plunged in the grossest ignorance of their true interests, and abandoned to so incorrigible an apathy that they seem to vegetate rather than to live; when, on the other hand, I observe the activity, the information, and the spirit of enterprise which keeps society in perpetual labor, in these American townships, whose budgets are drawn up with small method and with still less uniformity, — I am struck by the spectacle; *for, to my mind, the end of a good government is to insure the welfare of a people,* and not to establish order and regularity in the midst of its misery and its distress." [1]

The italics are my own; but it will be seen that he uses a phrase almost identical with Mr. Parkman's, and that he uses it to show that there is something to be looked at beyond good laws, — namely, the beneficial effect of self-government. In another place he comes back to the subject again : —

"It is incontestable that the people frequently conducts public business very ill; but it is impossible that the lower order should take a part in public business without extending the circle of their ideas, and without quitting the ordinary routine of their mental acquirements ; the humblest individual who is called upon to coöperate in the government of society acquires a certain degree of self-respect ; and, as he possesses authority, he can command the services of minds much more enlightened than his own. He is canvassed by a multitude of applicants, who seek to deceive him in a thousand different ways, but who instruct him by their deceit. . . . Democracy does not confer the most skilful kind of government upon the people ; but it produces that which the most skilful governments are frequently unable to awaken, namely, an all-pervading and restless activity, a superabundant force, and an energy which is inseparable from it, and which may, under favorable circumstances, beget the most

[1] Reeves's translation, London, 1838, vol. i. p. 97, note.

amazing benefits. These are the true advantages of democracy." [1]

These passages and others like them are worth careful study. They clearly point out the two different standards by which we may criticise all political systems. One class of thinkers, of whom Froude is the most conspicuous, holds that the "good of the people" means good laws and good administration, and that, if these are only provided, it makes no sort of difference whether they themselves make the laws, or whether some Cæsar or Louis Napoleon provides them. All the traditions of the early and later Federalists point this way. But it has always seemed to me a theory of government essentially incompatible with American institutions. If we could once get our people saturated with it, they would soon be at the mercy of some Louis Napoleon of their own.

When President Lincoln claimed, following Theodore Parker, that ours was not merely a government for the people, but of the people, and by the people as well, he recognized the other side of the matter, — that it is not only important what laws we have, but who makes the laws; and that "the end of a good government is to insure the welfare of a people," in

[1] De Tocqueville, vol. ii. pp. 74, 75.

this far wider sense. That advantage which
the French writer admits in democracy, that it
develops force, energy, and self-respect, is as
essentially a part of "the good of the governed" as is any perfection in the details of
government. And it is precisely these advantages which we expect that women, sooner or
later, are to share. For them, as for men, " the
good of the governed " is not genuine unless it
is that kind of good which belongs to the self-
governed.

RULING AT   In the last century the bitter sa-
SECOND-   tirist, Charles Churchill, wrote a
HAND   verse which will do something to
keep alive his name.   It is as follows : —

"Women ruled all; and ministers of state
    Were at the doors of women forced to wait, —
    Women, who 've oft as sovereigns graced the land,
    But never governed well at second-hand."

He touches the very kernel of the matter,
and all history is on his side. The Salic Law
excluded women from the throne of France, —
" the kingdom of France being too noble to be
governed by a woman," as it said. Accordingly
the history of France shows one long line of
royal mistresses ruling in secret for mischief ;
while more liberal England points to the reigns
of Elizabeth and Anne and Victoria, to show
how usefully a woman may sit upon a throne.

It was one of the merits of Margaret Fuller Ossoli, that she always pointed out this distinction. "Any woman can have influence," she said, "in some way. She need only to be a good cook or a good scold, to secure that. Woman should not merely have a share in the power of man, — for of that omnipotent Nature will not suffer her to be defrauded, — but it should be a *chartered* power, too fully recognized to be abused." We have got to meet, at any rate, this fact of feminine influence in the world. Demosthenes said that the measures which a statesman had meditated for a year might be overturned in a day by a woman. How infinitely more sensible then, to train the woman herself in statesmanship, and give her open responsibility as well as concealed power!

The same demoralizing principle of subordination runs through the whole position of women. Many a husband makes of his wife a doll, dresses her in fine clothes, gives or withholds money according to his whims, and laughs or frowns if she asks any questions about his business. If only a petted slave, she naturally develops the vices of a slave ; and when she wants more money for more fine clothes, and finds her husband out of humor, she coaxes, cheats, and lies. Many a woman half ruins her husband by her extravagance, simply because he has never told her frankly what his income is, or treated her, in money matters, like a rational being. Bankruptcy, perhaps, brings both to their senses; and thenceforward the husband discovers that his wife is a woman, not a child. But for want of this whole families and generations of women are trained to deception. I knew an instance where a fashionable dressmaker in New York urged an economical young girl, about to be married, to buy of her a costly *trousseau* or wedding outfit. "But I have not the money," said the maiden. "No matter," said the complaisant tempter: "I will wait four years, and send in the bill to your husband by degrees. Many ladies do it." Fancy the position of a pure young girl, wishing innocently to make herself beautiful in the eyes of her husband, and persuaded to go into his house with a trick like this upon her conscience! Yet it grows directly out of the whole theory of life which is preached to many women, — that all they seek must be won by indirect manœuvres, and not by straightforward living.

It is a mistaken system. Once recognize woman as born to be the equal, not inferior, of man, and she accepts as a right her share of the family income, of political power, and of all else that is capable of distribution. As it is, we are in danger of forgetting that woman, in mind as in body, was born to be upright. The women of Charles Reade — never by any possibility moving in a straight line where it is possible to find a crooked one — are distorted women ; and Nature is no more responsible for them than for the figures produced by tight lacing and by high-heeled boots. These physical deformities acquire a charm, when the taste adjusts itself to them ; and so do those pretty tricks and those interminable lies. But after all, to make a noble woman you must give a noble training.

VIII

SUFFRAGE

"No such phrase as virtual representation was ever known in law or constitution. It is altogether a subtlety and illusion, wholly unfounded and absurd. We must not be cheated by any such phantom or any other trick of law and politics." — James Otis, quoted by Charles Sumner in speech, March 7, 1866.

DRAWING THE LINE When in Dickens's "Nicholas Nickleby" the coal-heaver calls at the fashionable barber's to be shaved, the barber declines that service. The coal-heaver pleads that he saw a baker being shaved there the day before. But the barber points out to him that it is necessary to draw the line somewhere, and he draws it at bakers.

It is, doubtless, an inconvenience, in respect to woman suffrage, that so many people have their own theories as to drawing the line, and deciding who shall vote. Each has his hobby; and as the opportunity for applying it to men has passed by, each wishes to catch at the last remaining chance, and apply it to women. One believes in drawing an educational line; another,

in a property qualification; another, in new restrictions on naturalization; another, in distinctions of race; and each wishes to keep women,
for a time, as the only remaining victims for
his experiment.

Fortunately the answer to all these objections, on behalf of woman suffrage, is very brief
and simple. It is no more the business of its
advocates to decide upon the best abstract
basis for suffrage, than it is to decide upon the
best system of education, or of labor, or of marriage. Its business is to equalize, in all these
directions; nothing more. When that is done,
there will be plenty still left to do, without
doubt; but it will not involve the rights of women, as such. Simply to strike out the word
"male" from the statute, — that is our present
work. "What is sauce for the goose " — but
the proverb is somewhat musty. These educational and property restrictions may be of value;
but wherever they are already removed from
the men they must be removed from women
also. Enfranchise them equally, and then begin afresh, if you please, to legislate for the
whole human race. What we protest against
is that you should have let down the bars for
one sex, and should at once become conscientiously convinced that they should be put up
again for the other.

When it was proposed to apply an educational qualification at the South after the war, the Southern white loyalists all objected to it. If you make it universal, they said, it cuts off many of the whites. If you apply it to the blacks alone, it is manifestly unjust. The case is the same with women in regard to men. As woman needs the ballot primarily to protect herself, it is manifestly unjust to restrict the suffrage for her, when man has it without restriction. If she needs protection, then she needs it all the more from being poor, or ignorant, or Irish, or black. If we do not see this, the freedwomen of the South did. There is nothing like personal wrong to teach people logic.

We hear a great deal said in dismay, and sometimes even by old abolitionists, about "increasing the number of ignorant voters." In Massachusetts, there is an educational restriction for men, such as it is; in Rhode Island, a property qualification is required for voting on certain questions. Personally, I believe with "Warrington," that, if ignorant voting be bad, ignorant non-voting is worse; and that the enfranchised "masses," which have a legitimate outlet for their political opinions, are far less dangerous than disfranchised masses, which must rely on mobs and strikes. I will go farther, and say that I believe our republic is, on the whole, in less danger from its poor men, who have got to stay in it and bring up their children, than from its rich men, who have always Paris and London to fall back upon. I do not see that even a poll-tax or registry-tax is of any use as a safeguard; for if men are to be bought the tax merely offers a more indirect and palatable form in which to pay the price. Many a man consents to have his poll-tax paid by his party or his candidate, when he would reject the direct offer of a dollar bill.

But this is all private speculation, and has nothing to do with the woman-suffrage movement. All that we can ask, as advocates of this reform, is that the inclusion or the exclusion should be the same for both sexes. We cannot put off the equality of woman till that time, a few centuries hence, when the Social Science Association shall have succeeded in agreeing on the true basis of "scientific legislation." It is as if we urged that wives should share their husbands' dinners, and were told that the physicians had not decided whether beefsteak were wholesome. The answer is, "Beefsteak or tripe, yeast or saleratus, which you please. But, meanwhile, what is good enough for the wife is good enough for the husband."

FOR SELF-
PROTEC-
TION I remember to have read, many years ago, the life of Sir Samuel Romilly, the English philanthropist. He was the author of more beneficent legal reforms than any man of his day, and there was in that very book a long list of the changes he still meant to bring about. It struck me very much, that among these proposed reforms not one of any importance referred to the laws about women.

It shows — what all experience has shown — that no class or race or sex can safely trust its protection in any hands but its own. The laws of England in regard to woman were then so bad that Lord Brougham afterwards said they needed total reconstruction, if they were to be touched at all. Yet it is only since woman suffrage began to be talked about, that the work of law-reform has really taken firm hold. In many cases in America the beneficent measures are directly to be traced to some appeal from feminine advocates. Even in Canada, as was once stated by Dr. Cameron of Toronto, the bill protecting the property of married women was passed under the immediate pressure of Lucy Stone's eloquence. And even where this direct agency could not be traced, the general fact that the atmosphere was full of the agitation had much to do with all the reforms that took place. Legislatures, unwilling to give woman the ballot, were shamed into giving her something. The chairman of the judiciary committee in Rhode Island told me that until he heard women argue before the committee he had not reflected upon their legal disabilities, or thought how unjust these were. While the matter was left to the other sex only, even men like Sir Samuel Romilly forgot the wrongs of woman. When she began to advocate her own cause men also waked up.

But now that they are awake they ask, Is not this sufficient ? Not at all. If an agent who has cheated you surrenders reluctantly one half your stolen goods, you do not stop there and say, " It is enough. Your intention is honorable. Please continue my agent with increased pay." On the contrary, you say, " Your admission of wrong is a plea of guilty. Give me the rest of what is mine." There is no defence like self-defence, no protection like self-protection.

All theories of chivalry and generosity and vicarious representation fall before the fact that woman has been grossly wronged by man. That being the case, the only modest and honest thing for man to do is to say, " Henceforward have a voice in making your own laws." Till this is done, she has no sure safeguard, since otherwise the same men who made the old barbarous laws may at any time restore them.

It is common to say that woman suffrage will make no great difference; that women will think very much as men do, and it will simply double the vote without varying the result. About many matters this may be true. To be sure, it is probable that on questions of conscience, like slavery and temperance, the woman's vote would by no means coincide with man's. But grant that it would. The fact remains, — and all history shows it, — that on all that concerns her own protection a woman needs her own vote. Would a woman vote to give her husband the power of bequeathing her children to the control and guardianship of somebody else? Would a woman vote to sustain the law by which a Massachusetts chief justice bade the police take those crying children from their mother's side in the Boston court-room a few years ago, and hand them over to a comparative stranger, because that mother had married again? You might as well ask whether the colored vote would sustain the Dred Scott decision. Tariffs or banks may come or go the same, whether the voters be white or black, male or female; but when the wrongs of an oppressed class or sex are to be righted the ballot is the only guaranty. After they have

gained a potential voice for themselves, the Sir
Samuel Romillys will remember them.

WOMANLY   The newspapers periodically ex-
STATES-   press a desire to know whether
MANSHIP
             women have given evidence, on the
whole, of superior statesmanship to men. There
are constant requests that they will define their
position as to the tariff and the fisheries and
the civil-service question. If they do not speak,
it is naturally assumed that they will forever
after hold their peace. Let us see how that
matter stands.

It is said that the greatest mechanical skill
in America is to be found among professional
burglars who come here from England. Suppose one of these men were in prison, and we
were to stand outside and taunt him through
the window : " Here is a locomotive engine :
why do you not mend or manage it ? Here is
a steam printing-press : if you know anything,
set it up for me ! You a mechanic, when you
have not proved that you understand any of
these things ? Nonsense ! "

But Jack Sheppard, if he condescended to
answer us at all, would coolly say, " Wait a
while, till I have finished my present job. Being in prison, my first business is to get out of
prison. Wait till I have picked this lock, and

mined this wall; wait till I have made a saw
out of a watch-spring, and a ladder out of a pair
of blankets.   Let me do my first task, and get
out of limbo, and then see if your little printing-
presses and locomotives are too puzzling for my
fingers."

Politically speaking, woman is in jail, and
her first act of skill must be in getting through
the wall.   For her there is no tariff question,
no problem of the fisheries.   She will come to
that by and by, if you please; but for the present her statesmanship must be employed nearer
home.   The "civil-service reform" in which
she is most concerned is a reform which shall
bring her in contact with the civil service.   Her
political creed, for the present, is limited to that
of Sterne's starling in the cage, — "I can't get
out."   If she is supposed to have any common-
sense at all, she will best show it by beginning
at the point where she is, instead of at the point
where somebody else is.   She would indeed be
as foolish as these editors think her if she now
spent her brains upon the tariff question, which
she cannot reach, instead of upon her own enfranchisement, which she is gradually reaching.

The woman-suffrage movement in America,
in all its stages and subdivisions, has been the
work of woman.   No doubt men have helped
in it : much of the talking has been done by

them, and they have furnished many of the printed documents. But the energy, the methods, the unwearied purpose, of the movement, have come from women : they have led in all councils ; they have established the newspapers, got up the conventions, addressed the legislatures, and raised the money. Thirty years have shown, with whatever temporary variations, one vast wave of progress toward success, both in this country and in Europe. Now success is statesmanship.

I remember well the shouts of laughter that used to greet the anti-slavery orators when they claimed that the real statesmen of the country were not the Clays and Calhouns, who spent their strength in trying to sustain slavery, and failed, but the Garrisons, who devoted their lives to its overthrow, and were succeeding. Yet who now doubts this ? Tried by the same standard, the statesmanship of to-day does not lie in the men who can find no larger questions before them than those which concern the fisheries, but in the women whose far-reaching efforts will one day make every existing voting-list so much waste paper.

Of course, when the voting-lists with the women's names are ready to be printed, it will be interesting to speculate as to how these new monarchs of our destiny will use their power.

For myself, a long course of observation in the anti-slavery and woman - suffrage movements has satisfied me that women are not idiots, and that, on the whole, when they give their minds to a question, whether moral or practical, they understand it quite as readily as men. In the anti-slavery movement it is certain that a woman, Elizabeth Heyrick, gave the first impulse to its direct and simple solution in England; and that another woman, Mrs. Stowe, did more than any man, except perhaps Garrison and John Brown, to secure its right solution here. There was never a moment, I am confident, when any great political question growing out of the anti-slavery struggle might not have been put to vote more safely among the women of New England than among the clergy, or the lawyers, or the college professors. If they did so well in that great issue, it is fair to assume that, after they have a sufficient inducement to study out future issues, they at least will not be very much behind the men.

But we cannot keep it too clearly in view, that the whole question, whether women would vote better or worse than men on general questions, is a minor matter. It was equally a minor matter in case of the negroes. We gave the negroes the ballot, simply because they needed it for their own protection; and we shall

by and by give it to women for the same reason. Tried by that test, we shall find that their
statesmanship will be genuine. When they
come into power, drunken husbands will no
longer control their wives' earnings, and a chief
justice will no longer order a child to be removed
from its mother, amid its tears and outcries,
merely because that mother has married again.
And if, as we are constantly assured, woman's
first duty is to her home and her children, she
may count it a good beginning in statesmanship
to secure to herself the means of protecting
both. That once settled, it will be time enough
to "interview" her in respect to the proper
rate of duty on pig-iron.

TOO MUCH "Seek not to proticipate," says
PREDIC-
TION Mrs. Gamp, the venerable nurse in
"Martin Chuzzlewit" — "but take
'em as they come, and as they go." I am persuaded that our woman-suffrage arguments
would be improved by this sage counsel, and
that at present we indulge in too many bold
anticipations.

Is there not altogether too much tendency
to predict what women will do when they vote?
Could that good time come to-morrow, we
should be startled to find to how many different
opinions and "causes" the new voters were

already pledged. One speaker wishes that women should be emancipated, because of the fidelity with which they are sure to support certain desirable measures, as peace, order, freedom, temperance, righteousness, and judgment to come. Then the next speaker has his or her schedule of political virtues and is equally confident that women, if once enfranchised, will guarantee clear majorities for them all. The trouble is that we thus mortgage this new party of the future, past relief, beyond possibility of payment, and incur the ridicule of the unsanctified by committing our cause to a great many contradictory pledges.

I know an able and high-minded woman of foreign birth, who courageously, but as I think mistakenly, calls herself an atheist, and who has for years advocated woman suffrage as the only antidote to the rule of the clergy. On the other hand, an able speaker in a Boston convention soon after advocated the same thing as the best way of defeating atheism, and securing the positive assertion of religion by the community. Both cannot be correct : neither is entitled to speak for woman. That being the case, would it not be better to keep clear of this dangerous ground of prediction, and keep to the argument based on rights and needs ? If our theory of government be worth any-

thing, woman has the same right to the ballot
that man has : she certainly needs it as much
for self-defence. How she will use it, when
she gets it, is her own affair. It may be that
she will use it more wisely than her brothers ;
but I am satisfied to believe that she will use it
as well. Let us not attribute infallible wisdom
and virtue, even to women ; for, as dear Mrs.
Poyser says in "Adam Bede," "God Almighty
made some of 'em foolish, to match the men."

It is common to assume, for instance, that all
women by nature favor peace ; and that, even if
they do not always seem to promote it in their
social walk and conversation, they certainly will
in their political. When we consider how all the
pleasing excitements, achievements, and glories
of war, such as they are, accrue to men only,
and how large a part of the miseries are brought
home to women, it might seem that their vote
on this matter, at least, would be a sure thing.
Thus far the theory : the fact being that we
have been through a civil war which convulsed
the nation, and cost half a million lives ; and
which was, from the very beginning, fomented,
stimulated, and applauded, at least on one side,
by the united voice of the women. It will be
generally admitted by those who know, that,
but for the women of the seceding States, the
war of the Rebellion would have been waged

more feebly, been sooner ended, and far more
easily forgotten. Nay, I was told a few days
since by an able Southern lawyer, who was
long the mayor of one of the largest Southern
cities, that in his opinion the practice of duelling
— which is an epitome of war — owes its continued existence at the South to a sustaining
public sentiment among the fair sex.

Again, where the sympathy of women is
wholly on the side of right, it is by no means
safe to assume that their mode of enforcing that
sentiment will be equally judicious. Take, for
instance, the temperance cause. It is quite
common to assume that women are a unit on
that question. When we look at the two extremes of society, — the fine lady pressing wine
upon her visitors, and the Irishwoman laying in
a family supply of whiskey to last over Sunday,
— the assumption seems hasty. But grant it.
Is it equally sure, that when woman takes hold
of that most difficult of all legislation, the
license and prohibitory laws, she will handle
them more wisely than men have done? Will
her more ardent zeal solve the problem on
which so much zeal has already been lavished
in vain? In large cities, for instance, where
there is already more law than is enforced,
will her additional ballots afford the means to
enforce it? It may be so ; but it seems wiser

not to predict nor to anticipate, but to wait and hope.

It is no reproach on woman to say that she is not infallible on particular questions. There is much reason to suppose that in politics, as in every other sphere, the joint action of the sexes will be better and wiser than that of either singly. It seems obvious that the experiment of republican government will be more fairly tried when one half the race is no longer disfranchised. It is quite certain, at any rate, that no class can trust its rights to the mercy and chivalry of any other, but that, the weaker it is, the more it needs all political aids and securities for self-protection. Thus far we are on safe ground; and here, as it seems to me, the claim for suffrage may securely rest. To go farther in our assertions seems to me unsafe, although many of our wisest and most eloquent may differ from me; and the nearer we approach success, the more important it is to look to our weapons. It is a plausible and tempting argument, to claim suffrage for woman on the ground that she is an angel; but I think it will prove wiser, in the end, to claim it for her as being human.

FIRST-
CLASS
CARRIAGES
In a hotly contested municipal election, the other day, an active political manager was telling me his tactics. " We have to send carriages for some of the voters," he said. " First-class carriages ! If we undertake to wait on 'em, we must do it in good shape, and not leave the best carriages to be hired by the other party."

I am not much given to predicting just what will happen when women vote ; but I confidently assert that they will be taken to the polls, if they wish, in first-class carriages. If the best horses are to be harnessed, and the best cushions selected, and every panel of the coach rubbed till you can see your face in it, merely to accommodate some elderly man who lives two blocks away, and could walk to the polls very easily, then how much more will these luxuries be placed at the service of every woman, young or old, whose presence at the polls is made doubtful by mud, or snow, or the prospect of a shower.

But the carriage is only the beginning of the polite attentions that will soon appear. When we see the transformation undergone by every ferryboat and every railway station, so soon as it comes to be frequented by women, who can doubt that voting-places will experience the same change ? They will soon have — at least in the "ladies' department" — elegance instead of discomfort, beauty for ashes, plenty of rocking-chairs, and no need of spittoons. Very possibly they may have all the modern conveniences and inconveniences, — furnace registers, teakettles, Washington pies, and a young lady to give checks for bundles. Who knows what elaborate comforts, what queenly luxuries, may be offered to women at voting-places, when the time has finally arrived to sue for their votes?

The common impression has always been quite different from this. People look at the coarseness and dirt now visible at so many voting-places, and say, "Would you expose women to all that?" But these places are not dirtier than a railway smoking-car; and there is no more coarseness than in any ferryboat which is, for whatever reason, used by men only. You do not look into those places, and say with indignation, "Never, if I can help it, shall my wife or my beloved great-grandmother travel by steamboat or by rail!" You know that with these exemplary relatives will enter order and quiet, carpets and curtains, brooms and dusters. Why should it be otherwise with ward rooms and town halls?

There is not an atom more of intrinsic difficulty in providing a decorous ladies' room for a voting-place, than for a post-office or a railway station ; and it is as simple a thing to vote a ticket as to buy one. This being thus easily practicable, all men will desire to provide it. And the example of the first-class carriages shows that the parties will vie with each other in these pleasing arrangements. They will be driven to it, whether they wish it or not. The party which has most consistently and reso- lutely kept woman away from the ballot-box will be the very party compelled, for the sake of self-preservation, to make her " rights " agreeable to her when once she gets them. A few stupid or noisy men may indeed try to make the polls unattractive to her, the very first time ; but the result of this little experi- ment will be so disastrous that the offenders will be sternly suppressed by their own party leaders, before another election day comes. It will soon become clear, that of all possible ways of losing votes the surest lies in treating women rudely.

Lucy Stone tells a story of a good man in Kansas who, having done all he could to prevent women from being allowed to vote on school questions, was finally comforted, when that measure passed, by the thought that he should at least secure his wife's vote for a pet school- house of his own. Election day came, and the newly enfranchised matron showed the most culpable indifference to her privileges. She made breakfast as usual, went about her housework, and did on that perilous day precisely the things that her anxious husband had always predicted that women never would do under such circumstances. His hints and advice found no response; and nothing short of the best pair of horses and the best wagon finally sufficed to take the farmer's wife to the polls. I am not the least afraid that women will find voting a rude or disagreeable arrangement. There is more danger of their being treated too well, and being too much attacked and allured by these cheap cajoleries. But women are pretty shrewd, and can probably be trusted to go to the polls, even in first-class carriages.

EDUCATION *via* SUF-FRAGE   I know a rich bachelor of large property who fatigues his friends by perpetual denunciations of everything American, and especially of universal suffrage. He rarely votes; and I was much amazed, when the popular vote was to be taken on building an expensive schoolhouse, to see him go to the polls, and vote in the affirmative. On being asked his reason, he explained that, while we labored under the calamity of universal (male) suffrage, he thought it best to mitigate its evils by educating the voters. In short, he wished, as Mr. Lowe said in England when the last Reform Bill passed, "to prevail upon our future masters to learn their alphabets."

These motives may not be generous; but the schoolhouses, when they are built, are just as useful. Even girls get the benefit of them, though the long delay in many places before girls got their share came in part from the want of this obvious stimulus. It is universal male suffrage that guarantees schoolhouse and school. The most selfish man understands that argument : "We must educate the masses, if it is only to keep them from our throats."

But there is a wider way in which suffrage guarantees education. At every election time political information is poured upon the whole voting community till it is deluged. Presses run night and day to print newspaper extras; clerks sit up all night to send out congressional speeches; the most eloquent men in the community expound the most difficult matters to the ignorant. Of course each party affords only its own point of view; but every man has a neighbor who is put under treatment by some other party, and who is constantly attacking all who will listen to his provoking and pestilent counter-statements. All the common school education of the United States does not equal the education of election day; and as in some

States elections are held very often, this popular university seems to be kept in session almost the whole year round. The consequence is a remarkable average popular knowledge of political affairs, — a training which American women now miss, but which will come to them with the ballot.

And in still another way there will be an education coming to woman from the right of suffrage. It will come from her own sex, proceeding from highest to lowest. We often hear it said that after enfranchisement the more educated women will not vote, while the ignorant will. But Mrs. Howe admirably pointed out, at a Philadelphia convention, that the moment women have the ballot it will become the pressing duty of the more educated women, even in self-protection, to train the rest. The very fact of the danger will be a stimulus to duty, with women, as it already is with men.

It has always seemed to me rather childish, in a man of superior education, or talent, or wealth, to complain that when election day comes he has no more votes than the man who plants his potatoes or puts in his coal. The truth is that under the most thorough system of universal suffrage the man of wealth or talent or natural leadership has still a disproportionate influence, still casts a hundred votes where the

poor or ignorant or feeble man throws but one.
Even the outrages of New York elections
turned out to be caused by the fact that the
leading rogues had used their brains and energy, while the men of character had not.
When it came to the point, it was found that a
few caricatures by Nast and a few columns of
figures in the "Times" were more than a match
for all the repeaters of the ring.   It is always
so.   Andrew Johnson, with all the patronage
of the nation, had not the influence of "Nasby"
with his one newspaper.   The whole Chinese
question was perceptibly and instantly modified
when Harte wrote " The Heathen Chinee."

These things being so, it indicates feebleness
or dyspepsia when an educated man is heard
whining, about election time, with his fears of
ignorant voting.   It is his business to enlighten
and control that ignorance.   With a voice and
a pen at his command, with a town hall in
every town for the one, and a newspaper in
every village for the other, he has such advantages over his ignorant neighbors that the only
doubt is whether his privileges are not greater
than he deserves.   For one, in writing for the
press, I am impressed by the undue greatness,
not by the littleness, of the power I wield.   And
what is true of men will be true of women.   If
the educated women of America have not brains

or energy enough to control, in the long run, the votes of the ignorant women around them, they will deserve a severe lesson, and will be sure, like the men in New York, to receive it. And thenceforward they will educate and guide that ignorance, instead of evading or cringing before it.

But I have no fear about the matter. It is a libel on American women to say that they will not go anywhere or do anything which is for the good of their children and their husbands. Travel West on any of our great lines of railroad, and see what women undergo in transporting their households to their new homes. See the watching and the feeding, and the endless answers to the endless questions, and the toil to keep little Sarah warm, and little Johnny cool, and the baby comfortable. What a hungry, tired, jaded, forlorn mass of humanity it is, as the sun rises on it each morning, in the soiled and breathless railway-car! Yet that household group is America in the making ; those are the future kings and queens, the little princes and princesses, of this land. Now, is the mother who has undergone for the transportation of these children all this enormous labor to shrink at her journey's end from the slight additional labor of going to the polls to vote whether those little ones shall have schools or rumshops? The thought is an absurdity. A few fine ladies in cities will fear to spoil their silk dresses, as a few foppish gentlemen now fear for their broadcloth. But the mass of intelligent American women will vote, as do the mass of men.

FOLLOW YOUR LEADERS   "There go thirty thousand men," shouted the Portuguese, as Wellington, with a few staff-officers, rode along the mountain-side. The action of the leaders' minds, in any direction, has a value out of all proportion to their numbers. In a campaign there is a council of officers, — Grant and Sherman and Sheridan perhaps. They are but a trifling minority, yet what they plan the whole army will do; and such is the faith in a real leader, that, were all the restraints of discipline for the moment relaxed, the rank and file would still follow his judgment. What a few general officers see to be the best to-day, the sergeants and corporals and private soldiers will usually see to be best to-morrow.

In peace, also, there is a silent leadership; only that in peace, as there is more time to spare, the leaders are expected to persuade the rank and file, instead of commanding them. Yet it comes to the same thing in the end. The movement begins with certain guides, and if you wish to know the future, keep your eye on them. If you wish to know what is already decided, ask the majority; but if you wish to find out what is likely to be done next, ask the leaders.

It is constantly said that the majority of women do not yet desire to vote, and it is true. But to find out whether they are likely to wish for it, we must keep our eyes on the women who lead their sex. The representative women, — those who naturally stand for the rest, those most eminent for knowledge and self-devotion, — how do they view the thing? The rank and file do not yet demand the ballot, you say; but how is it with the general officers?

Now, it is a remarkable fact, about which those who have watched this movement for twenty years can hardly be mistaken, that almost any woman who reaches a certain point of intellectual or moral development will presently be found desiring the ballot for her sex. If this be so, it predicts the future. It is the judgment of Grant and Sherman and Sheridan as against that of the average private soldier of the Two Hundredth Infantry. Set aside, if you please, the specialists of this particular agitation, — those who were first known to the public through its advocacy. There is no just reason why they should be set aside, yet con-

cede that for a moment.   The fact remains that
the ablest women in the land — those who were
recognized as ablest in other spheres, before
they took this particular duty upon them — are
extremely apt to assume this cross when they
reach a certain stage of development.

When Margaret Fuller first came forward
into literature, she supposed that literature was
all she wanted.   It was not till she came to
write upon woman's position that she discovered
what woman needed.   Clara Barton, driving
her ambulance or her supply wagon at the battle's edge, did not foresee, perhaps, that she
should make that touching appeal, when the
battle was over, imploring her own enfranchisement from the soldiers she had befriended.
Lydia Maria Child, Julia Ward Howe, Harriet
Beecher Stowe, Louisa Alcott, came to the
claim for the ballot earlier than a million others,
because they were the intellectual leaders of
American womanhood.   They saw farthest, because they were in the highest place.   They
were the recognized representatives of their sex
before they gave in their adhesion to the new
demand.   Their judgment is as the judgment
of the council of officers, while Flora McFlim-
sey's opinion is as the opinion of John Smith,
unassigned recruit.   But if the generals make
arrangements for a battle, the chance is that

John Smith will have to take a hand in it, or else run away.

It is a rare thing for the petition for suffrage from any town to comprise the majority of women in that town. It makes no difference: if there are few women in the town who want to vote, there is as much propriety in their voting as if there were ten millions, so long as the majority are equally protected in their right to stay at home. But when the names of petitioners come to be weighed as well as counted, the character, the purity, the intelligence, the social and domestic value of the petitioners is seldom denied. The women who wish to vote are not the idle, the ignorant, the narrow-minded, or the vicious; they are not "the dangerous classes:" they represent the best class in the community, when tried by the highest standard. They are the natural leaders. What they now see to be right will also be perceived even by the foolish and the ignorant by and by.

In a poultry-yard in spring, when the first brood of ducklings goes toddling to the water-side, no doubt all the younger or feebler broods, just hatched out of similar eggs, think these innovators dreadfully mistaken. "You are out of place," they feebly pipe. "See how happy we are in our safe nests. Perhaps, by and by, when properly introduced into society, we may run

about a little on land, but to swim! — never!"
Meanwhile their elder kindred are splashing
and diving in ecstasy; and, so surely as they
are born ducklings, all the rest will swim in
their turn. The instinct of the first duck solves
the problem for all the rest. It is a mere
question of time. Sooner or later, all the
broods in the most conservative yard will follow
their leaders.

HOW TO MAKE WOMEN UNDERSTAND POLITICS   An English member of Parliament said in a speech, some years ago, that the stupidest man had a clearer understanding of political
questions than the brightest woman. He did
not find it convenient to say what must be the
condition of a nation which for many years has
had a woman for its sovereign; but he certainly
said bluntly what many men feel. It is not indeed very hard to find the source of this feeling.
It is not merely that women are inexperienced
in questions of finance or administrative practice, for many men are equally ignorant of
these. But it is undoubtedly true of a large
class of more fundamental questions, — as, for
instance, of some now pending at Washington,
— which even many clear-headed women find
it hard to understand, while men of far less
general training comprehend them entirely.

Questions of the distribution of power, for instance, between the executive, judicial, and legislative branches of government, — or between the United States government and those of the separate States, — belong to the class I mean. Many women of great intelligence show a hazy indistinctness of views when the question arises whether it is the business of the general government to preserve order at the voting-places at a congressional election, for instance, as the Republicans hold; or whether it should be left absolutely in the hands of the state officials, as the Democrats maintain. Most women would probably say that so long as order was preserved, it made very little difference who did it. Yet, if one goes into a shoe-shop or a blacksmith's shop, one may hear just these questions discussed in all their bearings by uneducated men, and it will be seen that they involve a principle. Why is this difference? Does it show some constitutional inferiority in women, as to this particular faculty?

The question is best solved by considering a case somewhat parallel. The South Carolina negroes were considered very stupid, even by many who knew them; and they certainly were densely ignorant on many subjects. Put face to face with a difficult point of finance legislation, I think they would have been found to

know even less about it than I do. Yet the
abolition of slavery was held in those days by
many great statesmen to be a subject so difficult that they shrank from discussing it ; and
nevertheless I used to find that these ignorant
men understood it quite clearly in all its bearings. Offer a bit of sophistry to them, try to
blind them with false logic on this subject, and
they would detect it as promptly, and answer it
as keenly, as Garrison or Phillips would have
done ; and, indeed, they would give very much
the same answers. What was the reason?
Not that they were half wise and half stupid ;
but that they were dull where their own interests had not trained them, and they were sharp
and keen where their own interests were concerned.

I have no doubt that it will be so with women when they vote. About some things they
will be slow to learn ; but about all that immediately concerns themselves they will know
more at the very beginning than many wise
men have learned since the world began. How
long it took for English-speaking men to correct, even partially, the iniquities of the old
common law! — but a parliament of women
would have set aside at a single sitting the
alleged right of the husband to correct his wife
with a stick no bigger than his thumb. It took

the men of a certain State of this Union a good many years to see that it was an outrage to confiscate to the State one half the property of a man who died childless, leaving his widow only the other half; but a legislature of women would have annihilated that enormity by a single day's work. I have never seen reason to believe that women on general questions would act more wisely or more conscientiously, as a rule, than men: but self-preservation is a wonderful quickener of the brain; and in all questions bearing on their own rights and opportunities as women, it is they who will prove shrewd and keen, and men who will prove obtuse, as indeed they have usually been.

Another point that adds force to this is the fact that wherever women, by their special position, have more at stake than usual in public affairs, even as now organized, they are apt to be equal to the occasion. When the men of South Carolina were ready to go to war for the "State-Rights" doctrines of Calhoun, the women of that State had also those doctrines at their fingers'-ends. At Washington, where politics make the breath of life, you will often find the wives of members of Congress following the debates, and noting every point gained or lost, because these are matters in which they and their families are personally concerned;

and as for that army of women employed in the "departments" of the government, they are politicians every one, because their bread depends upon it.

The inference is, that if women as a class are now unfitted for politics it is because they have not that pressure of personal interest and responsibility by which men are unconsciously trained. Give this, and self-interest will do the rest, aided by that power of conscience and affection which is certainly not less in them than in men, even if we claim no more. A young lady of my acquaintance opposed woman suffrage in conversation on various grounds, one of which was that it would, if enacted, compel her to read the newspapers, which she greatly disliked. I pleaded that this was not a fatal objection; since many men voted "early and often" without reading them, and in fact without knowing how to read at all. She said, in reply, that this might do for men, but that women were far more conscientious, and, if they were once compelled to vote, they would wish to know what they were voting for. This seemed to me to contain the whole philosophy of the matter; and I respected the keenness of her suggestion, though it led me to an opposite conclusion.

INFERIOR TO MAN, AND NEAR TO ANGELS   If it were anywhere the custom to disfranchise persons of superior virtue because of their virtue, and to present others with the ballot, simply because they had been in the state prison, — then the exclusion of women from political rights would be a high compliment, no doubt. But I can find no record in history of any such legislation, unless so far as it is contained in the doubtful tradition of the Tuscan city of Pistoia, where men are said to have been ennobled as a punishment for crime. Among us crime may often be a covert means of political prominence, but it is not the ostensible ground ; nor are people habitually struck from the voting-lists for performing some rare and eminent service, such as saving human life, or reading every word of a presidential message. If a man has been President of the United States, we do not disfranchise him thenceforward ; if he has been governor, we do not declare him thenceforth ineligible to the office of United States senator. On the contrary, the supposed reward of high merit is to give higher civic privileges. Sometimes these are even forced on unwilling recipients, as when Plymouth Colony in 1633 imposed a fine of twenty pounds on any one who should refuse the office of governor.

It is utterly contrary to all tradition and precedent, therefore, to suppose that women have been hitherto disfranchised because of any supposed superiority. Indeed, the theory is self-annihilating, and has always involved all supporters in hopeless inconsistency. Thus the Southern slaveholders were wont to argue that a negro was only blest when a slave, and there was no such inhumanity as to free him. Then, if a slave happened to save his master's life, he was rewarded by emancipation immediately, amid general applause. The act refuted the theory. And so, every time we have disfranchised a rebel, or presented some eminent foreigner with the freedom of a city, we have recognized that enfranchisement, after all, means honor, and disfranchisement implies disgrace.

I do not see how any woman can avoid a thrill of indignation when she first opens her eyes to the fact that it is really contempt, not reverence, that has so long kept her sex from an equal share of legal, political, and educational rights. In spite of the duty paid to individual women as mothers, in spite of the reverence paid by the Greeks and the Germanic races to certain women as priestesses and sibyls, the fact remains that this sex has been generally recognized, in past ages of the human race, as stamped by hopeless inferiority, not by angelic superiority. This is carried so far that a certain taint of actual inferiority is held to attach to women, in barbarous nations. Among certain Indian tribes, the service of the gods is defiled if a woman but touches the implements of sacrifice; and a Turk apologizes to a Christian physician for the mention of the women of his family, in the very phrases used to soften the mention of any degrading creature. Mr. Leland tells us that among the English gypsies any object that a woman treads upon, or sweeps with the skirts of her dress, is destroyed or made away with in some way, as unfit for use. In reading the history of manners, it is easy to trace the steps from this degradation up to the point now attained, such as it is. Yet even the habit of physiological contempt is not gone, and I do not see how any one can read history without seeing, all around us, in society, education, and politics, the tradition of inferiority. Many laws and usages which in themselves might not strike all women as intrinsically worth striving for — as the exclusion of women from colleges or from the ballot-box — assume great importance to a woman's self-respect, when she sees in these the plain survival of the same contempt that once took much grosser forms.

And it must be remembered that in civilized communities the cynics, who still frankly express this utter contempt, are better friends to women than the flatterers, who conceal it in the drawing-room, and only utter it freely in the lecture-room, the club, and the "North American Review." Contempt at least arouses pride and energy. To be sure, in the face of history, the contemptuous tone in regard to women seems to me untrue, unfair, and dastardly ; but, like any other extreme injustice, it leads to reaction. It helps to awaken women from that shallow dream of self-complacency into which flattery lulls them. There is something tonic in the manly arrogance of Fitzjames Stephen, who derides the thought that the marriage contract can be treated as in any sense a contract between equals ; but there is something that debilitates in the dulcet counsel given by an anonymous gentleman, in an old volume of the "Ladies' Magazine" that lies before me, — "She ought to present herself as a being made to please, to love, and to seek support ; *a being inferior to man, and near to angels.*"

IX

OBJECTIONS TO SUFFRAGE

"When you were weak and I was strong, I toiled for you. Now you are strong and I am weak. Because of my work for you, I ask your aid. I ask the ballot for myself and my sex. As I stood by you, I pray you stand by me and mine." —CLARA BARTON.

[Appeal to the returned soldiers of the United States, written from Geneva, Switzerland, by Clara Barton, invalided by long service in the hospitals and on the field during the civil war.]

THE FACT OF SEX It is constantly said that the advocates of woman suffrage ignore the fact of sex. On the contrary, they seem to me to be the only people who do not ignore it.

Were there no such thing as sexual difference, the wrong done to woman by disfranchisement would be far less. It is precisely because her traits, habits, needs, and probable demands are distinct from those of man, that she is not, never was, never can, and never will be, justly represented by him. It is not merely that a vast number of human individuals are disfranchised; it is not even because in many of our States the disfranchisement extends to a majority, that the evil is so great; it is not merely that we disfranchise so many units and tens: but we exclude a special element, a peculiar power, a distinct interest, — in a word, a sex.

Whether this sex is more or less wise, more or less important, than the other sex, does not affect the argument: it is a sex, and, being such, is more absolutely distinct from the other than is any mere race from any other race. The more you emphasize the fact of sex, the more you strengthen our argument. If the white man cannot justly represent the negro, — although the two races are now so amalgamated that not even the microscope can always decide to which race one belongs, — how impossible that one sex should stand in legislation for the other sex!

This is so clear that, so soon as it is stated, there is a shifting of the ground. "But consider the danger of introducing the sexual influence into legislation!" . . . Then we are sure to be confronted with the case of Miss Vinnie Ream, the sculptor. See how that beguiling damsel cajoled all Congress into buying poor statues! they say. If one woman could do so much, how would it be with one hundred? Precisely the Irishman's argument against the use of pillows: he had put one feather on a rock, and found it a very uncomfortable support. Grant, for the sake of argument, that Miss Ream gave us poor art; but what gave her so much power? Plainly that she was but a single feather. Congress being composed exclusively of men, the mere fact of her sex gave her an exceptional and dangerous influence. Fill a dozen of the seats in Congress with women, and that danger at least will be cancelled. The taste in art may be no better; but an artist will no more be selected for being a pretty girl than now for being a pretty boy. So in all such cases. Here, as everywhere, it is the advocate of woman suffrage who wishes to recognize the fact of sex, and guard against its perils.

It is precisely so in education. Believing boys and girls to be unlike, and yet seeing them to be placed by the Creator on the same planet and in the same family, we hold it safer to follow his method. As they are born to interest each other, to stimulate each other, to excite each other, it seems better to let this impulse work itself off in a natural way, — to let in upon it the fresh air and the daylight, instead of attempting to suppress and destroy it. In a mixed school, as in a family, the fact of sex presents itself as an unconscious, healthy, mutual stimulus. It is in the separate schools that the healthy relation vanishes, and the thought of sex becomes a morbid and diseased thing. This observation first occurred to me when a pupil and a teacher in boys' boarding-schools years ago : there was such marked superiority as to sexual refinement in the day-scholars, who saw their sisters and the friends of their sisters every day. All later experience of our public-school system has confirmed this opinion. It is because I believe the distinction of sex to be momentous, that I dread to see the sexes educated apart.

The truth of the whole matter is that Nature will have her rights — innocently if she can, guiltily if she must ; and it is a little amusing that the writer of an ingenious paper on the other side, called " Sex in Politics," in an able New York journal, puts our case better than I can put it, before he gets through, only that he is then speaking of wealth, not women : " Anybody who considers seriously what is meant by the conflict between labor and capital, of which we are only just witnessing the beginning, and what is to be done *to give money legitimately that influence on legislation which it now exercises illegitimately*, must acknowledge at once that the next generation will have a thorny path to travel." The italics are my own. Precisely what this writer wishes to secure for money, we claim for the disfranchised half of the human race, — open instead of secret influence; the English tradition instead of the French; women as rulers, not as kings' mistresses; women as legislators, not merely as lobbyists; women employing in legitimate form that power which they will otherwise illegitimately wield. This is all our demand.

HOW WILL   "It would be a great convenience,
IT RESULT? my hearers," said old Parson Withington of Newbury, "if the moral of a fable could only be written at the beginning of it, instead of the end. But it never is." Commonly the only thing to be done is to get hold of a few general principles, hold to those, and trust that all will turn out well. No matter how thoroughly a reform may have been discussed, — negro emancipation or free-trade, for instance, — it is a step in the dark at last, and the detailed results never turn out to be precisely according to the programme.

An " esteemed correspondent," who has written some of the best things yet said in America in behalf of the enfranchisement of woman, writes privately to express some solicitude, since, as she thinks, we are not ready for it yet. "I am convinced," she writes, " of the abstract right of women to vote; but all I see of the

conduct of the existing women, into whose
hands this change would throw the power, in-
clines me to hope that this power will not be
conceded till education shall have prepared a
class of women fit to take the responsibilities."

Gradual emancipation, in short ! — for fear of
trusting truth and justice to take care of themselves.   Who knew, when the negroes were set
free, whether they would at first use their freedom well, or ill ?   Would they work ? would
they avoid crimes ? would they justify their
freedom ? The theory of education and preparation seemed very plausible.   Against that, there
was only the plain theory which Elizabeth Heyrick first announced to England, — " Immediate,
unconditional emancipation."   " The best preparation for freedom is freedom."   What was
true of the negroes then is true of women now.

" The lovelier traits of womanhood," writes
earnestly our correspondent, " simplicity, faith,
guilelessness, unfit them to conduct public
affairs, where one must deal with quacks and
charlatans. . . . We are not all at once 'as gods,
knowing good and evil ; ' and the very innocency
of our lives, and the habits of pure homes, unfit
us to manage a certain class who will flock to
this standard."

But the basis of all republican government
is in the assumption that good is ultimately

stronger than evil. If we once abandon this, our theory has gone to pieces, at any rate. If we hold to it, good women are no more helpless and useless than good men. The argument that would here disfranchise women has been used before now to disfranchise clergymen. I believe that in some States they are still disfranchised ; and, if they are not, it is partly because good is found to be as strong as evil, after all, and partly because clergymen are not found to be so angelically good as to be useless. I am very confident that both these truths will be found to apply to women also.

Whatever else happens, we may be pretty sure that one thing will. The first step towards the enfranchisement of women will blow to the winds the tradition of the angelic superiority of women. Just so surely as women vote, we shall occasionally have women politicians, women corruptionists, and women demagogues. Conceding, for the sake of courtesy, that none such now exist, they will be born as inevitably, after enfranchisement, as the frogs begin to pipe in the spring. Those who doubt it ignore human nature ; and, if they are not prepared for this fact, they had better consider it in season, and take sides accordingly. In these pages, at least, they have been warned.

What then ? Suppose women are not "as

gods, knowing good and evil : " they are not to
be emancipated as gods, but as fallible human
beings.   They are to come out of an ignorant
innocence, that may be only weakness, into a
wise innocence that will be strength.   It is too
late to remand American women into a Turkish
or Jewish tutelage : they have emerged too far
not to come farther.   In a certain sense, no
doubt, the butterfly is safest in the chrysalis.
When the soft thing begins to emerge, the world
certainly seems a dangerous place ; and it is
hard to say what will be the result of the
emancipation.   But when she is once half out,
there is no safety for the pretty creature but to
come the rest of the way, and use her wings.

I HAVE
ALL THE
RIGHTS I
WANT
When Dr. Johnson had published
his English Dictionary, and was
asked by a lady how he chanced to
make a certain mistake that she
pointed out, he answered, " Ignorance, madam,
pure ignorance."   I always feel disposed to
make the same comment on the assertion of
any woman that she has all the rights she wants.
For every woman is, or may be, or might have
been, a mother.   And when she comes to know
that even now, in many parts of the Union, a
married mother has no legal right to her child,
I should think her tongue would cleave to her

mouth before she would utter those foolish words again.

All the things I ever heard or read against slavery did not fix in my soul such a hostility to it as a single scene in a Missouri slave-jail many years ago. As I sat there, a purchaser came in to buy a little girl to wait on his wife. Three little sisters were brought in, from eight to twelve years old : they were mulattoes, with sweet, gentle manners; they had evidently been taken good care of, and their pink calico frocks were clean and whole. The gentleman chose one of them, and then asked her, good-naturedly enough, if she did not wish to go with him. She burst into tears, and said, "I want to stay with my mother." But her tears were as powerless, of course, as so many salt drops from the ocean.

That was all. But all the horrors of "Uncle Tom's Cabin," the stories told me by fugitive slaves, the scarred backs I afterwards saw by dozens among colored recruits, did not impress me as did that hour in the jail. The whole probable career of that poor, wronged, motherless, shrinking child passed before me in fancy. It seemed to me that a man must be utterly lost to all manly instincts who would not give his life to overthrow such a system. It seemed to me that the woman who could tolerate, much less defend it, could not herself be true, could not be pure, or must be fearfully and grossly ignorant.

You acquiesce, fair lady. You say it was horrible indeed, but, thank God! it is past. Past? Is it so? Past, if you please, as to the law of slavery, but as to the legal position of woman still a fearful reality. It is not many years since a scene took place in a Boston court-room, before Chief Justice Chapman, which was worse, in this respect, than that scene in St. Louis, inasmuch as the mother was present when the child was taken away, and the wrong was sanctioned by the highest judicial officer of the State. Two little girls, who had been taken from their mother by their guardian, their father being dead, had taken refuge with her against his wishes; and he brought them into court under a writ of habeas corpus, and the court awarded them to him as against their mother. "The little ones were very much affected," says the "Boston Herald," "by the result of the decision which separated them from their mother; and force was required to remove them from the court-room. The distress of the mother was also very evident."

There must have been some special reason, you say, for such a seeming outrage: she was a bad woman. No: she was "a lady of the highest respectability." No charge was made against her; but, being left a widow, she had married again; and for that, and that only, so far as appears, the court took from her the guardianship of her own children, — bone of her bone, and flesh of her flesh, the children for whom she had borne the deepest physical agony of womanhood, — and awarded them to somebody else.

You say, "But her second husband might have misused the children." Might? So the guardian might, and that where they had no mother to protect them. Had the father been left a widower, he might have made a half-dozen successive marriages, have brought stepmother after stepmother to control these children, and no court could have interfered. The father is recognized before the law as the natural guardian of the children. The mother, even though she be left a widow, is not. The consequence is a series of outrages of which only a few scattered instances come before the public; just as in slavery, out of a hundred little girls sold away from their parents, only one case might ever be mentioned in any newspaper.

This case led to an alteration of the law in Massachusetts, but the same thing might yet happen in some States of the Union. The possibility of a single such occurrence shows that there is still a fundamental wrong in the legal position of woman. And the fact that most women do not know it only deepens the wrong — as Dr. Channing said of the contentment of the Southern slaves. The mass of men, even of lawyers, pass by such things, as they formerly passed by the facts of slavery.

There is no lasting remedy for these wrongs, except to give woman the political power to protect herself. There never yet existed a race, nor a class, nor a sex, which was noble enough to be trusted with political power over another sex, or class, or race. It is for self-defence that woman needs the ballot. And in view of a single such occurrence as I have given, I charge that woman who professes to have "all the rights she wants," either with a want of all feeling of motherhood, or with "ignorance, madam, pure ignorance."

SENSE ENOUGH TO VOTE   There is one special point on which men seem to me rather insincere toward women. When they speak to women, the objection made to their voting is usually that they are too angelic. But when men talk to each other, the general assumption is, that women should not vote because they have not brains enough — or, as old Theophilus Parsons wrote a century ago, have not "a sufficient acquired discretion."

It is an important difference. Because, if women are too angelic to vote, they can only be fitted for it by becoming more wicked, which is not desirable. On the other hand, if there is no objection but the want of brains, then our public schools are equalizing that matter fast enough. Still, there are plenty of people who have never got beyond this objection. Listen to the first discussion that you encounter among men on this subject, wherever they may congregate. Does it turn upon the question of saintliness, or of brains? Let us see.

I travelled the other day upon the Boston and Providence Railroad with a party of mechanics, mostly English and Scotch. They were discussing this very question, and, with the true English habit, thought it was all a matter of property. Without it a woman certainly should not vote, they said; but they all favored, to my surprise, the enfranchisement of women of property. "As a general rule," said the chief speaker, "a woman that's got property has got sense enough to vote."

There it was! These foreigners, who had found their own manhood by coming to a land which not only the Pilgrim Fathers but the Pilgrim Mothers had settled, and subdued, and freed for them, were still ready to disfranchise most of the daughters of those mothers, on the ground that they had not "sense enough to vote." I thanked them for their blunt truthfulness, so much better than the flattery of most of the native-born.

My other instance shall be a conversation overheard in a railway station near Boston, between two intelligent citizens, who had lately listened to Anna Dickinson. "The best of it was," said one, "to see our minister introduce her." "Wonder what the Orthodox churches would have said to that ten years ago?" said the other. "Never mind," was the answer. "Things have changed. What I think is, it's all in the bringing up. If women were brought up just as men are, they'd have just as much brains." (Brains again!) "That's what Beecher says. Boys are brought up to do business, and take care of themselves: that's where it is. Girls are brought up to dress and get married. Start 'em alike! That's what Beecher says. Start 'em alike, and see if girls haven't got just as much brains."

"Still harping on my daughter," and on the condition of her brains! It is on this that the whole question turns, in the opinion of many men. Ask ten men their objections to woman suffrage. One will plead that women are angels. Another fears discord in families. Another points out that women cannot fight, — he him-

self being very likely a non-combatant. Another
quotes St. Paul for this purpose, — not being,
perhaps, in the habit of consulting that authority on any other point. But with the others,
very likely, everything will turn on the question of brains. They believe, or think they believe, that women have not sense enough to
vote. They may not say so to women, but they
habitually say it to men. If you wish to meet
the common point of view of masculine voters,
you must find it here.

It is fortunate that it is so. Of all points,
this is the easiest to settle ; for every intelligent
woman, even if she be opposed to woman suffrage, helps to settle it. Every good lecture
by a woman, every good book written by one,
every successful business enterprise carried on,
helps to decide the question. Every class of
girls that graduates from every good school
helps to pile up the argument on this point.
And the vast army of women, constituting nine
out of ten of the teachers in our American
schools, may appeal as logically to their pupils,
and settle the argument based on brains. " If
we had sense enough to educate you," they
may say to each graduating class of boys, "we
have sense enough to vote beside you."

"The ladies actively working to secure the coöperation of their sex in caucuses and citizens' conventions are not actuated by love of notoriety, and are not, therefore, to be classed with the absolute woman suffragists." — Boston Daily Transcript, Sept. 1, 1879.

AN INFELI- CITOUS EPITHET When the eloquent colored abolitionist, Charles Remond, once said upon the platform that George Washington, having been a slaveholder, was a villain, Wendell Phillips remonstrated by saying, "Charles, the epithet is not felicitous." Reformers are apt to be pelted with epithets quite as ill-chosen. How often has the charge figured in history, that they were "actuated by love of notoriety"! The early Christians, it was generally believed, took a positive pleasure in being thrown to the lions, under the influence of this motive; and at a later period there was a firm conviction that the Huguenots consented readily to being broken on the wheel, or sawed in pieces between two boards, and felt amply rewarded by the pleasure of being talked about. During the whole anti-slavery movement, while the abolitionists were mobbed, fined, and imprisoned, — while they were tabooed by good society, depleted of their money, kept out of employment, by the mere fact of their abolitionism, — there never was a moment when their motive was not considered by many persons to be the love of notoriety. Why should the advocates of woman suffrage expect any different treatment now?

It is not necessary, in order to dispose of this charge, to claim that all reformers are heroes or saints. Even in the infancy of any reform, it takes along with it some poor material; and unpleasant traits are often developed by the incidents of the contest. Doubtless many reformers attain to a certain enjoyment of a fight, at last: it is one of the dangerous tendencies which those committed to this vocation must resist. But, so far as my observation goes, those who engage in reform for the sake of notoriety generally hurt the reform so much that they render it their chief service when they leave it; and this happy desertion usually comes pretty early in their career. The besetting sin of reformers is not, so far as I can judge, the love of notoriety, but the love of power and of flattery within their own small circle, — a temptation quite different from the other, both in its origin and its results.

Notoriety comes so soon to a reformer that its charms, whatever they may be, soon pall upon the palate, just as they do in case of a popular poet or orator, who is so used to seeing himself in print that he hardly notices it. I suppose there is no young person so modest that he does not, on first seeing his name in a newspaper, cut out the passage with a certain tender solicitude, and perhaps purchase a few extra copies of the fortunate journal. But when the same person has been battered by a score or two of years in successive unpopular reforms, I suppose that he not only would leave the paper uncut or unpurchased, but would hardly take the pains even to correct a misstatement, were it asserted that he had inherited a fortune or murdered his grandmother. The moral is that the love of notoriety is soon amply filled, in a reformer's experience, and that he will not, as a rule, sacrifice home and comfort, money and friends, without some stronger inducement. This is certainly true of most of the men who have interested themselves in this particular movement, the "weak-minded men," as the reporters, with witty antithesis, still describe them; and it must be much the same with the "strong-minded women" who share their base career.

And it is to be remembered, above all, that, considered as an engine for obtaining notoriety, the woman-suffrage agitation is a great waste of energy. The same net result could have been won with far less expenditure in other ways. There is not a woman connected with it who could not have achieved far more real publicity as a manager of charity fairs or as a sensation letter-writer. She could have done this, too, with far less trouble, without the loss of a single genteel friend, without forfeiting a

single social attention, without having a single
ill-natured thing said about her — except perhaps that she bored people, a charge to which
the highest and lowest forms of prominence
are equally open. Nay, she might have done
even more than this, if notoriety was her sole
aim : for she might have become a "variety"
minstrel or a female pedestrian ; she might have
written a scandalous novel ; she might have got
somebody to aim at her that harmless pistol,
which has helped the fame of so many a wan-
dering actress, while its bullet somehow never
hits anything but the wall. All this she might
have done, and obtained a notoriety beyond
doubt. Instead of this, she has preferred to
prowl about, picking up a precarious publicity
by giving lectures to willing lyceums, writing
books for eager publishers, organizing schools,
setting up hospitals, and achieving for her sex
something like equal rights before the law.
Either she has shown herself, as a seeker after
notoriety, to be a most foolish or ill-judging
person, — or else, as was said of Washington's
being a villain, "the epithet is not felicitous."

THE
ROB ROY
THEORY
"The Saturday Review," in an
article which denounces all equality
in marriage laws and all plans of
woman suffrage, admits frankly the practical

obstacles in the way of the process of voting.
"Possibly the presence of women as voters
would tend still further to promote order than
has been done by the ballot." It plants itself
wholly on one objection, which goes far deeper,
thus : —

"If men choose to say that women are not their
equals, women have nothing to do but to give in.
Physical force, the ultimate basis of all society and
all government, must be on the side of the men ;
and those who have the key of the position will not
consent permanently to abandon it."

It is a great pleasure when an opponent of
justice is willing to fall back thus frankly upon
the Rob Roy theory : —

"The good old rule
Sufficeth him, the simple plan
That they should take who have the power,
And they should keep who can."

It is easy, I think, to show that the theory is
utterly false, and that the basis of civilized society is not physical force, but, on the contrary,
brains.

In the city where the "Saturday Review"
is published, there are three regiments of
"Guards" which are the boast of the English
army, and are believed by their officers to be
the finest troops in the world. They have dete-
riorated in size since the Crimean war ; but I

believe that the men of one regiment still average six feet two inches in height; and I am
sure that nobody ever saw them in line without
noticing the contrast between these magnificent
men and the comparatively puny officers who
command them. These officers are from the
highest social rank in England, the governing
classes; and if it were the whole object of this
military organization to give a visible proof of
the utter absurdity of the "Saturday Review's"
theory, it could not be better done. There is
no country in Europe, I suppose, where the
hereditary aristocracy is physically equal to
that of England, or where the intellectual class
has so good a physique. But set either the
House of Lords or the "Saturday Review"
contributors upon a hand-to-hand fight against
an equal number of "navvies" or "coster-
mongers," and the patricians would have about
as much chance as a crew of Vassar girls in a
boat-race with Yale or Harvard. Take the men
of England alone, and it is hardly too much to
say that physical force, instead of being the
basis of political power in any class, is apt to be
found in inverse ratio to it. In case of revolution, the strength of the governing class in any
country is not in its physical, but in its mental
power. Rank and money, and the power
to influence and organize and command, are

merely different modifications of mental training, brought to bear by somebody.

In our country, without class distinctions, the
same truth can be easily shown. Physical
power lies mainly in the hands of the masses :
wherever a class or profession possesses more
than its numerical share of power, it has usually
less than its proportion of physical vigor. This
is easily shown from the vast body of evidence
collected during our civil war. In the volume
containing the medical statistics of the Provost
Marshal General's Bureau, we have the tabu-
lated reports of about 600,000 persons subject to draft, and of about 500,000 recruits,
substitutes, and drafted men ; showing the precise physical condition of more than a million
men.

It appears that, out of the whole number
examined, rather more than 257 in each 1000
were found unfit for military service. It is
curious to see how generally the physical power
among these men is in inverse ratio to the social and political prominence of the class they
represent. Out of 1000 unskilled laborers, for
instance, only 348 are physically disqualified ;
among tanners, only 216 ; among iron-workers,
189. On the other hand, among lawyers, 544
out of 1000 are disqualified ; among journalists,
740 ; among clergymen, 954. Grave divines

are horrified at the thought of admitting women
to vote, since they cannot fight; though not
one in twenty of their own number is fit for
military duty, if he volunteered. Of the editors
who denounce woman suffrage, only about one
in four could himself carry a musket; while of
the lawyers who fill Congress, the majority
could not be defenders of their country, but
could only be defended. If we were to dis-
tribute political power with reference to the
"physical basis" which the "Saturday Review"
talks about, it would be a wholly new distribution, and would put things more hopelessly up-
side down than did the worst phase of the
French Commune. If, then, a political theory
so utterly breaks down when applied to men,
why should we insist on resuscitating it in order
to apply it to women? The truth is that as
civilization advances the world is governed
more and more unequivocally by brains; and
whether those brains are deposited in a strong
body or a weak one becomes a matter of less
and less importance. But it is only in the very
first stage of barbarism that mere physical
strength makes mastery; and the long head
has controlled the long arm since the beginning
of recorded time.

And it must be remembered that even these
statistics very imperfectly represent the case.

They do not apply to the whole male sex, but actually to the picked portion only, to the men presumed to be of military age, excluding the very old and the very young. Were these included, the proportion unfit for military duty would of course be far greater. Moreover, it takes no account of courage or cowardice, patriotism or zeal. How much all these considerations tell upon the actual proportion may be seen from the fact that in the town where I am writing, for instance, out of some twelve thousand inhabitants and about three thousand voters, there are only some three hundred who actually served in the civil war, — a number too small to exert a perceptible influence on any local election. When we see the community yielding up its voting power into the hands of those who have actually done military service, it will be time enough to exclude women for not doing such service. If the alleged physical basis operates as an exclusion of all non-combatants, it should surely give a monopoly to the actual combatants.

THE VOTES OF NON-COM-BATANTS The tendency of modern society is not to concentrate power in the hands of the few, but to give a greater and greater share to the many. Read Froissart's Chronicles, and Scott's novels of chivalry, and you will see how thoroughly the difference between patrician and plebeian was then a difference of physical strength. The knight, being better nourished and better trained, was apt to be the bodily superior of the peasant, to begin with; and this strength was reinforced by armor, weapons, horse, castle, and all the resources of feudal warfare. With this greater strength went naturally the assumption of greater political power. To the heroes of "Ivanhoe," or "The Fair Maid of Perth," it would have seemed as absurd that yeomen and lackeys should have any share in the government, as it would seem to the members in an American legislature that women should have any such share. In a contest of mailed knights, any number of unarmed men were but so many women. As Sir Philip Sidney said, "The wolf asketh not how many the sheep may be."

But time and advancing civilization have tended steadily in one direction. "He giveth power to the weak, and to them who have no might He increaseth strength." Every step in the extension of political rights has consisted in opening them to a class hitherto humbler. From kings to nobles, from nobles to burghers, from burghers to yeomen; in short, from strong to weak, from high to low, from rich to poor.

All this is but the unconscious following out of one sure principle, — that legislation is mainly for the protection of the weak against the strong, and that for this purpose the weak must be directly represented. The strong are already protected by their strength : it is the weak who need all the vantage-ground that votes and legislatures can give them. The feudal chiefs were stronger without laws than with them. "Take care of yourselves in Sutherland," was the anxious message of the old Highlander : "the law has come as far as Tain." It was the peaceful citizen who needed the guaranty of law against brute force.

But can laws be executed without brute force ? Not without a certain amount of it, but that amount under civilization grows less and less. Just in proportion as the masses are enfranchised, statutes execute themselves without crossing bayonets. "In a republic," said De Tocqueville, "if laws are not always respectable, they are always respected." If every step in freedom has brought about a more peaceable state of society, why should that process stop at this precise point ? Besides, there is no possibility in nature of a political division in which all the men shall be on one side and all the women on the other. The mutual influence of the sexes forbids it. The

very persons who hint at such a fear refute
themselves at other times, by arguing that
"women will always be sufficiently represented
by men," or that "every woman will vote as
her husband thinks, and it will merely double
the numbers." As a matter of fact, the law
will prevail in all English-speaking nations: a
few men fighting for it will be stronger than
many fighting against it; and if those few
have both the law and the women on their side,
there will be no trouble.

The truth is that in this age *cedant arma
togæ:* it is the civilian who rules on the throne
or behind it, and who makes the fighting-men
his mere agents. Yonder policeman at the
corner looks big and formidable: he protects
the women and overawes the boys. But away
in some corner of the City Hill there is some
quiet man, out of uniform, perhaps a consump-
tive or a dyspeptic or a cripple, who can over-
awe the burliest policeman by his authority as
city marshal or as mayor. So an army is but
a larger police; and its official head is that
plain man at the White House, who makes or
unmakes, not merely brevet-brigadiers, but ma-
jor-generals in command, — who can by the
stroke of the pen convert the most powerful
man of the army into the most powerless.
Take away the occupant of the position, and

put in a woman, and will she become impotent
because her name is Elizabeth or Maria Theresa? It is brains that more and more govern
the world; and whether those brains be on the
throne, or at the ballot-box, they will soon make
the owner's sex a subordinate affair. If woman
is also strong in the affections, so much the
better. "Win the hearts of your subjects,"
said Lord Burleigh to Queen Elizabeth, "and
you will have their hands and purses."

War is the last appeal, and happily in these
days the rarest appeal, of statesmanship. In
the multifarious other duties that make up
statesmanship we cannot spare the brains, the
self-devotion, and the enthusiasm of woman.
One of the most important treaties of modern
history, the peace of Cambray, in 1529, was
negotiated, after previous attempts had failed,
by two women, — Margaret, aunt of Charles V.,
and Louisa, mother of Francis I. Voltaire said
that Christina of Sweden was the only sovereign of her time who maintained the dignity
of the throne against Mazarin and Richelieu.
Frederick the Great said that the Seven Years'
War was waged against three women, — Elizabeth of Russia, Maria Theresa, and Mme. Pom-
padour. There is nothing impotent in the
statesmanship of women when they are admitted to exercise it: they are only powerless

for good when they are obliged to obtain by
wheedling and flattery a sway that should be
recognized, responsible, and limited.

MANNERS   There is in Boswell's "Life of
REPEAL   Johnson" a correspondence which
LAWS   is well worth reading by both advocates and opponents of woman suffrage. Boswell, who was of an old Scotch family, had a
difference of opinion with his father about an
entailed estate which had descended to them.
Boswell wished the title so adjusted as to cut
off all possibility of female heirship. His father, on the other hand, wished to recognize
such a contingency. Boswell wrote to Johnson
in 1776 for advice, urging a series of objections, physiological and moral, to the inheritance of a family estate by a woman; though,
as he magnanimously admits, "they should be
treated with great affection and tenderness,
and always participate of the prosperity of the
family."

Dr. Johnson, for a wonder, took the other
side, defended female heirship, and finally
summed up thus : "It cannot but occur that
women have natural and equitable claims as
well as men, and these claims are not to be
capriciously or lightly superseded or infringed.
When fiefs inspired military service, it is easily

discerned why females could not inherit them ; but the reason is at an end. *As manners make laws, so manners likewise repeal them.*"

This admirable statement should be carefully pondered by those who hold that suffrage should be only coextensive with military duty. The position that woman cannot properly vote because she cannot fight for her vote efficiently is precisely like the position of feudalism and of Boswell, that she could not properly hold real estate because she could not fight for it. Each position may have had some plausibility in its day, but the same current of events has made each obsolete. Those who in these days believe in giving woman the ballot argue precisely as Dr. Johnson did in 1776. Times have changed, manners have softened, education has advanced, public opinion now acts more forcibly ; and the reference to physical force, though still implied, is implied more and more remotely. The political event of the age, the overthrow of American slavery, would not have been accomplished without the "secular arm" of Grant and Sherman, let us agree : but neither would it have been accomplished without the moral power of Garrison the non-resistant, and Harriet Beecher Stowe the woman. When the work is done, it is unfair to disfranchise any of the participants. Dr. Johnson was right : " When fiefs [or votes] implied military service, it is easily discerned why women should not inherit [or possess] them ; but the reason is at an end. As manners make laws, so manners likewise repeal them."

Under the feudal system it would have been absurd that women should hold real estate, for the next armed warrior could dispossess her. By Gail Hamilton's reasoning, it is equally absurd now : "One man is stronger than one woman, and ten men are stronger than ten women ; and the nineteen millions of men in this country will subdue, capture, and execute or expel the nineteen millions of women just as soon as they set about it." Very well : why, then, do not all the landless men in a town unite, and take away the landed property of all the women ? Simply because we now live in civilized society and under a reign of law ; because those men's respect for law is greater than their appetite for property ; or, if you prefer, because even those landless men know that their own interest lies, in the long-run, on the side of law. It will be precisely the same with voting. When any community is civilized up to the point of enfranchising women, it will be civilized up to the point of sustaining their vote, as it now sustains their property rights, by the whole material force of the community. When the thing is once established, it will no more occur to anybody that a woman's vote is power-less because she cannot fight, than it now occurs to anybody that her title to real estate is invalidated by the same circumstance.

Woman is in the world ; she cannot be got rid of : she must be a serf or an equal ; there is no middle ground. We have outgrown the theory of serfdom in a thousand ways, and may as well abandon the whole. Women have now a place in society : their influence will be ex-erted, at any rate, in war and in peace, legally or illegally ; and it had better be exerted in direct, legitimate, and responsible methods, than in ways that are dark, and by tricks that have not even the merit of being plain.

DANGER-OUS VOTERS   One of the few plausible objec-tions brought against women's vot-ing is this : that it would demoralize the suffrage by letting in very dangerous voters ; that virtuous women would not vote, and vicious women would. It is a very unfounded alarm.

For, in the first place, our institutions rest — if they have any basis at all — on this principle, that good is stronger than evil, that the majority of men really wish to vote rightly, and that only time and patience are needed to get the worst abuses righted. How any one can doubt this,

who watches the course of our politics, I do not
see. In spite of the great disadvantage of having masses of ignorant foreign voters to deal
with, — and of native black voters, who have
been purposely kept in ignorance, — we certainly see wrongs gradually righted, and the
truth by degrees prevail. Even the one great,
exceptional case of New York city has been
reached at last ; and the very extent of the
evil has brought its own cure. Now, why should
this triumph of good over evil be practicable
among men, and not apply to women also?

It must be either because women, as a class,
are worse than men, — which will hardly be asserted, — or because, for some special reason,
bad women have an advantage over good women
such as has no parallel in the other sex. But I
do not see how this can be. Let us consider.

It is certain that good women are not less
faithful and conscientious than good men. It is
generally admitted that those most opposed to
suffrage will very soon, on being fully enfranchised, feel it their duty to vote. They
may at first misuse the right through ignorance, but they certainly will not shirk it. It is
this conscientious habit on which I rely without
fear. Never yet, when public duty required,
have American women failed to meet the emergency ; and I am not afraid of it now. More-

over, when they are once enfranchised and their votes are needed, all the men who now oppose or ridicule the demand for suffrage will begin to help them to exercise it.   When the wives are once enfranchised, you may be sure that the husbands will not neglect those of their own household : they will provide them with ballots, vehicles, and policemen, and will contrive to make the voting-places pleasanter than many parlors, and quieter than some churches.

On the other hand, it seems altogether probable that the very worst women, so far from being ostentatious in their wickedness upon election day, will, on the contrary, so disguise and conceal themselves as to deceive the very elect, and, if it were possible, the very police-men.   For whatever party they may vote, they will contribute to make the voting-places as orderly as railway stations.   These covert ways are the very habit of their lives, at least by day-light ; and the women who have of late done the most conspicuous and open mischief in our community have done it, not in their true character as evil, but, on the contrary, under a mask of elevated purpose.

That women, when they vote, will commit their full share of errors I have always main-tained.   But that they will collectively misuse their power seems to me out of the question ;

and that the good women are going to stay at home, and let bad women do the voting, appears quite as incredible. In fact, if they do thus, it is a fair question whether the epithets "good" and "bad" ought not, politically speaking, to change places. For it naturally occurs to every one, on election day, that the man who votes, even if he votes wrong, is really a better man, so far as political duties go, than the very loftiest saint who stays at home and prays that other people may vote right. And it is hard to see why it should be otherwise with women.

HOW WOMEN WILL LEGISLATE It is often said that when women vote their votes will make no difference in the count, because they will merely duplicate the votes of their husbands and brothers. Then these same objectors go on and predict all sorts of evil things for which women will vote quite apart from their husbands and brothers. Moreover, the evils thus predicted are apt to be diametrically opposite. Thus Goldwin Smith predicts that women will be governed by priests, and then goes on to predict that women will vote to abolish marriage; not seeing that these two predictions destroy each other.

On the other hand, I think that the advocates of woman suffrage often err by claiming too much, — as that all women will vote for peace, for total abstinence, against slavery, and the rest. It seems better to rest the argument on general principles, and not to seek to prophesy too closely. The only thing which I feel safe in predicting is that woman suffrage will be used, as it should be, for the protection of woman. Self-respect and self-protection, — these are, as has been already said, the two great things for which woman needs the ballot.

It is not in the nature of things, I take it, that a class politically subject can obtain justice from the governing class. Not the least of the benefits gained by political equality for the colored people of the South is that the laws now generally make no difference of color in penalties for crime. In slavery times there were dozens of crimes which were punished more severely by the statute if committed by a slave or a free negro than if done by a white. I feel very sure that under the reign of impartial suffrage we should see fewer such announcements as this, which I cut from a late New York "Evening Express:" —

"Last night Capt. Lowery, of the Twenty-seventh Precinct, made a descent upon the dance-house in the basement of 96 Greenwich Street, and arrested fifty-two men and eight women. The entire batch was brought before Justice Flammer, at the Tombs

Police Court, this morning. Louise Maud, the proprietoress, was held in five hundred dollars bail to answer at the Court of General Sessions. *The fifty-two men were fined three dollars each, all but twelve paying at once; and the eight women were fined ten dollars each, and sent to the Island for one month.*"

The italics are my own. When we reflect that this dance-house, whatever it was, was unquestionably sustained for the gratification of men, rather than of women ; when we consider that every one of these fifty-two men came there, in all probability, by his own free will, and to spend money, not to earn it ; and that probably a majority of the women were driven there by necessity or betrayal, or force or despair, — it would seem that even an equal punishment would have been cruel injustice to the women. But when we observe how trifling a penalty was three dollars each to these men, whose money was likely to go for riotous living in some form, and forty of whom had the amount of the fine in their pockets ; and how hopelessly large an amount was ten dollars each to women who did not, probably, own even the clothes they wore, and who were to be sent to prison for a month in addition, — we see a kind of injustice which would stand a fair chance of being righted, I suspect, if women came into power. Not that they would punish their own sex less severely ; probably they would not : but they would put men more on a level as to the penalty.

It may be said that no such justice is to be expected from women ; because women in what is called "society" condemn women for mere imprudence, and excuse men for guilt. But it must be remembered that in "society" guilt is rarely a matter of open proof and conviction, in case of men : it is usually a matter of surmise ; and it is easy for either love or ambition to set the surmise aside, and to assume that the worst reprobate is "only a little wild." In fact, as Margaret Fuller pointed out years ago, how little conception has a virtuous woman as to what a dissipated young man really is! But let that same woman be a Portia, in the judgment-seat, or even a legislator or a voter, and let her have the unmistakable and actual offender before her, and I do not believe that she will excuse him for a paltry fine, and give the less guilty woman a penalty more than quadruple.

Women will also be sure to bring special sympathy and intelligent attention to the wrongs of children. Who can read without shame and indignation this report from "The New York Herald"?

THE CHILD-SELLING CASE.

Peter Hallock, committed on a charge of abducting Lena Dinser, a young girl thirteen years old, whom, it was alleged, her father, George Dinser, had sold to Hallock for purposes of prostitution, was again brought yesterday before Judge Westbrook in the Supreme Court Chambers, on the writ of habeas corpus previously obtained by Mr. William F. Howe, the prisoner's counsel. Mr. Howe claimed that Hallock could not be held on either section of the statute for abduction. Under the first section the complaint, he insisted, should set forth that the child was taken contrary to the wish and against the consent of her parents. On the contrary, the evidence, he urged, showed that the father was a willing party. Under the second section, it was contended that the prisoner could not be held, as there was no averment that the girl was of previous chaste character. Judge Westbrook, a brief counter argument having been made by Mr. Dana, held that the points of Mr. Howe were well taken, and ordered the prisoner's discharge.

Here was a father who, as the newspapers allege, had previously sold two other daughters, body and soul, and against whom the evidence seemed to be in this case clear. Yet through the defectiveness of the statute, or the remissness of the prosecuting attorney, he goes free, without even a trial, to carry on his infamous

traffic for other children. Grant that the points
were technically well taken and irresistible, —
though this is by no means certain, — it is very
sure that there should be laws that should reach
such atrocities with punishment, whether the
father does or does not consent to his child's
ruin; and that public sentiment should compel
prosecuting officers to be as careful in framing
their indictments where human souls are at
stake as where the question is of dollars only.
It is upon such matters that the influence of
women will make itself felt in legislation.

INDIVID-   As the older arguments against
UALS *vs.*   woman suffrage are abandoned, we
CLASSES   hear more and more of the final objection, that the majority of women have not
yet expressed themselves on the subject.   It is
common for such reasoners to make the remark,
that if they knew a given number of women —
say fifty, or a hundred, or five hundred — who
honestly wished to vote, they would favor it.
Produce that number of unimpeachable names,
and they say that they have reconsidered the
matter, and must demand more, — perhaps ten
thousand. Bring ten thousand, and the demand
again rises. "Prove that the majority of women wish to vote, and they shall vote." "Precisely," we say: "give us a chance to prove it

by taking a vote;" and they answer, "By no means."

And, in a certain sense, they are right. It ought not to be settled that way, — by dealing with woman as a class, and taking the vote. The agitators do not merely claim the right of suffrage for her as a class : they claim it for each individual woman, without reference to any other. If there is only one woman in the nation who claims the right to vote, she ought to have it. In Oriental countries all legislation is for classes, and in England it is still mainly so. A man is expected to remain in the station in which he is born ; or, if he leaves it, it is by a distinct process, and he comes under the influence, in various ways, of different laws. If the iniquities of the "Contagious Diseases" act in England, for instance, had not been confined in their legal application to the lower social grades, the act would never have passed. It was easy for men of the higher classes to legislate away the modesty of women of the lower classes ; but if the daughter of an earl could have been arrested, and submitted to a surgical examination at the will of any policeman, as the daughter of a mechanic might be, the law would not have stood a day. So, through all our slave States, there was class legislation for every person of negro blood : the laws of crime, of punishment, of testimony, were all adapted to classes, not individuals. Emancipation swept this all away, in most cases : classes ceased to exist before the law, so far as men at least were concerned ; there were only individuals. The more progress, the less class in legislation. We claim the application of this principle as rapidly as possible to women.

Our community does not refuse permission for women to go unveiled till it is proved that the majority of women desire it ; it does not even ask that question : if one woman wishes to show her face, it is allowed. If a woman wishes to travel alone, to walk the streets alone, the police protects her in that liberty. She is not thrust back into her house with the reproof, "My dear madam, at this particular moment the overwhelming majority of women are indoors : prove that they all wish to come out, and you shall come." On the contrary, she comes forth at her own sweet will : the policeman helps her tenderly across the street, and waves back with imperial gesture the obtrusive coal-cart. Some of us claim for each individual woman, in the same way, not merely the right to go shopping, but to go voting ; not merely to show her face, but to show her hand.

There will always be many women, as there are many men, who are indifferent to voting.

For a time, perhaps always, there will be a larger percentage of this indifference among women. But the natural right to a share in the government under which one lives, and to a voice in making the laws under which one may be hanged, — this belongs to each woman as an individual; and she is quite right to claim it as she needs it, even though the majority of her sex still prefer to take their chance of the penalty, without perplexing themselves about the law. The demand of every enlightened woman who asks for the ballot — like the demand of every enlightened slave for freedom — is an individual demand; and the question whether they represent the majority of their class has nothing to do with it. For a republic like ours does not profess to deal with classes, but with individuals; since "the whole people covenants with each citizen, and each citizen with the whole people, for the common good," as the constitution of Massachusetts says.

And, fortunately, there is such power in an individual demand that it appeals to thousands whom no abstract right touches. Five minutes with Frederick Douglass settled the question, for any thoughtful person, of that man's right to freedom. Let any woman of position desire to enter what is called "the lecture-field," to support herself and her children, and at once all abstract objections to women's speaking in public disappear : her friends may be never so hostile to "the cause," but they espouse her individual cause ; the most conservative clergyman subscribes for tickets, but begs that his name may not be mentioned. They do not admit that women, as a class, should speak, — not they ; but for this individual woman they throng the hall. Mrs. Dahlgren abhors politics : a woman in Congress, a woman in the committee-room, — what can be more objectionable ? But I observe that when Mrs. Dahlgren wishes to obtain more profit by her husband's inventions all objections vanish : she can appeal to Congressmen, she can address committees, she can, I hope, prevail. The individual ranks first in our sympathy : we do not wait to take the census of the "class." Make way for the individual, whether it be Mrs. Dahlgren pleading for the rights of property, or Lucy Stone pleading for the rights of the mother to her child.

DEFEATS BEFORE VICTORIES After one of the early defeats in the War of the Rebellion, the commander of a Massachusetts regiment wrote home to his father : " I wish people would not write us so many letters of condolence. Our defeat seemed to trouble them much more than it troubles us. Did people suppose there

were to be no ups and downs? We expect to
lose plenty of battles, but we have enlisted for
the war."

It is just so with every successful reform.
While enemies and half-friends are proclaiming
its defeats, those who advocate it are rejoicing
that they have at last got an army into the field
to be defeated. Unless this war is to be an
exception to all others, even the fact of having
joined battle is a great deal. It is the first step.
Defeat first; a good many defeats, if you please:
victory by and by.

William Wilberforce, writing to a friend in
the year 1817, said, "I continue faithful to the
measure of Parliamentary reform brought forward by Mr. Pitt. I am firmly persuaded that
at present a prodigious majority of the people
of this country are adverse to the measure. In
my view, so far from being an objection to the
discussion, this is rather a recommendation."
In 1832 the reform bill was passed.

In the first Parliamentary debate on the
slave trade, Colonel Tarleton, who boasted to
have killed more men than any one in England,
pointing to Wilberforce and others, said, "The
inspiration began on that side of the house;"
then turning round, "The revolution has reached
to this also, and reached to the height of fanat-
icism and frenzy." The first vote in the House

of Commons, in 1790, after arguments in the affirmative by Wilberforce, Pitt, Fox, and Burke, stood, ayes, 88 ; noes, 163 : majority against the measure, 75. In 1807 the slave trade was abolished, and in 1834 slavery in the British colonies followed ; and even on the very night when the latter bill passed, the abolitionists were taunted by Gladstone, the great Demerara slaveholder, with having toiled for forty years and done nothing. The Roman Catholic relief bill, establishing freedom of thought in England, had the same experience. It passed in 1829 by a majority of a hundred and three in the House of Lords, which had nine months before refused by a majority of forty-five to take up the question at all.

The English corn laws went down a quarter of a century ago, after a similar career of failures. In 1840 there were hundreds of thousands in England who thought that to attack the corn laws was to attack the very foundations of society. Lord Melbourne, the prime minister, said in Parliament, that "he had heard of many mad things in his life, but, before God, the idea of repealing the corn laws was the very maddest thing of which he had ever heard." Lord John Russell counselled the House to refuse to hear evidence on the operation of the corn laws. Six years after, in 1846, they were abolished forever.

How Wendell Phillips, in the anti-slavery meetings, used to lash pro-slavery men with such formidable facts as these, — and to quote how Clay and Calhoun and Webster and Everett had pledged themselves that slavery should never be discussed, or had proposed that those who discussed it should be imprisoned, — while, in spite of them all, the great reform was moving on, and the abolitionists were forcing politicians and people to talk, like Sterne's starling, nothing but slavery!

We who were trained in the light of these great agitations have learned their lesson. We expect to march through a series of defeats to victory. The first thing is, as in the anti-slavery movement, so to arouse the public mind as to make this the central question. Given this prominence, and it is enough for this year or for many years to come. Wellington said that there was no such tragedy as a victory, except a defeat. On the other hand, the next best thing to a victory is a defeat, for it shows that the armies are in the field. Without the unsuccessful attempt of to-day, no success to-morrow.

When Mrs. Frances Anne Kemble came to this country, she was amazed to find Americans celebrating the battle of Bunker Hill, which she had always heard claimed as a victory for

King George. Such it was doubtless called;
but what we celebrated was the fact that the
Americans there threw up breastworks, stood
their ground, fired away their ammunition, —
and were defeated. Thus the reformer, too,
looking at his failures, often sees in them such
a step forward, that they are the Bunker Hill
of a new revolution. Give us plenty of such
defeats, and we can afford to wait a score of
years for the victories. They will come.

INDEX

INDEX

INDEX

American Women: Images and Realities
An Arno Press Collection

[Adams, Charles F., editor]. **Correspondence between John Adams and Mercy Warren Relating to Her "History of the American Revolution," July-August, 1807.** With a new appendix of specimen pages from the "History." 1878.

[Arling], Emanie Sachs. **"The Terrible Siren": Victoria Woodhull, (1838-1927).** 1928.

Beard, Mary Ritter. **Woman's Work in Municipalities.** 1915.

Blanc, Madame [Marie Therese de Solms]. **The Condition of Woman in the United States.** 1895.

Bradford, Gamaliel. **Wives.** 1925.

Branagan, Thomas. **The Excellency of the Female Character Vindicated.** 1808.

Breckinridge, Sophonisba P. **Women in the Twentieth Century.** 1933.

Campbell, Helen. **Women Wage-Earners.** 1893.

Coolidge, Mary Roberts. **Why Women Are So.** 1912.

Dall, Caroline H. **The College, the Market, and the Court.** 1867.

[D'Arusmont], Frances Wright. **Life, Letters and Lectures: 1834, 1844.** 1972.

Davis, Almond H. **The Female Preacher, or Memoir of Salome Lincoln.** 1843.

Ellington, George. **The Women of New York.** 1869.

Farnham, Eliza W[oodson]. **Life in Prairie Land.** 1846.

Gage, Matilda Joslyn. **Woman, Church and State.** [1900].

Gilman, Charlotte Perkins. **The Living of Charlotte Perkins Gilman.** 1935.

Groves, Ernest R. **The American Woman.** 1944.

Hale, [Sarah J.] **Manners; or, Happy Homes and Good Society All the Year Round.** 1868.

Higginson, Thomas Wentworth. **Women and the Alphabet.** 1900.

Howe, Julia Ward, editor. **Sex and Education.** 1874.

La Follette, Suzanne. **Concerning Women.** 1926.

Leslie, Eliza . **Miss Leslie's Behaviour Book: A Guide and Manual for Ladies.** 1859.

Livermore, Mary A. **My Story of the War.** 1889.

Logan, Mrs. John A. (Mary S.) **The Part Taken By Women in American History.** 1912.

McGuire, Judith W. (A Lady of Virginia). **Diary of a Southern Refugee, During the War.** 1867.

Mann, Herman . **The Female Review: Life of Deborah Sampson.** 1866.

Meyer, Annie Nathan, editor.**Woman's Work in America.** 1891.

Myerson, Abraham. **The Nervous Housewife.** 1927.

Parsons, Elsie Clews. **The Old-Fashioned Woman.** 1913.

Porter, Sarah Harvey. **The Life and Times of Anne Royall.** 1909.

Pruette, Lorine. **Women and Leisure: A Study of Social Waste.** 1924.

Salmon, Lucy Maynard. **Domestic Service.** 1897.

Sanger, William W. **The History of Prostitution.** 1859.

Smith, Julia E. **Abby Smith and Her Cows.** 1877.

Spencer, Anna Garlin. **Woman's Share in Social Culture.** 1913.

Sprague, William Forrest. **Women and the West.** 1940.

Stanton, Elizabeth Cady. **The Woman's Bible** Parts I and II. 1895/1898.

Stewart, Mrs. Eliza Daniel . **Memories of the Crusade.** 1889.

Todd, John. **Woman's Rights.** 1867. [Dodge, Mary A.] (Gail Hamilton, pseud.) **Woman's Wrongs.** 1868.

Van Rensselaer, Mrs. John King. **The Goede Vrouw of Mana-ha-ta.** 1898.

Velazquez, Loreta Janeta. **The Woman in Battle.** 1876.

Vietor, Agnes C., editor. **A Woman's Quest: The Life of Marie E. Zakrzewska, M.D.** 1924.

Woodbury , Helen L. Sum n er. **Equal Suffrage.** 1909.

Young, Ann Eliza. **Wife No. 19.** 1875.